Bollywood Gay

'A help yourself book to living an authentic life.'

Manjinder Singh Sidhu

Bollywood Gay

Copyright © 2016 Manjinder Singh Sidhu

www.myspiritualsoul.com

ISBN 978-0-9954590-0-7

First published in Great Britain in 2016 by My Spiritual Soul.

Cover design by Adì Aviram

Printed in the United Kingdom

To My Parents, Sisters & Partner

Who have always tried to understand and support me.

FOLLOW MANJINDER SINGH SIDHU

WEBSITE
MySpiritualSoul.com

FACEBOOK
Facebook.com/MySpiritualSoul

TWITTER
@ManjinderSidhu, #BollywoodGay

YOUTUBE
YouTube.com/ManjinderSidhu

INSTAGRAM
Instagram.com/MySpiritualSoul

'Your birth is a revolution. You chose to be born like this.'

CONTENTS

PART 3: COMING OUT

PART 4: LET'S CHANGE THIS

PART 5: THE BIGGER PICTURE

'My aim, to raise a conscious army of gay men, fuelled by love, weapon of choice meditation, who first rectify their own issues, thereby escaping the perils of third dimension consciousness (which locks them onto physical desires, ego and suffering), elevating them, to eventually bring ripple effects to the world.'

INTENTION

This is my first book called 'Bollywood Gay' a self-help for LGBTI South Asians. It is a help yourself book which aims to benefit society in a bigger way through the ripple effect. There is no such book written for this group; however, it's also relevant to any person wanting to live an authentic life. Spiritual contexts are woven throughout it raising the vibrational frequency of its reader. The chapters are written in simple entertaining but purposeful spirit in the easiest of fashions. It's hip, trendy, relevant and new.

The reason why I have decided to write this book is due to the complete lack of positive role models and governmental support for this minority. Having worked around the globe as a support worker, human rights activist (UNHCR, UNICEF, Governments, NGOs), documentary maker (including on LGBTI topics) and being gay myself I know of the complete lack of positive literature for this group. I have literally been asked by higher forces to be a channel for this book so it can be written in the physical dimension to raise the consciousness of those who read it.

Currently, I provide life coaching and spiritual counselling, workshops and one on one sessions to LGBTI South Asians and have appeared on various TV (Sikh Channel, Zee TV, Sky News) and radio platforms (BBC Asian Network, BBC India) advocating rights for LGBTI.

My intention is to help as many LGBTI individuals residing in the sub-continent of India, Pakistan and Bangladesh. I have lived in India and understood the pain LGBTI feel with the illegality of homosexuality through the Penal Code Section 377. I am collaborating with LGBTI activists there and would love for you to also rise with me, hand in hand. This book adds to my workshops and campaigning work. I also see it helping the South Asian LGBTI diaspora around the world. I have a real presence with this group globally and I'm expanding this with my social media and weekly YouTube videos. The book is also for anyone, any minority, any under-represented group and not just for the LGBTI community. The book has an activist slant, urging people first to sort their own issues before moving onto the bigger task of bringing LGBTI rights in South Asia. This would, in turn, give room for South Asians to come out and be who they are, and give permission to others to be themselves too.

Revolutionary, necessary and fiery.

The way in which this book is orchestrated and written is with great purpose. There has been great intention to use only positive language and imagery within the work. The reason being that words, in fact, have a frequency. As per angel therapist Doreen Virtue's research, positive words hold a higher frequency and thus resonate higher energy than negative words. The usage of these words either in thought form or language has a direct influence on your frequency. Your feelings and thoughts literally assimilate to the language you use.

I want your experience with this book to be positive, motivational, inspirational and eye opening. I want to remove the years of self-victimisation and external blame so you can reclaim your inner power. I want you to realise that you are the change and can do it in an instant with each and every thought, feeling and word you use.

The book is based predominantly on the Law of Attraction principles as explained in Chapter 3. It was written whilst listening to the likes of the Law of Attraction experts Abraham Hicks and spiritual teacher Teal Swan as well as using binaural beats and love frequency inducing music. There is great intention with all of this. The receiving of this book should be done so in the same manner in which it was intended and in the manner it was written, love.

The book is also written with the chakra system underlying it unconsciously. A chakra is a centre of the seven main spiritual powers we have in our body (more in Chapter 14). As we move from the lower chakras of survival, up to our heart chakra of compassion and finally to our enlightenment chakra, the purpose of the book is to secure you firstly in your foundations and then allow you to rise and support the whole, the collective, the Universe, etc. As a reader, I expect great things from you. For expectation is the greatest driving force. Expect as though you already are that which I hope you to be: secure, balanced, happy, supported and motivated to help all.

Plenty of examples are put inside each chapter to enable newbies to grasp and understand topics. Examples are also good for those who already understand the basic spiritual and the Law of Attraction principles, as we all need re-reminding. Every chapter finishes with Action Sheets, intended to dive into your mind, to allow you to pierce through blockages, limiting beliefs, feelings, goals and desires. Do you want the man of your dreams? Do you want to come out to your family? Do you want to live a happier life? All the Action sheets will spearhead you on to that effect. Do them at your leisure and in whichever manner you would like. I am neither a disciplinarian nor someone who believes in rules and regulations.

Be free, be loving, be one.

PART 1: INTRODUCTION

'My birth was a political statement. A statement I knew nothing of. I was told I was wrong. A sin. My mere existence unnatural. My love for a man disgusting. My kisses a revolution. Centre stage my relationship. Standing out my walk. Forced onto a platform. Outsider. And then I took on that stage. Put on my best clothes. And shone. Just like you did.'

1) WHO AM I?

'I think my whole birth was to bring peace. First within myself and then outside, to my family and in a larger sense to the entire world. All that I had seen, heard and experienced had geared me up to that point.'

So how did I get here? Writing a book called 'Bollywood Gay', having my mum appear on a viral video and my dad speaking on Zee TV? Let me tell you; it's been a bumpy ride, and if I can do it, and am doing it, then you can do it too!

I grew up in a traditional, conservative, Sikh family. My dad was the man of the house and my mum enjoyed to direct us. My childhood was less than idyllic. Troubled, arguments, unease and a lot of fighting. My parents, until recently, argued a lot. Despite the constant disharmony within my home, we were however, well fed and looked after. We knew we mattered greatly to our parents and were loved unconditionally. There were the usual Indian family pressures of having good grades, getting a well-paid job and marriage to someone of the opposite sex was of course expected.

'Let me assure you, I have had it tough, and if I can make it, so can you.'

How did I internalise this? I was continuously anxious. My psychologist said it was like living in a war zone, which led to my anxiety and irritable bowel syndrome. Growing up I had a lot of health issues. I had a heart murmur, a hole in my heart, which according to author Louise Hay, is caused by a lack of joy, and internalised anger, which I guess seems about right. I had epileptic fits, seizures, psoriasis, coeliac 'dis-ease' and many other auto-immune 'dis-eases' (I refer to disease as 'dis-ease' due to Louise Hay's reasoning that all illness is due to the unease one feels in the body). I believe all these 'dis-eases' were created by my subconscious mind, which attacked itself due to guilt, shame and lack of self-love.   I used to count all the illnesses I had as a child repeatedly in my head, but will spare you the pain of that now. For I believe what we focus on grows and as it stands I focus on good health.

I lived on edge. I didn't know when I needed to be on guard, alert, or run downstairs. The disharmony within my home affected me to the core. I could not fathom why people would argue and cause so much pain. I wanted to change this. I used to try to change the situation by intervening, just like the UN Peacekeepers do, unsuccessfully. I tried to calm conflicts using a wooden spoon as a means of causing dialogue- i.e. you can only speak when you are holding the spoon. No one ever listened to the spoon or me, and quite often I sat alone at the kitchen table with my spoon. Whenever I would try to have a dialogue with my dad, he would walk out of the house, or get defensive and angry. My mother would never accept her faults or apologise either.

It turned into a daily habit of my sisters and I having a go at my mum for what had happened and blaming her for everything, as we could not confront our dad.

I've always been spiritual. Growing up I was known as the 'Baba' (wise old man) at home. I used to do peace prayers (Sukhmani Sahib) every Sunday to bring about harmony. I used to do my twice daily prayers (Jap Ji Sahib and Reharas Sahib), morning and evening. This all sprung from that which was going on around me combined with my deep fascination for all that was unseen and unknown. I loved Indian mythology about Gods, Goddesses and ancient civilisations. I would revel in the Hindu epics 'Mahabharat' and 'Ramayan'.

That all changed, when I started going through puberty at the young age of 8. Hair began to grow around my private regions. I didn't know what was happening to me, as sex education hadn't been taught at school yet. The boys would salivate about all the girls in school, whereas I preferred to look at the male underwear section of the clothing catalogues sent to my home. I tried looking at the bra and panty sections of those magazines, but they did nothing for me, and when I imagined them, I just saw a hot guy in the picture. Then one day I turned the page to the men's underwear section, and I was hooked to the muscly bodies, chiselled jawlines and protruding packages. Yes please, I thought! I didn't know what it meant; I was too young to realise. I knew that society around me thought it was wrong, however, deep down it felt so right. I also remember travelling with my dad in the car, whilst he focused on getting to the destination; I would sneakily stare at the boys ;-)

Now I did not know much about sex. My first encounter with a condom was when I was in primary school (age 6 or so)! A boy had brought it with him and was messing about with it in the playground, throwing it at us. My eldest sister later informed me of what it was, after spotting the same thing on the floor on the way to the doctors. She said it prevented people from having babies. I questioned, 'Oh no, I've touched it now, does that mean I won't have any kids?' That was the extent of my knowledge on these things. My first encounter of seeing a real penis was also at this school, where a boy in the playground whilst dancing, with everyone watching proceeded to take his willy out and shake it at everyone! 'Ew gross', I thought but at the same time, it intrigued me. A similar incidence happened in secondary school where a guy I had a bit of a crush on, as did many of the girls, proceeded to take his penis out and shake it at me in the locker rooms!

One day I asked my eldest sister what sex meant, as it was scribbled on the xylophone at school (shows what kind of classy schools I grew up in) and she shoved the dictionary at me. I was horrified. Man inserts penis in vagina :-O Obviously even before that, social conditioning and the environment around me had shown me that marriage was between man and woman, and that was the basis of a family. Thus having feelings for men, though they felt so good, also felt so wrong and bad. Guilt and shame quickly took over.

I began removing myself from members of my family and focused on my studies. Religion became a thing of the past after I hit puberty. I neither knew what Sikhism thought about homosexuality nor felt connected to 'God'. I felt like God had forsaken me. I hid my deep secret within me and threw away the key.

'Holding onto anger is like drinking poison and expecting the other person to die.' Buddha

I still, however, wanted to bring peace within my home. I had been feeling quite angry and upset about all that had and was going on around me. The process started with forgiveness. To forgive all that had happened, by removing it from my consciousness. I used to find it hard to be in the presence of my father; we had never hugged or exchanged meaningful conversation. I wanted to rectify that. I started experimenting. I understood the importance of having a good relationship with him and also knowing that it would, in turn, help me have a good relationship in the future with someone I loved. I began at the age of 15 or so to start giving my dad hugs. First, they were just pats on the back, which then progressed into full blown hugs. I wanted to bring love where there was fear. I wanted to be an example to my sisters on how to forgive and heal. I spent time with my father and sat down with him to converse. And slowly things got better and better.

Being the only son from an Asian family, I was expected to marry a woman, provide offspring and continue the family name. I worried I would be disowned, forced to marry a woman or kicked out of the house or worse, especially given the household I was brought up in. My parents themselves had had an arranged marriage. Brought up in India, they did as they were told as children. Once they arrived in the UK, like most Indians in the 70s, they shied away from British culture and held on tightly to the values of the village back home.

This meant that we as children we were not allowed outside. We were expected to go to school and come straight back home to study. No playing out on the street or with friends, mind my friends lived further away from me. I used to spend my afternoons with homework and evenings playing on my bike with my middle sister. Even as I grew older, and started college and started working part time the voice of my mother echoed in my ears:

'Home to school, school to home, home to work, work to home. Bas (that's it).'

I think my parent's lived in fear. Fear of the West, fear of British culture, fear that their children would be corrupted by sex, drugs and rock 'n' roll. For a gay son like me, it made the flight to freedom even more desperate.

SCHOOL LIFE

I grew up in an ethnic neighbourhood that was ghettoised and poor. Most if not all of the children in my school were black or South Asian. We only had one or two white children in the whole school. I didn't get bullied as such apart from one reoccurring incident, which I remember from primary school (age 8). A boy called Daniel (who ironically came out as gay a few years later) used to kick me whilst I stood in line. He would also tell me to turn around so he could punch me in the back, for no reason. He vented out his pent up anger on me, and I would go home with bruises. I guess deep down I held the vibrational energy of anger and violence and hence the Law of Attraction matched us up quite nicely (explained in Chapter 3). Then in secondary school, luckily Daniel and I were not in the same class, and he could go about beating other boys in his class, as I focused on my studies.

In secondary school I did experience some incidents of name-calling. Sometimes the boys would call me 'Woman-Gender' instead of Manjinder. I found it quite amusing due to the ingenuity of it; however every time I heard it in the hallways I looked sideways to see if a teacher was around. I did not want to be 'outed' to the adults at school for fear they would believe the name-callers. The typical 'batty man', 'gay boy' and 'chi chi man' colloquial was, of course, administered to me from time to time, as a way of the other kids saying we see your difference. Apart from that, I managed to escape real homophobic name-calling by being studious, funny and independent!

I was a funny geek. I would get top marks, rebel and make people laugh. It was at this time I started to feel awkward around boys, especially in the changing rooms, during Physical Education (P.E.) lessons. I'm sure most gay men experienced anxiety going to P.E. classes. Macho boys would try to outdo one another by being the best at football, and I was always the last one to be picked for the team. Perhaps, I was seen as a liability, with my inability to be good at certain sports (I was however great at hitting a ball with a bat). The girls would play hockey, and I resorted to playing with them, along with a few other boys. To be honest, I was frightened of the competitive show of manliness, which I felt was forced, fake, and from a place of lack. I would skip P.E. by giving forged illness notes, to which teachers were none, the wiser. I do feel teachers should realise why certain children repeatedly skip P.E. lessons and try to figure out other healthier ways of incorporating physical exercise into their lives. It is traumatic enough going to school, let alone being gay and then forced to exercise with the macho boys. Gender is totally thrown out of the window.

For my A Levels, I went to an all boys Grammar school, which was one of the most isolating experiences I went through during my teenage years. My sisters had left home, one was married, and one was working away, and I was left at home with my parents. My dad worked late as did my mum, and dark nights trying to read history books, made me very depressed. I used to skip certain classes and stay home. I managed to get good grades, after retaking my first-year exams in my second year in January. However, after that, I lost all motivation and didn't even revise for my examinations. A straight A* GCSE student getting B's and C's for A Levels, made my Grammar school Head of Year speak very discouragingly to me, hoping I would be ok. Luckily University College London (one of the top universities in the world) confirmed my place the same day, and the rest was history.

University was a time of liberation. I could be myself, whilst away from home; by telling people I was gay and by going to gay clubs. I remember the first few weeks of Uni. Everyone I met, I would say 'Hi, my name is Mani, and I'm gay'. I could barely stop myself, and I would play up to the stereotypes of what being gay was meant to look like. I remember going to the gay clubs in Central London and noticing that I would be the only South Asian there. The gay scene in 2005 Central London was predominantly white. I mean it still is, with a sprinkling of a few South Asian nights each month. I was a bit of a coconut then. I did not hang out with Indians, or listen to and watch Bollywood movies and songs. I preferred to have friends from other nationalities, for I assumed all South Asians were homophobic, narrow-minded and judgemental, just as the ones I had experienced back at home. I wanted to distance myself from them and steer towards the white culture, which I thought was more accepting. How wrong I was. I felt even more marginalised and discriminated in white gay spaces, as the only brown person there. I got ignored by men in clubs for my white friends and felt like an outsider.

I had thought as soon as I was away from home, at Uni, I would walk into a gay bar or club and meet the man of my dreams. This, unfortunately, or fortunately did not happen. I was single for a good decade after this, partly due to work, and partly due to my unconscious guilt and shame of being who I was. I had short-term flings here and there and an open relationship for a few months. But my actual real monogamous relationship came at the age of 28. How I did it, I will explain in Chapter 15.

On top of this, there were no diverse gay role models growing up. I mean yes we had a few drag queens or feminine and flamboyant homosexuals on TV, but all of them were white and did not represent the person I was. I guess I ran away from my femininity for it made me stand out and the likes of those role models on TV were the ones that echoed all the name-calling I used to hear at school. I did not for a second feel safe and connected.

COMING OUT

I first came out to my form teacher at the age of 15. I had a crush on him, and he was new to the school. The response was shockingly negative and not what I expected. He told me he could not discuss it, as it was illegal to do so. It was seen as encouraging homosexuality. As you can see in the last few years, LGBTI rights in the West have improved drastically, with schools having to talk about these issues. However, until date, out ethnic LGBTI role models are rarely seen in the community.

I came out to one of my sisters at the age of 18 via a phone call. The coming out again did not go to plan. Initially, she was ok with it and then she freaked out and denied it by shutting off from me altogether. This scared me further from telling my parents. I understand now, that she reacted this way because she was worried for my mum and wanted to protect her. I told my other sister when I was 21. Again my timing was not great. I had blurted out I was gay to my first sister after she had an argument with her husband, and told my second sister when she was in her final year exams at university. My second sister thankfully was less fearful and thus more accepting of who I was. They both told me to keep my secret with me and not to tell our parents.

I had always told myself that I would get educated and find a well-paid job before telling my parents. But as I finished my short-term project with the United Nations (UNHCR) in Israel I felt compelled to tell them. I was depressed, lonely and disconnected to who I really was. I felt the history of trauma and closetedness was preventing me from an authentic relationship with someone I loved. I had read many online articles instructing me that coming out was the only solution. I also felt that being gay was pointless if I couldn't get into a loving, romantic relationship. It was with this intention I told my parents. I had been distancing myself from them for many years, living in various countries or cities pursuing my education and career. I did not enjoy speaking to them on the phone, and they knew something was up but could not put their finger on it. Initially, they thought I didn't love them anymore and hence were relieved when I told them I was gay over SMS. Their reaction was positive, loving and understanding from the onset. I could not have asked for a better coming out.

All these years I had worried myself sick for no reason. I do have to give credit to my own inner mind for this. I had been trying to accept myself as a gay man for a couple of years before this. Using the examples in the book 'The Secret' to inform people that my parents knew who I was and accepted me fully, even before I had told them. It helped me feel good about the situation and myself to an extent where I could open up to them. I returned home soon after coming out to them and spent quality time with them. I have to give them a lot of credit for all that they have done for me since. They have come leaps and bounds ahead from what I could ever have envisaged. This is my hope for you too. That through reading this book and the principles contained within it, you too can fine-tune your internal dialogue so that your coming out is as smooth as mine.

How did I manage to get my parents to support me to such an extent that they would be willing to be filmed for the world to see it? I had been working in prestigious human rights offices around the world, desperately trying to get the approval of my parents. But I realised that working in Human Rights for poverty consciousness, stale, ego driven and logical environs was not my best forte. I needed expansion, abundance, and creative divine feminine energy. I need to be free. I needed to bring spiritualism back to the forefront and lead. Hand in hand, with my LGBTI friends and family from all walks of life. Take them on the path. Or rather help them realign to their true self by echoing their essence through me. It is my deepest wish for you all to be happy. For what you do onto others you do onto yourself. There is no separation. You can do this by identifying, accepting, forgiving and then finally releasing all that you went through. I will explain this in detail in Part 4.

TO SUMMARISE MY JOURNEY:

'I had to be cracked open to be of service. I was stubborn. I was wild. I needed taming and training. I needed to listen to my inner solace. My silence to know who I was and why I was here. For many years I ran away from home, to cities and far away exotic places. I wished to be of service. That had always been a seed within me. But I also wished to take my shame away from others. From those who knew me. I wanted to be anonymous and unknown. I was the light and laughter in the eyes of others, but in the eyes of my own, I was a stranger. A distant memory. I worked for various prestigious organisations trying to prove my worth and trying to be validated. But inside I was empty and all alone. The work did not fill me, and I withered with pain. I sought out a remedy. Self-help books were my lifeline. As was meditation, prayer and yoga. I became an astute student of asceticism. I lived with the Tibetans. I did course after course. Alternative became my lifestyle. Chanting, crystals and compassion my pathway. Obsessed with happiness. How to obtain it and remain within it. As I grew, I realised many things, past lives, the emptiness of life, not in a pessimistic sense but in a liberating sense, and deep love and acceptance for all. I was now ready and people came to me for advice.'

Help others remember who they are. Spread the following message on social media. Facebook, Tweet, Pin, Instagram and Email:

Bollywood Gay Message #1:
I am pure love energy.
#BollywoodGay

Action Sheet 1: Who Are You?

Write down your biography in the space below. It will help us piece together and discover hidden patterns in your psyche and allow us to work on how to release and heal them:

MY CHILDHOOD WAS LIKE:

_____
_____
_____
_____
_____
_____
_____
_____

MY RELATIONSHIP WITH MY:

Dad:

_____
_____

Mum:

_____
_____

Siblings:

_____
_____

Extended Family:

_____
_____

School Friends:

_____
_____

When I found out I was LGBTI, the **struggle** I went through and the **acceptance issues** were:

_____
_____
_____
_____
_____
_____

My **coming out** story was: (if you're in the closet, jot down your fears of being LGBTI)

_____
_____
_____
_____
_____

How did **people react** or how do you think they will react to your coming out?

_____
_____
_____
_____

What do you **love** about **yourself**?

_____
_____
_____

What do you **love** about your **parents**?

_____
_____
_____

What **miracle** would you want to happen in your **family**?

_____
_____
_____

How would you **feel** if that came **true**?

_____
_____
_____
_____

'You are Universal consciousness. Your job is to teach the world unconditional love and break out of gender norms and stereotypes.'

2) LABELS ARE SO LAST SEASON. LET'S TALK ABOUT THE SOUL.

LGBTI. Top. Bottom. Versatile. Jock. Twink. Bear. Cub. Otter.

What do all these labels mean and more importantly do we need them? After all, we are pure infinite Source energy.

What do I mean by Source? Source means the Source from where we all came from. You may refer to it as God, Nature, Universe or Creation. I use these terms interchangeably for to me they all mean the same. They are again labels to describe the unknown power that created the Universe to which we belong. Use whichever term feels most comfortable to you.

So what is LGBTI? Lesbian, Gay, Bisexual, Transgender and Intersex. We could also add queer, pansexual, asexual or many other terms to the list to describe someone's sexual orientation or gender.

Lesbian and gay (also referred to as homosexual), are those who are sexually attracted to someone of their own sex. So a gay man is sexually attracted to men, and a gay woman or lesbian is sexually attracted to other women.

Bisexual people are sexually attracted to both men and women but not necessarily in an equal ratio. Indeed most bisexual people I speak to say their sexual attraction to either gender can change according to their mood or taste that particular day.

Transgender are those who are assigned a certain gender at birth by a doctor but who do not self-identify with it. They could be born anatomically male or female but feel that they are either another gender on the gender spectrum or agender (without gender). Transgender individuals do not have a specific sexual orientation and therefore may identify with a variety of sexual identities as well.

Intersex individuals are not distinctly identified as male or female. This is due to a variation in their sex characteristics including chromosomes, gonads, or genitals. Often during birth, intersex babies are given sex reassignment surgeries to make them more acceptable to society as a whole.

This is now regarded as a violation of their human rights and genital mutilation as it is nonconsensual and dangerous. Intersex individuals may thus identify with varying degrees of gender or sexual identities, which may evolve as they grow.

MSM means men who have sex with men. It is a term used especially in South Asia by those who do not want to be labelled as gay. These men may choose to have sexual relationships with men but still be married to women. It also refers to straight men that have sex with other men for mere sexual gratification in an environment where women are not allowed to date or be in relationships with other men before marriage.

Then we have top, bottom, versatile, jocks, twinks, bears, cubs, otters, daddies etc. I will spare you the definitions of these. If you are really curious, you can Google them. (Top, bottom and versatile will be explained in Chapter 6). The definitions explain sexual preferences and body types, which have now become a norm in the gay world. You will find people labelling themselves or others into these small categories or even changing their bodies to fit into another category. Some say bears will only date other bears, and muscly guys only other muscly guys. Twinks are assumed to be skinny petite types who are feminine and bottom. We limit our spiritual selves greatly by being serious with these terms. Use them in jest or better not at all.

Currently, the rights for lesbians or gays and bisexuals to a lesser degree are widely accepted in the western hemisphere of our world. Transgender and intersex individuals however, experience the most discrimination. This is partly due to their non-conformation to gender stereotypes (lesbian, gay and bisexual people also do this, but to a lesser extent). The lifespan of most transgender in the Western world is very low. Most experience violence, exclusion and even murder. This is especially true of ethnic trans people.

Now, what is gender? According to the Oxford Dictionary the definition of gender is:

> ***'The state of being male or female (typically used with reference to social and cultural differences rather than biological ones).'***

Gender is often misinterpreted to mean the biological sex, which is determined by the physical, sexual organs a person was born with. However, it is more complex then that. A person can be born with male sexual organs but feel inherently female inside. Their mannerism, way of seeing themselves and perception can be of the divine feminine, and they may deeply desire to be physically female.

Thus gender is actually the relationship between an individual's biological sex (gender biology), their internal sense of self as male, female, both or neither (gender identity) as well as their outward presentations and behaviours (gender expression). Gender, like sexuality, is not a binary system but a spectrum on which each person sits and can change over time. It is with that intention the pronoun 'they' is used throughout the book instead of s/he to encompass the totality of the gender spectrum.

Gender is socially constructed and therefore reinforced by society from birth. As soon a child is born it is categorised. Blue for boys and pink for girls. This is a new system, in the recent past newborn boys wore pink. However nearly everything in society is assigned a gender: toys, colours, clothing and behaviour. So by the time a child is three through social conditioning most display preferences to activities and exhibit behaviours typically associated with their sex. Due to the entrenchment of social gender roles and expectations in our culture, most of us can't imagine anything different. As a result, individuals who fit into these expectations rarely if ever question what gender is.

I am male and female. Just like you.

However, there are prominent examples of individuals who live outside of these typical identities all around the globe. For South Asia, the most prominent are the Hijra community. In India, they were revered and even feared. When a newborn son was born, they would come to check if the baby was one of their own (intersex) and take him away with them. If he were not, they would ask for money. Not giving money to them meant a curse on the family. The Hijra community nowadays, unfortunately, resorts to begging and prostitution. They are often abused or raped by police and local populations. Despite this, they do represent the most complex understanding of gender and have been able to maintain a third gender tick box on most Indian government forms. It is with this stance that lobbyists against Section 377 are campaigning.

Is being LGBTI a choice?

'There is deliberate intention from the non-physical perception for being gay.'
Abraham Hicks

Yes being LGBTI is a choice, as is gender, but it's a choice made before being born on this planet. You choose it before you incarnate in your physical body in order to see a different perspective and grow as a being. You cannot consciously change your gender or sexuality once you are born. It is set to the way you intended before incarnating and only through full acceptance of who you are may this move up or down the gender/sexuality spectrum. Gender is unimportant from an energy perspective. It's only in the physical form where it expresses itself as one polarity or the other. Beyond the physical dimension, the soul is genderless.

Your spirit is neither male nor female, but male and female energy combined (Shiv Shakti energy) and thus it can manifest in either. That is why some of us choose to incarnate as LGBTI in order to learn lessons needed for our souls to grow and to embody femininity and masculinity within ourselves.

For our souls to understand gender properly, we need to be outside social norms, to feel excluded or different enough so that we can grow. As LGBTI people we have chosen to incarnate on this earth to challenge gender stereotypes and norms.

Our higher self is void of gender for energy is genderless. This is why the human race is en route spiritually to be gender androgynous. Androgynous people are closer to the truth of who they really are. They understand both the divine feminine and masculine energies that are contained within us all. Humanity is therefore heading towards being a race with no gender. Where we realise our unity and not our duality. In order to do this we need to release resistance to gender and embrace it. We can do this by acknowledging both male and female aspects within us. If we resist them then we will be a match to gender and gender issues will continue.

Society: 'I cannot love you because you are not the way I need you to be so I can love you.'

Response: 'I am not a condition that you can force into conformity to serve your purpose of loving conditionally.'

You have come forth into this physical realm to say I am, that which I am and I won't change to please you. And if you don't like it, it's not my problem it's yours. See happiness is an internal, independent task. It's not up to you to help someone to be happy or to love you as a result. They, themselves must realise that it is only their own connection to Source energy that will make them feel loved. When we are in a state of oneness, we don't expect or ask others to conform to what we deem acceptable, and we love unconditionally. Personal alignment with Source is what most of the world lacks, as it blames others for their unhappiness.

From Source perspective, you have chosen to be different enough from the norm so that society is not able to change you to please them. You say, 'I will be different enough to give them an opportunity to open up their thinking about life. If they care enough about loving me, they may be guided back to their Source, their joy.'

If anyone tells you otherwise, it comes from their disconnection from Source, and that's why you experience the pain in the words when they say your life is a sin.

You come for variety, expansion and diversity. Our consciousness wants a different kind of experience so that it can learn how to come back to alignment with our true self. In a society that is based on conformity, it's our variety that is the balance and strength for expansion. We incarnate declaring to be different enough so that laws won't be able to contain us, not to teach a lesson to the world but to tell others they are barking up the wrong tree when their happiness depends on our conformity. You come forth as an angel to want others to understand that they will never find joy by trying to change you. They cannot control you; indeed there are not enough resources to control everyone.

Those who do not conform to binary concepts of gender are powerful teachers. We are powerful teachers of unconditional love, compassion and authenticity. We come, wanting to be different than most, a difference that cannot be socialised. So many people have been square pegs rammed into round holes. So now energies come with a greater difference. You are born with something that can't please society. It's up to them to please themselves. Find alignment with who you are first. Your purpose is stronger, and you are not influenced by what others think. You come with deliberate intention; your consciousness wants a different kind of contrast to expand. Diversity is the platform from where all evolution comes forth. To acknowledge ideas that exist and expand them further. This is happening in large numbers now, where people are being born into bodies or situations where they have driving impulses very different from everyone else.

Being gay and lesbian does come with its challenges. This allows our consciousness to expand. Expansion helps the whole Universe understand a different perspective and grow. In a way, we are helping the whole living, breathing organism of the Universe to learn and develop. From a reincarnation perspective we all choose the lesson we want to learn on earth in order to help the 'all', that from where we come from, to expand. We are all interconnected as one being. We are droplets of water in the huge expanse of the ocean of life. We are not separate from one another. It is a holographic illusion, which makes us think as such. Energetically, atomically you and I are not separate. Thus whatever I experience, learn, expand upon, ultimately helps you.

Being LGBTI also brings with it some spiritual advantages. We get the opportunity to question gender stereotypes, go outside the gender box altogether and ultimately get to know the soul. We learn to transcend the physical to fall in love with the 'all'. See love should not be restricted. If both parties practice sex whilst in alignment, love backs the sexual connection. Growth also comes from experiencing the pain of being told what we are doing is wrong as it creates extreme expansion for us. We have to face ourselves and be honest about what we are which allows us to evolve spiritually and align with our true self.

WHY ARE SOME PEOPLE TRANSGENDER?

Being born transgender again is a pre-birth intention to search for identity. A transgender person's main intention for this life is authenticity. To find authenticity you have to be inauthentic. You have to live a life where you are lying to yourself and experience an identity crisis by feeling void of identity or in the wrong identity. Gender identity is second to choosing to be human. Transgender people spiritually chose to experience contrast through their self-image, self-reflection and self-expression. They are here to learn that they can only be truly happy if they accept who they really are.

With transgender individuals, they come into the physical form with the gender they initially chose but do not feel they fit into it. They incarnate as male but don't identify with that gender and vice versa. This causes resistance. The first step of the healing process is to release resistance to the gender you were born in.   Resistance to your gender keeps you stuck in that gender. Whereas focusing positively towards your gender enables you to release it. Then you can choose a body and lifestyle that reflects the real you. This is not the same thing as trying to force yourself to be that thing you want to change. Forcing yourself can be detrimental to your health.

The decision to change your gender should come from a positive mental space. From feeling happy about it and not running away from something else which is from a negative mental space. You can figure this out by paying attention to how you feel about the gender you no longer want to be. Do you want to change to allow yourself to be who you were meant to be or is it due to resistance to your current gender? If you want to change your gender because of resistance, it is important to release the resistance, because then you might not want a sex change after all. However, if you still want to change your gender identity after releasing the resistance, it means you are aligned with your authentic self, and your sex change is for the right reasons. You release resistance to your current gender by observing your core belief patterns on being male or female, and accepting them. Core beliefs and how to release them are discussed in Chapter 11.

It's important to reaffirm that nothing about you needs to be fixed. Being transgender does not mean you have mental issues. You are here to have an identity crisis to realise who your authentic self is, and be a teacher of authenticity to others.

You may try to bring me down, clip my wings, and cage me up. But I will fly. I was born to soar, to rise and shine. I am light and this life is mine.

Trying to figure out why people are the way they are only takes us out of alignment with who we really are. We can never fully understand someone else, as we are not in their shoes. Also as nothing is permanent people are always evolving and changing. So don't try to understand why others live or think the way they do, simply sync up with who you are and why you are here. Your job is you and your own individual connection to Source. Focus on that.

No one comes on this planet to conform. We are all so unique in ourselves. So go live happily on your own terms and let other people deal with it or not as it's none of their business. Simply love yourself unconditionally.

Let others know that they are beyond labels. That their soul cannot be contained. Facebook, Tweet, Pin, Instagram, and Email the message below:

Bollywood Gay Message #2:
My soul knows no labels.
#BollywoodGay

Action Sheet 2: What's Your Label?

Do you *label* yourself?

_____

_____

Does labelling yourself *limit* who you really are?

_____

_____

_____

How would you more *accurately* describe yourself, which takes in the *totality* of who you really are?

_____

_____

_____

Why do you *believe* you were *born* LGBTI?

_____

_____

_____

_____

Having read this chapter do you believe you have a *certain purpose* on earth? That you were born this way for a particular reason? If so what is it?

_____

_____

_____

_____

What things *confuse*, *scare*, *annoy* or cause *angst* within you about being LGBTI?

_____

_____

_____

_____

What *lessons* or *blessings* have come about from being who you are? I.e. do you see the world in a different light? How is that *positive*?

_____

_____

_____

_____

'What you are living is the evidence of what you are thinking and feeling- every single time.' Abraham Hicks

3) WHAT IS THE LAW OF ATTRACTION?

'You are the creator of your own experience. You live in a vibrational Universe. You have control of the signal that you emit.'

We are all made of atoms. These atoms vibrate at very high velocity. Essentially, our essence is one of vibrational energy. That is what we are made of.

The Law of Attraction says, 'that which is vibrationally likened to itself will match up with that which is likened to itself. Whatever you are vibrationally offering is coming to you and will be reflected fully in your experience.' See the Law of Attraction is the law of mirroring. The only way we are going to become self-aware is that every time we have a feeling or thought, it is reflected back at us. Each time we think a good or a bad thought we offer a vibrational frequency. Good feelings or thoughts produce high-frequency energy, and bad feelings or thoughts produce low-frequency energy. We are literally creating by what we are paying attention to.

What we give our attention to grows. When we say, we want something we attract that. When we say, we don't want something we attract that also. The Universe does not distinguish between do and don't, but it focuses on the object of your attention. So saying I do want a cake, or I don't want a cake means the same thing to the Universe. What the Universe tunes into is your feeling about that situation. So if you feel strongly about a situation even if it's a situation that you no longer want in your life you will bring it into your experience. You may not want a cake, as you think you will put on extra pounds on your waist. However, all that you are thinking and feeling is 'cake, cake, cake'. It is the object of your attention. The Universe tunes into that vibrational feeling and gives you more cake. Thus it's very important to be careful about how you feel about specific situations you do want to manifest, as the Universe is impartial as a mirror!

For instance, you have to smile in order to see the reflection of yourself in the mirror smile back at you. You can't expect the reflection in the mirror to smile first before you smile back at it. In the same way with life, you have to change your perception first for the Universe to manifest it as your reality. You have to feel as though you already have it. Then it will manifest.

Just as feelings attract feelings, thoughts attract thoughts. It takes about 17 seconds to create momentum. Like a car on a hill, as it starts rolling down (without the hand break on) it gains momentum. What I mean by momentum is that more of the same thoughts and feelings will come after you have been focusing on those thoughts for a prolonged time. For a thought to attract some sort of physical manifestation in time, space reality takes about a minute. So you have to think good thoughts for at least this amount of time to create a momentum and attract that which you want.

Can we all do this? We are always doing this, whether we know it or not. We are manifesting all day, every day. We are living in a time space reality that functions like a mirror, a mirror hologram made for our learning.

The first manifestations on an instinctual level are emotions such as excitement, eagerness, and anticipation. These let you know you are in the vibrational vicinity of that expectant place. Then good ideas, inspiration and imaginative thoughts come to you. Most people are used to acting their way into what they want, pushing against the resistance that they have already set up. But if you spend most of your time working on your emotions, feeling good about yourself, you will be in the receiving of your vision. Then you will naturally be in the right place at the right time when someone rendezvous with you.

When you take care of your emotions (the way you feel) people, situations and events naturally start mirroring what you are thinking and come to support you. You receive never-ending universal support if you first prepare the atmosphere within you to receive it. Quite simply you need to get on the same wavelength of what you want and then allow it to manifest for you.

'What you think you become, what you feel you attract, what you imagine you create.'

When you ask for something, the thing you want is automatically available to you in the non-physical. Meaning it's already vibrationally present in the Universe. All you have to do is to be in the same vibrational frequency as it long enough for it to physically manifest. The path is always coming to you, but you have to be in the right place to realise it. Even the visualisation of it in the first place is an unfolding of it for you. So before it is vibrationally observable in the physical, it has to be vibrationally observable in your emotional feelings. Fear repels the thing you want, but love brings it to you.

We have to be careful as we have multiple vibrations to every subject such as money, career and relationships. If you have a negative feeling vibration (you feel bad about a subject), the vibration of what you want, and how you feel about it are in two different places. Our feelings are the best indicators of how close we are to manifesting our desire. Therefore to be a deliberate creator, it is important to feel as good as possible for as often as you can.

The reason why most people don't manifest their desires or dreams is because they have been thinking about the absence of their desire more than the having of it. You have to realise that every topic is actually two topics. Just like a stick has two ends, the one end is of having the thing, and the other end is the absence of it. So depending on how you are feeling about a topic that is the vibration you will activate. Say for instance you want more money in your life, but you focus on the feeling of not having enough money, as opposed to feeling abundant, you then manifest the lack feeling instead. Thus it is crucial, especially when trying to manifest specific desires, to hold the vibration of the having of the thing as opposed to the absence of it. Otherwise, it is strongly recommended to go general. Meaning stop focusing on the specifics of your desire, but start appreciating all those things that are going well for you in your life. Be grateful for having lungs to breath, legs that allow you to travel, food to nourish your body, a mother and father who love you, etc. Thinking in a generic way has less momentum and thus you will still attract your desire, be it more slowly.

You have the power to reprogramme your mind and reconnect to Source.

Let's take an example. You want to manifest a particular car. However, you keep focusing on you not having the car. You keep focusing on the banged out motor you have. The flat tyres of your car, the rusty engine and peeling metal work. In this mental state, it is advisable to start listing all the positive aspects of your life generally to increase your momentum and vibrational energy to that of allowing, abundance and positivity. Only once you are in that mental space can you really manifest what you want. Your job is to allow. The Universe will bring it to you.

Once you are feeling good about yourself, you can go specific about your dream car. Start imagining the final stage of having the car. Choose the car you want, imagine it, draw it and put it on your vision board (a piece of paper where you place all the things you want to manifest in your life as described in Action Sheet 4). Feel the feeling of already having the car. Imagine how you would feel whilst sitting in the driver's seat, with the plush leather seats, the air con soothing you whilst the music is blasting. As you sit in your current banged out motor, carry on imagining the wonderful feeling of already having acquired the car of your dreams. You thank your old car for its job, excitedly expectant of the new vehicle that is on its way. Do this 5 minutes a day. Then allow the Universe to match it up for you. The 'how' is not our job. The Universe does that for us. The 'what' is our job.

Many people get caught up in the how. How it will happen. How it is possible. We just have to focus on what we want, and the Universe will provide it for us if we believe and feel as though it's true. For example, there is an insect in your home. The insect can only see the floor it is on. However, you can see that the insect needs to go outside. You can see a different broader perspective. The Universe is like that. We can only see what is right in front of us, but the Universe sees a broader perspective. The physical action of you moving the insect from inside to outside is as effortless as the Universe bringing your soulmate from their country to yours. So trust that the Universe will figure out the 'how' for you and just focus on 'what' you want.

You are worthy beyond description. You are Source.

Your feelings are the most important thing. We come on this planet to have fun, to enjoy and live in joy. Once in this vibrational energy state of knowing, comfort and safety, life unfolds like magic! Be watchful of your feelings for they become thoughts, which in turn become words, actions and momentum!

Good ideas come to you when you are aligned and connected to Source. We are so used to the tangible to want to see it, hear it, smell it, taste it and touch it. However, manifestations first appear in the non-physical. Source knows where you stand in relationship to everything you want and knows many paths to get to where you want to be. For you to be aware of how far you are from your desire you need to be aware of your feelings, the better you feel, the higher your vibrational mindset, the more awareness you get of the path that is already there.

Ultimately the reason why we want anything in the first place is that we believe, in having it, we will feel better. So why not feel good now, and let all those desires which you have already asked for to come to you in time.

The better you feel, the better things will work out for you. Just feel good. Do things that feel good. I've been a victim of not doing this. I would say, 'I don't have time to have fun I have to work instead. I don't have time to meditate; I don't have time to go for a walk.' But the reality is that we don't have the time not to. There is leverage in alignment, meaning that being connected to Source is the best possible way to get the things you want. Always start the day feeling good. Whether that's by meditating, dancing or singing about all the things great about your life as you shower. Feeling good is the most important part and the whole point of life!

A good daily practice of mine is to make a consistent effort to think about things that feel good. Far too often society gets into this judgemental, negative, critical mode, where people congregate to have a good old go at all things they dislike and all the negative stories they have heard. Whether this is about health, wealth, world affairs, local affairs or scandals. This kind of behaviour limits you. It literally traps you into a prison or cage where only impurities and negativities manifest. The unconscious mind is like an empty canvass, as you speak or think, those things are imprinted on the canvas. At first, the depth and darkness of the imprint is light as a pencil, but the more you keep beating the drum of what you don't want and what you don't like, the deeper and darker the imprint becomes. As you think negative thoughts, you attract more of the same.

So tell the story you want to tell. When asked by someone about your current situation, always reminisce on the wonderful future that is coming to you and not the bad past or current hardships you face. Smile and focus on all the exciting opportunities you have or want as though they are already coming towards you. You are the master of your story. Victim or Success? You decide. Meditation can help you halt your negative mind and thus prevent further negative manifestations. When you meditate, you stop all thoughts, which also means you stop all resistance thoughts, and therefore you are connected and allow that what you want, to come to you.

Expectation = desire + belief.

The Universe does not care about what you say. It cares about your feelings which reflect the vibration you hold. Most of the time your words represent the feeling you are experiencing. Affirmations are a wonderful thing to do. Declaring aloud and to yourself that you are 'an amazing bolt of light' is uplifting and energising. However, we need to be careful. When doing affirmations, the reason why they don't always work is because we are pretending to feel a certain way. If you are saying you are happy when you actually feel sad, the positive affirmation becomes worthless. Declaring that 'I feel good' or 'I am loved' is great but the important thing is to feel good whilst saying them. The Universe does not hear what you are saying rather; it hears what you feel. So if you feel weak, and you proclaim you are strong, the Universe responds with weakness. No matter how loud you speak, the Universe hears what you are feeling every time. There is no good in trying too hard. You need to feel the emotion you declare. So feel good and then do affirmations.

When bad things happen, it is actually a good thing. The contrast of not getting what you want forces you to ask for a better alternative. All the crap that happens to you in life actually helps you to firm up and know what you actually do want. You can't spend it, sleep with it or have fun with it yet. You still have to prepare for it to come. The Universe is, in fact, protecting you and re-directing you down the path that has the least resistance and most ease for you. We don't have foresight and thus can never know what will happen. But if we expect the best, the best will surely manifest. So regardless if you are in a shitty situation right now, if you think the best, it will all work out for you.

Things you set your mind to are more likely to occur. A positive expectation will have a higher chance of a positive outcome.

Resistance and doubt are manifestations of your self-disbelief. When faced with them, correct your thoughts and feelings and reaffirm what you want as though you believe it is possible. It's not about trying to change old beliefs because every time you look at negative beliefs, they don't change but get stronger. Your intention has to go onto the beliefs that you actually want. So focus on what you want and believe it is possible!

YOU WANT TO MANIFEST MORE MONEY?

Earlier I spoke about manifesting more financial abundance into your life. To do this, you have to get into the alignment of abundance. Even if you live in poor housing on welfare, you have to maintain an abundant mindset. Focus on all the areas of your life where there is abundance and the feeling of the abundance that you want will manifest in your coming future. Check out the

Action Sheet at the end of this chapter for a game you can play to exercise your abundance muscles.

However, it is important to remember that the Universe manifests abundance in different ways. You can have abundance in love, friends, health, finances or having your dreams manifest at will. Thus try not to get caught up on just receiving abundance from the Universe in one manner or the other. Keep your mind open to all the other possibilities of abundance. For abundance in good health is more important than a few extra coins in your pocket. Even if you are in abject poverty, abundance can come in the form of shelter, food or a kind gesture from a passerby. When we pick up cues from the Universe more of what we want will flow easily into our lives.

You are infinite Source energy, pure, loving and kind.

There are all sorts of people in the world. But you attracted them to yourself in the first place. It is easy to say clean yourself up energetically by returning to positive thoughts, however, when caught up in negativity it can be difficult. Therefore a good coping technique for those unbalanced times would be either to change the subject that is causing you pain, breathe and let it go or to move away from the situation/person altogether. Accept that right now this is what is and all you can do is manage your response.

There will, of course, be rejections, disappointments, failures and misgivings in life and they happen due to personal misalignment with Source. You can't expect to be connected to Source, 100% of the time. Forgive yourself for these times and refuse to be rattled.

HOW DO YOU ASK THE UNIVERSE FOR CHANGE, ESPECIALLY FOR THE LGBTI MOVEMENT?

Every day I receive many emails, comments and messages on my social media. Most of the emails are based on fear. Fear of coming out, fear of family and fear of society. As you fear, so you manifest. The thoughts, feelings and vibrations you echo literally carve out your reality. Turn this around. Base your life on love and trust. Think thoughts of love. Imagine the best possible scenarios. And you will see, the Universe sculpts exactly that kind of life for you.

Let me give you an example. When you see injustice in the world, your inner being asks for something that feels better- justice. However, when we expect others to mirror this justice and they don't, we hold ourselves apart from the very change we want. We are pushing against this resistance. This way change happens very slowly, when the resistant ones die, and non-resistant ones come forward.

A better way would be to see the injustice, desire it to be different and live as though it's different.

Because every time you look back at what is, you defy your own dream, tear yourself apart from it and blame those who do not act as though you want them. So instead look at that dream, live it, be it. Don't look for evidence that proves against it. Don't use contrary evidence to split yourself from your vision. Behave, speak and act as though your family, the community, and country you live in already has LGBTI rights.

By doing this, not only will you manifest the type of future you want: one where there are LGBTI rights for all but also you line up to those who think the same way as you do. You release resistance to what is, the negativity that surrounds you and attract those who share the same vision as you. As you feel, think, speak and act out of your dream, as though it is already in existence you have far greater chance of manifesting it in your lifetime. We live in parallel Universes, where each person is living life according to the way they see the world around them. Those who think good thoughts and feel great about their current reality live wonderful lives. They are not burying their head in the sand; they are simply vibrating at a high level with others who live their vision. You see in life; there are all sorts of people. Liberal, accepting, loving folks and those who are not that way inclined. I know the kind I would rather share a dinner table with. It's not about converting people to your message, but it is a simple case of living your message. Eventually, through time the leverage will come in your favour and the masses will either succumb through legislation, protests or simple realisation that we are all one, and thus all of us deserve the same rights.

Everything with Ease.

Once you can grasp this concept, which you can understand further by checking out Abraham Hicks on YouTube, you will understand how important it is to feel good. Abraham Hicks explain exactly why things happen, why you attract them into your life and how your feelings and thoughts literally carve out and manifest your future.

That's why if you want a loving, peaceful and happy life, it's in your best interest to feel that way as often as possible. You need to raise your vibration. To raise one's vibration means that one is in a higher frequency of love, joy, or abundance and thus in alignment with whatever we want to attract. By simply changing your perspective when you feel bad to feeling good easily remedies this.

'Keep your thoughts positive because your thoughts become your words.
Keep your words positive because your words become your behaviour.
Keep your behaviour positive because your behaviour becomes your habits.
Keep your habits positive because your habits become your values.
Keep your values positive because your values become your destiny.'
Mahatma Gandhi

Historically the Universe was designed differently. Our collective consciousness would instantly manifest in the physical reality. The Vedas (Hindu religious texts) speak of pious people who lived for hundreds of years, very similarly to Atlantean times (Atlanteans are believed to have been a highly spiritually advanced race that lived on Atlantis). People would simply think a thought and manifest it. But the problem was as people became less pious, they would think negative thoughts and manifest them straight away. When in the vicinity of powerlessness they would manifest powerless thoughts. If afraid of dying, they manifested death immediately. If afraid their child would fall down the stairs, their child instantly did. That is why the current matrix of this holographic Universe allows for a buffer time, whereby you have to think a thought for a prolonged time before it manifests in our reality. Science is toying with the idea that the Universe is indeed a hologram and spirituality states that our current perception determines what version of this hologram we experience which is referred to as different spiritual dimensions or realms (more in Chapter 13). Indeed if you are seriously interested in spirituality, then watch out for my subsequent books that will focus on Indian, African and South American indigenous and tribal spiritualties. Otherwise, if you're a novice, and you only care about coming out and having a good life just ignore this. Only take from this book what makes sense for you. Adapt it to your own thinking and be very critical.

Now share the message below. Facebook, Tweet, Pin, Instagram, and Email the powerful lesson that the Law of Attraction teaches us.

Bollywood Gay Message #3:
I attract everything into my life.
#BollywoodGay

Action Sheet 3: How Have You Attracted Your Current Situation?

What is your current situation with your **family**, **friends**, **career**, **relationship**, **health** and **finances**?

_____

_____

_____

How do you think you **attracted** these into your life? List both the **negative** and **positive** mental attributes that contributed to their manifestation?

_____

_____

_____

_____

Do you generally live in the **moment**, are **positive** and **upbeat**?

_____

_____

What is the overall **habit pattern** of your mind? Are you a **worrier** or a **relaxed** person?

_____

_____

What's your **coping strategy** when things go wrong?

_____

_____

_____

How would you like to **feel**?

_____

_____

What **goals** or **desires** would you like to manifest in the next **three**, **six** and **twelve** months of your life? Relationship, career, money, etc.?

_____

_____

_____

_____

_____

_____

Imagine that you already have **accomplished** these. How do you **feel** now that you have **achieved** them?

_____

_____

How do you **envision** yourself in the **future**? What kind of person do you want to become?

_____

_____

_____

What **negative** habit patterns would you like to **release**?

_____

_____

What **positive** emotions would you like to **encompass**?

_____

_____

What makes you **happy**, **act silly** and have **fun**?

_____

_____

_____

Do you have a **regular spiritual** or **religious practice** or anything that brings you joy such as a specific dance workout, health regime or routine?

_____

_____

What is **positive** in your life **right now**? What can you be **grateful** and **appreciative** for?

_____

_____

_____

GAME: _Imagine that you live in a social housing scheme. Compare your life to someone who lives in abject poverty in sub-Saharan Africa. Would they be happy to live in your apartment? List the things in your home that they would be grateful to have in theirs such as running water, gas, a bed to sleep in, heating, etc._

_____

_____

_____

_____

_____

PART 2: LGBTI EXPLAINED

'Everything is a direct reflection of you.'

4) BEING GAY & SOUTH ASIAN

'Great freedom and relief come in accepting oneself and living in accordance to one's dreams.'

Being gay and South Asian is not something that is talked about in the Asian community. Asian families, due to culture can be less accepting of homosexuality, as they don't see it as normal. People are born into a tradition, which is bound by honour, submission and cultural norms.

For instance, the Punjabi culture is very heteronormative (the assumption that heterosexuality is the norm). The gender norms dictate that men should be masculine and women feminine without much room for anything else. I used to feel like an outsider at family events all the time; I still do, but not as much. Weddings were and can still be painful experiences for me. Aunties and uncles asking about my marriage and boys doing the Punjabi bhangra dance acting macho and manly. I would feel uncomfortable dancing with everyone watching, especially with the film crew around. Now, I realise that most people feel like outsiders at these events. Insecurities and jealousy are all too common with everyone trying to prove their self-worth and gain validation from the rest. Exhausting. That is why I choose whether I will go to these events or not.

I am afraid of being disowned.

It is understandable then that most of my clients if not all, are bound by fear. It imprisons them. They negatively think of the outcome they do not want. I hear these words regularly, 'My parents will disown me, there is no life being gay, I will be alone forever.' If you also think like this, you are more likely to manifest it into your life because what you focus on becomes. Whatever you have in your periphery vision multiplies. This leads to unnecessary worry, tension, depression or worse. I always ask my clients to focus on the present moment where they are. To know they are safe and loved. In this minute they are speaking to me, and trying to work on themselves, just as you are reading this book, means they are on the right path. The path to being a better version of themselves. I encourage them to visualise and feel how they would like their life to be in the next couple of months or years. The sights, smells, sounds, tastes and feelings. I want them to dream the best life possible and imagine it is coming to them, if not already here. The way the Law of Attraction works is quite simple. We are frequencies of energy. As we tune our frequency to another dial, just like a radio station, what we bring into our life is matched to that frequency. Thus thinking in a positive manner not only removes tonnes of fear from your shoulders but also relaxes you into the infinite possibilities of the Universe. I imagine it like a person wearing a hoodie looking down at the dark street in front of them unable to see what is around them, to the person without a hoodie looking straight ahead confidently able to see what possibilities surrounds them. We are but energy after all.

CAN I BE STRAIGHT?

Some of my clients ask me if I can make them straight. To which I reply no. Sexuality can be fluid like a scale and may evolve through time. But if you are purposely trying to change your sexuality to gain validation or acceptance, it just won't happen. When we reject aspects of our self, we are not truly connected to our higher self. In the state of total alignment to Source, we are happy and content. We accept all aspects of ourselves and do not want to become anything else. When we are at this stage, we have no need to change who we are for we accept ourselves fully. We realise the benefits of being who we are and the lesson(s) we have come to learn to expand our consciousness. Then, only if in this state of total alignment with Source, our sexuality changes, it does. But we cannot force it to do so.

Life can be harder for Asian LGBTI females. As women, their freedom can be restricted. They may not be allowed out of the house late. They have to be careful of being seen in certain places in fear someone they know may inform their family. We have to realise gender suppression exists, especially in South Asian families. Fathers and brothers can be overbearing to women, with mothers being even worse. Women may have to get married at an earlier age without having the choice for higher education.

If you are transgender, you may feel like you cannot express yourself at all. You may fear being misunderstood or seen as a spectacle. In India, the transgender or Hijra community as they are known are tolerated to an extent. However, people are scared believing they will be cursed if they do not give them money when they do their infamous tali (clap). In the Pakistani culture Mujra dance (a form of dance originated by courtesans in the Mughal era) does hold space for transgender people. However, here too they are seen as objects of desire and used for the sexual gratification of so-called heterosexual men.

DO SURVIVORS OF SEXUAL ABUSE ATTRACT IT?

Being in tight-knit extended families also gives rise to the probability of sexual abuse. It is quite common for some LGBTI to experience rape as a child in the hands of uncles and male cousins. It happens in Asian families but is rarely spoken about. People don't speak about these things as it is considered 'besti' (shame) and no real attempt is made to understand why this happens.

Abraham Hicks, the masters of the Law of Attraction, say we attract sexual abuse, not because we want it but because we are a vibrational match to it. They say it could happen because the environment we live in and the energy around us is so chaotic, filled with abuse, low vibe energy, brokenness and lack of self-love that we literally absorb that into our consciousness. We tell ourselves that we too are broken and attract similar people.

To combat this, we need to make sure that our families are vibrating at the highest vibration possible. Only when we see each other as pure Source energy, can we treat one another with utter most respect and dignity. When we lose our connection to who we really are, we don't see others or ourselves as whole.

From a spiritual perspective, as awful as it is, it can be said that survivors of sexual abuse choose to experience it as a life lesson. A traumatic thing such as this can crack open one's ego quicker and allow them to connect to Source much faster. It can allow greater spiritual expansion, allow a person to know what they do actually what from their life, grow and gain wisdom.

It may happen to gay people, due to the lack of comfort they feel from a male figure. They may seek comfort and acceptance in a man. Gay people are more vulnerable and may give off the vibe of vulnerability that others can pick up on. It could be a desire for love or connection and not to do with sex at all. Regardless of why it happens, we must remember that our first sexual experience is meant to be special. Your entire life can be affected due to sexual abuse. You may get flashbacks and suicidal tendencies blaming yourself and questioning 'Why did it happen to me?' I want to make it clear, I'm not saying you attracted your abuser, and therefore it is your fault. No, I am saying that there may be reasons as to why it happened, and let's get to the root of it so we can pluck it out and allow you to heal.

Most people feel uncomfortable talking about this subject. They rather just put the perpetrators in the bad people pile and forget about them. Lock away the key and not try to understand why it happens. Declaring 'I'm more comfortable hating you'. But as you do this, you are not connected to Source. The Source within you does not hate them. God is not a vengeful God. Source is love. Stories of condemnation may feel better than stories of forgiveness and understanding. However, these people are no different from us. They are Source energy but misaligned. They are vulnerable seeking the same love and acceptance we all are. Perhaps they haven't had the same comfort from their families or partner. Maybe they see themselves in the child, the vulnerability or wanting to be loved and cared for by someone. Whatever the reason we can improve the situation by providing help and support for perspective perpetrators. They need to be able to go to the doctor and discuss the root causes why this happens without fear of imprisonment. Everyone deserves compassion. We need to talk about this topic openly. If we have support groups, there would be less chance of it happening full stop. Let's remove the stigma from this topic both for the survivor and the perpetrator.

The reason why I write this is because of the deep self-loathing, hatred and shame LGBTI people feel towards their sexual abuse. I want you to rid yourself of this pain, which causes illness within you and prevents you from living your beautiful life. Perhaps through understanding a different perspective you can forgive the perpetrator, not because you are doing them a favour, but because you are releasing the pain from yourself. (More on forgiveness in Chapter 13).

We attract our parents.

From an energetic level before we incarnated in this physical form we attracted our parents because their energy matched our own. Their energy is perfect for our development. The Tibetan Book of Living and Dying talks about our soul as a light of energy. We literally gravitate towards parents who match our internal energy. The karma we have accumulated and the life lessons we have chosen are all in the home we selected before birth. So remove the resentment you have towards your parents.

Bless your parents for they only want what's best for you. They come from backgrounds of poverty consciousness, lack and fear. They react with control and anger. They try to dictate what you are doing and how you should be doing it. They want to know where you go, who with and why you are back so late. This is very typical South Asian diaspora antics. Indeed back in India, especially in the major cities friends of mine (typically male, but also female) have much more freedom than we do.

Asian parents also love to compare. They repeatedly compare you to so and so's daughter or son who is doing this or has a certain well paid profession. Comparison is likened to suicide. If you are an insecure person, which most LGBTI children are, being compared to other relatives or friends can make you feel even worse about yourself. You may try to compete to get better grades, higher salaried careers or give up altogether. A great technique I have gathered over the years is to be happy for those who are doing well. When we praise others, we align to their successful energy, bringing more of that to us.

Added to this, growing up in a family environment means you absorb what is happening around you. The fears and pleasures of those in your home literally imprint in your subconscious mind. Issues and behavioural patterns may embed themselves inside of you, and only if you are aware can you come about changing them. (You can learn more about this in Chapter 11).

SO HOW CAN YOU IMPROVE YOUR FAMILY SITUATION?

Ultimately, anything that happens around us is a direct reflection of what is going on within us. Look within yourself to see where you are manifesting these issues. Always reflect on the question, 'How am I attracting this?' What limiting beliefs bring up these emotions from those around you? We have to bring peace within ourselves first before it can manifest around us.

Preaching to your parents won't help a bit. They will simply get annoyed. You have to be the light and shine brightly. We are vibrational beings, and as our vibration increases to love, joy, and happiness, our interaction with others improves. Your family will become nicer people. So act as though they already accept you. Think about the positive outcome and reaction you want from them. Try not to react from anger. Centre and balance yourself and then act from a place of deep kindness.

Don't use imagery from past experiences about your parents or extended family's reactions to scare you. Fear is false evidence appearing real. If you think your parents will act a certain way, you will certainly manifest that. No matter their past, you need to live in the present and not assume your parents will always react negatively. Imagine the best outcome possible. This is exactly how I managed to have an easy coming out process. I used to tell people years before I came out that my parents already knew and accepted me. If you feel this is too false for you to believe, then say, 'My parents are coming around to my way of thinking and allowing me the space to find my own life partner.'

Let's take this example:

'My mum always gets annoyed when I come home late. So she will get annoyed again.'

With reflection:
'I am annoyed at coming home late because my mum has in the past expressed this and thus I don't want to get told off.'

But the reality is:
'I have absorbed certain habit patterns, traits and ideas from those around me: parents, siblings, friends and larger society. This mixes with my own inner insecurity and negativity. I then self-project past events into the present thus manifesting the reaction from my mother once I return home.'

If we realised this and worked on our limiting beliefs, insecurities and released what society has fed us and stopped projecting the past and reliving it, we could be free of the bondages we tie ourselves in.

Accept yourself first. You need not tell others, but accept and love yourself fully. Rid yourself from the limited mindset from past experiences. Truth is in the moment, and it is created. Connect to your higher self and allow the unlimited possibilities of the Universe to come to you. Ask for guidance from above; ask your Angels, Guardians, Universe, Nature, God, Ascended Masters, Enlightened Beings, and Guides of the highest compassion and truth to help you. Keep reassuring yourself that you accept yourself first and are accepted by others too.

WHAT ABOUT MY SHAADI (MARRIAGE)?

One of the biggest barriers to coming out as a South Asian is marriage. Heterosexual marriage. Most Asian families expect marriage. Even before the conception of their child, parents conceptualise the marriage and life they want their child to have. It comes from both a place of love and fear. Love because they want us to have the best life possible and fear because it is out of control and angst over what society will say.

Arranged marriages or assisted/introduced marriages are the norm in our culture as opposed to love marriages. Thus the pressure for such a marriage can be devastating, especially if you are not used to speaking openly and honestly with your parents from a young age about your thoughts, ideas and aspirations. Particularly if you have been living with them all this while. It can be hard, and a lot of personal courage is needed. You may feel trapped and want to do what's best for your family's izzat (honour).

This causes huge problems for us in 2016, for LGBTI and straight people alike. We want to fall in love with the partner of our dreams and wishes- Bollywood style and not the type our parents seek. For LGBTI this poses added difficulties because we love someone of the same sex, which is considered taboo. We would, well most perhaps, be happy if our parents found LGBTI rishtey (wedding proposals) for us to ponder over.

Let me make this point clear; I am against any forced or pressured marriage. I don't mind introductions made by relatives, but ultimately we should have the choice to make our own mind. If you are in a dire life-threatening situation you need to call the authorities. There are plenty of avenues of support available in the East and West.

Marrying someone of the opposite sex if you are gay can be quite damaging. Firstly to yourself. If you marry them, you will be unhappy, and those around you will pick up that energy too. It will cause an air of resentment and ill will. Your poor wife or husband who had no knowledge of your homosexuality will not get the life they dreamt of either. They deserve to be with a partner who loves and adores them. A partner who above all else is honest. Imagine if you are unable to perform sexually. Your whole life is a lie. I receive phone calls from men, telling me of their sham marriages. The marriages they had to have to save face and family honour. This leads to resentment and depression. It's not the life you were meant to live. I even know of guys I dated in the past who have married women and are pretending to be heterosexual. Yes, friends from the East, this kind of stuff is rampant in the West. We don't seem to be living a free life here either. I've dated bisexual men, who say they will only marry women, to satisfy society but never inform them of their past. What kind of inauthentic life is this? In purdah (secrecy/hiding), shame and guilt ten fold. We place lie over a lie, hoping it will cover up our desire for a man when it only festers and becomes more of our misery.

SHOULD I HAVE A MARRIAGE OF CONVENIENCE INSTEAD?

Due to this many South Asian LGBTI have resorted to marriages of convenience, whereby a LGBTI person marries another of the opposite sex for the sake of the family. They have Facebook groups and chat rooms where they meet and without informing their families resort to planning sham marriages so to avoid the shame of coming out. I have my own views on this. Personally, I would never do it, as I believe it is not living an authentic life. For whenever your parents come to visit, you have to live a lie, perhaps you have to have children and attend family functions as a couple. Imagine then how difficult it would be to have a proper same sex relationship. For me it is messy. However, I understand why people resort to this.

The guilt and shame that comes with the realisation that we are gay and South Asian is overwhelming. We keep quiet about it, try to change ourselves and try to please our parents. Depression and suicidal tendencies can arise if we think we are bad or wrong, especially as we realise that we cannot change ourselves. Added to this, family pressure and shame can leave us helpless.

SO HOW DO I COME OUT?

Therefore coming out as LGBTI and Asian can be tough. Yet it is not impossible. We are the pioneers of our generation. We need to be well equipped and stable minded to deal with this important and serious situation. The first task is to deal with being gay yourself. Accept it yourself. This is easy to say but how do you actually do that? Self-acceptance means self-love. It means loving all those parts of yourself that you don't want to. Your flaws, your annoying habits, or those aspects about you that society ridicules or does not understand. This can be done in many ways. I lay them out in Action Sheet 9: How much do you love yourself? Feel free to do that in your own time!

I understand the pain of coming out and being authentic especially if you live in a small village in rural India, Pakistan or Bangladesh. I get regular calls from clients who are in remote villages in India who don't even have basic knowledge of what their sexuality is. It's neither taught in schools nor by parents. They are lost and confused. When I ask them to Google it if they have access to a computer, they say they are too scared even to do that. No one can force you to come out. I understand the strength and power needed to do this. For you may fear losing your parents, your dignity and maybe even your own life. This is no laughing matter. I understand. Let's be clear. The collective consciousness of the locale where you live is at a stage of purdah, control and fear. This needs to be overcome. The only way I can suggest is to focus on the good, and the outcome you want without ever looking back. Don't fear the outcome, but think of the possibilities. Of course, if you want to marry a girl and live an inauthentic life just to please your parents and society I understand. Perhaps your role in this life is to pave the way for your children to come out.

We should not judge you for that. It is a certain kind of soul mission to truly come out proud and be who you are. Think what is best for you in your current environment and situation. Become a tolerant person who is loving and kind. Stand up for the rights of those who are less fortunate than yourself and educate those around you on basic rights. You are the change and no matter what, you can make a positive impact even in your small isolated village. Think Malala Yousafzai, the brave girl who fought for her basic rights. You don't even have to be as proactive or in the firing line as her. Oh no! Just focusing on positive actions and words is enough.

Also, it is important for me to tell you that you have the option of applying for asylum. If the country you live in is persecutory towards LGBTI people, in its refusal to accept LGBTI rights through law, lack of police protection or is actively mistreating LGBTI then you may have a claim for refugee status. To do this, you have to leave your country and arrive at the next safe country and apply for asylum. You need to have extensive evidence showing that you are LGBTI even to be considered. The system is discriminatory, judgemental and flawed and requires those who are persecuted to fund themselves to get to a safe nation. But where there is a will there is a way. For instance, LGBTI organisations in your country or another country may be able to provide for safe passage abroad.

Yes, thoughts about your family, culture, religion and what people are going to say will come up and bring up fear and anxiety. But you must rise above this. It takes great struggle and pains to rise and accept who you really are, no matter what your sexuality. To live in accordance to your own inner happiness is a great joy compared to living to please others so they are happy. Once you get this, life flows naturally like a sweet stream. The light at the end of the tunnel shines brightly as you close in on it. Create the life you want and you will be happy. But you must work in accordance to the greater good within. Act from a place of love and embody peace. Only then will you repel the negative forces that surround you. Only then will it be possible to be yourself and not get abused for it. Only then will you attract like-minded, loving folk and all the positive forces of the Universe will guide your every step. I cannot stress this enough. You cannot simply come out and feel anger and aggression to those around you and expect to live a peaceful life. Chapter 11 explains this in greater detail.

It is important to remind you that you don't have to come out straight away. Maybe you need a get out plan. You may need some space and may decide to move out, or keep quiet whilst you work on yourself. This is absolutely fine and somewhat cautious. I would suggest making sure you are financially secure before you decide to come out to your parents. That way you can support yourself and live the life you were meant to whilst your parents get comfortable with the idea of the real you.

Being gay and South Asian can be a blessing in disguise.

Once out, you don't have to conform to South Asian ideals and marry someone of the same caste, religion or colour as your family. You can leave your home and live your life authentically. If you need, you can leave home before coming out to firm your own self-identity and confidence. See straight people are stuck in social conventions. They are not pushed enough to break through the moulds parents place upon them. Many get good grades, a career in what their parents would approve and prod along without questioning their existence or the meaning of life itself. This leads to later life resentment, which manifests in physical and mental illness. If you can't live your truth, you will experience 'dis-ease'. That is why it is imperative to live life for yourself; your health depends upon it. Then straight people will look up to you, for your boldness and vigour. They will be inspired and jealous that you are living your personal life path. So help them along the way too. You are the light, show the way.

It's time to Facebook, Tweet, Pin, Instagram, and Email the message below:

Bollywood Gay Message #4:
I am proud to be South Asian & LGBTI.
#BollywoodGay

Action Sheet 4: Lay Out Your Fears As A South Asian Gay Man

What **negative belief patterns** do you hold about being LGBTI and South Asian?

_____

_____

How does that **limit** you?

_____

_____

What **self-supporting** thoughts would you rather have?

_____

_____

How would you like to **feel** in **3**, **6**, **9**, **12** months time?

_____

_____

_____

How can you **change** your **thoughts/feelings** to achieve this?

_____

_____

_____

Thinking about the past causes depression, worrying about the future causes anxiety. Learn to live in the present moment. To do this a simple **breath meditation** 10 minutes a day can bring great relief to you. Focus on the natural inhale and exhale of your breath returning your focus to your breath every time your mind wanders. Be gentle on yourself and don't get annoyed if you fall off the horse. You may react in anger. This is normal. I do it too. I get annoyed and frustrated. To change our habit patterns takes time and patience. Practice, practice, practice.

Creating a **vision board** is one of the best ways to remind yourself what you want on a regular basis. So grab a piece of plain paper, a white board or some space on your computer. Stick on it all the good things that you want in your life in the next 1, 5, 10 years time and put it up somewhere you can see it on a daily basis. Think about what you want to achieve regarding how you want to feel by acquiring the desire as opposed to just the goal. For instance, I want to feel connected, free, abundant, creative and conscious, so the goals I want need to reflect those feelings. The feelings are the most important part of the process.

What would you ideal life look like? Can you **draw** it using **colourful pens** and **pencils**? (The therapeutic benefits of colouring are similar to meditation and very beneficial in alleviating depression and low mood. Plus it's fun).

'At your essence you are energy- neither created nor destroyed. You can call this energy the soul, spirit or consciousness. Regardless your essence is pure love energy. It has no religion. For it is universal. Non-sectarian. You are Love.'

5) RELIGION OF MAN VS. RELIGION OF THE SOUL

'Religions wrongly reduce sexuality to the physical. However, when people are attracted to each other, it is due to their vibrational energetic match. It has nothing to do with their male or female exterior. Quite simply it is a mutual exchange of energy that brings them together as one.'

It is interesting to note that throughout history the stance on LGBTI issues has evolved, regressed or even stagnated. In ancient Roman, Greek, Indian and Middle Eastern times, homosexuality was revered. But the modern day story is quite different. Throughout time religion has been used as a method to control people. Control their sexuality, reproduction, physical movements, economy and mind. It has helped a lot of people of course, but it has also been a great profit maker too.

From a spiritual perspective, religion is seen as an ideology that is stagnant and still. As humans, we are constantly growing and expanding. Our connection to that which we call God is unique, individual and evolving. Thus spiritually, religion is seen as a map, with directions on it to all those who want to follow it. A guide. However, a real connection to God is and always has been a personal one. Spirituality cultivates this unique connection without dogma or regulation. It simply states: make your own rules.

We tend to absorb the religion that we were born into and follow its customs accordingly. There is thus great danger in blind faith. We need to use our intellect and logic to deduce whether this particular religion indeed reflects the person who we are. Does it serve me? Have I read the sacred texts and understood them? Do I believe them? Has what's been written inside been written by the founder themselves? Does it embody sacred rights for all? Surely God is a loving being who values and includes all? Does it include women's rights? Homosexual rights? Animal rights? Does it need to? Is all life sacred to you? There is no right or wrong answer, and only you can decide.

Certain religious texts were written many hundreds or thousands of years after the founder died. So has interpretation gotten in the way? Has the word of mouth been distorted? Do people who follow this particular religion embody it? Are they peaceful and loving?

Religion is complex and personal to me. I say create your own religion with your own connection to God. Know what feels right and wrong for you. When you connect to higher forces, love should pour from you. Judgement and ego should dissolve. Religion, however, is not evil. It gives plenty of people hope, faith and compassion. Religion is not the problem; it's people who misuse it. So I won't discount the value of it. Use your own gut, your internal GPS system to know your truth.

I'm sure all of us are well aware that the Abrahamic religions Christianity, Islam and Judaism consider homosexuality a sin. Well, at least that is what the generalised interpreted standpoint is. There are however others who say that this is a misinterpretation of sources that are taken out of context. They say that in the story of Lot, God punishes villagers due to their criminality, rape and violence towards one another and the Angels as opposed to homosexuality itself (the villagers rape male or female alike, without prejudice as a form of control and suppression). Either way, I would not let it be a defining point for myself at least. You are free to choose your own stance. I am neither religious nor entrenched into views of sin, fear and proscriptions on what to or not to do. I believe in love and freedom for all.

Today some denominations within these religions accept homosexuality and are inclusive of homosexual people. Some even welcome members regardless of same-sex sexual practices, allowing for the ordination of LGBTI clerics/rabbis, and affirmation of same-sex unions. They generally claim that people who are attracted to the same sex are acceptable, but the act of anal sex is not.

Indian religions like Hinduism, Buddhism, Jainism and Sikhism, however, do not specifically focus on sexuality; though there are strong historical references that homosexuality existed at the time of their compilation. These religions tend to be more fluid, open or unclear with regards to sexual orientation. The texts in which they are expressed are generally more tolerant or based on compassion, love and acceptance for all. They do not specify homosexuality as a sin. Although modern day culture, in reality, is less accepting.

In the past, Hindus were more open to variations in human sexuality than they are at present. Historically, Hinduism accommodated, institutionalised, or revered, same-sex love and sexuality as witnessed in its mythologies and religious imagery.

In some Hindu sects (especially among the hijra population), many divinities are androgynous. There are Hindu deities who are intersex, who manifest in all three genders or who switch from one gender to the next. There are also deities born from two males, two females, a single male or a single female. Deities who avoid the opposite sex or who partner with the same sex are also mentioned in Hindu mythology. Although, a majority of Hindus do not accept this and consider it heretical in nature. The ones who do accept it proclaim that for humans to grasp the diverse qualities of both God and nature is near impossible.

Many Hindu priests have performed same-sex marriages, arguing that marriage is a union of souls rather than gender and that love is the result of attachments from previous births. In 2009, the Hindu Council UK became one of the first major religious organisations to support LGBTI rights when they issued a statement **'Hinduism does not condemn homosexuality'**.

There is nothing stated against homosexuality in Sikhism. Indeed the Anand Karaj (marriage ceremony) states:

'The two female souls unite with the one male soul of the Lord.'

Thus you can even say that the scriptures advocate lesbian marriage. However, as we are well aware the soul in Sikhism is genderless, and thus this is only metaphorically written.

Sikhism stresses the importance of living a good life and passing good values onto one's children. Having children if you are physically able is considered a good thing. Of course, gay couples can adopt or have their own kids in different ways. However, the Akal Takht (Sikh governing body) has constructed one Rehat Maryada (Sikh Code of Conduct) which states that marriage is only between a man and a woman. Throughout time there had been many Rehat Maryada. However, unfortunately, the Akal Takht has described homosexuality as **'against the Sikh religion and the Sikh code of conduct and totally against the laws of nature,'** and called on Sikhs to support laws against gay marriage. It has to be noted that the Akhal Takht is made up of men, and always has been. No women, no one with different abilities, sexualities, or castes has ever been represented within it. Thus these men of power use philosophical reasoning to deduce the meaning of the Gurbani (Sikh Guru's words). Recently the Akal Takht has been in the firing line for its corruption and thus the sacrality and legitimacy in its rulings are questionable.

'Anyone who is angry in their religion is not living it.'

Through time, culture evolves; ways of living and thinking evolve too leading us to assume that religion would evolve alongside with it. However, this has not been the case for most world religions.

According to New Age spirituality, many decisions made by religious organisations were not inspired by Source; they were motivated by economic reasons, biases or opinions. The way to know if something is inspired by Source (God) is to see how it feels to you. If something feels bad, you can deduce that it Source did not inspire it. So when religious people tell you, you are wrong, a sinner or will go to hell, that bad feeling you experience helps you to deduce they are disconnected to Source. Source does not hate, judge or prejudge. Source is loving and pure. What happens in most world religions is that people who have not experienced God themselves reiterate the subjective Godly experience of another from the texts they read out to you. This is a greatly flawed premise because truth is subjective and when expressed to others is prone to distortion and misinterpretation.

'If you are trying to guide yourself with one piece of information, find what's right for you and live it, and the Law of Attraction will bring you the same.' Abraham Hicks

When someone tells you they know what is right, and you don't it means they are not connected to Source. Thinking there is a God with a final correct conclusion about everything is a flawed premise. Source is always expanding, evolving and does not have rules. When man is guarded or blameful, he is not connected to God energy. He simply bends the value of God according to his own needs. It is false to believe that there are absolute right or wrongs and by forcing people to do them we will have harmony on earth. People die to prove the right way of living saying they have approval from God. This is not the true definition of God. This life is full of variety, and it brings forth new ideas. To say only the founder of our religion can receive the right message from God and all other messages from other groups are false is incorrect.

Over time people modify religion to serve their own purposes. Copies of religious texts have been edited and re-translated many times. The integral basis and power are glossed over in the hundred re-translations. Money, power and control are behind this.

Unworthiness due to lack of connection to Source is the root of the issue with sexuality.

As children, we meet adults who are not connected with their own value or worthiness. From this lack, they pass their fears on to us. The subject of sexuality has changed countless times with the passing of new laws trying to control people and make them conform. They differ from cultures to society and religion. Sexual laws and rules have been made by those who are out of alignment with who they are. We are all vibrational beings and the Law of Attraction only brings us that which we are vibrationally a match to. We should not care what others do but should focus on our own connection to Source. Then we wouldn't fear the negative impact of other people's behaviour. But due to our ignorance and fear of what might come, we create laws that bring exactly that which we don't want towards us.

It is, of course, the case that those topics we push against are more likely to occur with vehemence. The topic of sexuality is the same. It is religious organisations that have pushed against sexuality the most and thus it is ironic that sex and sexuality are topics most prevalent in religious houses.

'Religion is belief in someone else's experience. Spirituality is having your own experience.' Deepak Chopra

Anyway, I believe in a spiritual perspective. We are who we are, and we need to accept that. There is divine order and reasoning behind this. Homosexuality has existed and always will exist in all species on this planet. The spirit itself is genderless and sexless. It neither craves nor needs love, affection, connection, or union to another, for it already understands its wholeness and interconnected nature.

Currently, we view God from our third dimension of consciousness, whereas God is a multi-dimension phenomenon. We make God into a 'he' whereas God is so much more. In spiritual terms and Indian religious terms, we are all God energy. All that is, is part of God consciousness, neither separate nor different. Therefore instead of conceptualising what God is, it is best to experience who God is. Talking about it simply theorises it.

There are no requirements for Source to appreciate you; for Source loves unconditionally. We are all extensions of Source and no matter how much you withhold yourself, what rules and regulations you follow, Source loves you regardless. Whether you fall in love with someone of the same gender, a different caste or whether you choose to fast, God loves you.

If religion holds the standpoint that being gay is wrong, then God really screwed up. It is a fear-based mechanism when we are told we are being strayed when we deviate from the supposed norm. Do not let others, who come in crowds dictating that what you feel is wrong to overcome you. Your life experience is what matters the most, if something feels right for you go with that.

SHOULD YOU GO AGAINST RELIGION?

By shouting no at a religion will cause resistance within you, stopping you from your own connection to God. Thus don't make going against a religion a life changing issue. By giving up resistance to religion, you will feel better as you have come into alignment with who you are. Religious people haven't changed their stance and nor have you. For the most part, religions are looking at conditions and needing to control those conditions to feel good. However, you cannot control conditions, and it's not your job to do so, as it will make you miserable. Identify your personal relationship with Source (which all religions talk about), and recognise the thoughts which have alignment within you and make you feel better. You have a right to choose for yourself what is of value for you and what is not. It's your God-given right to reason and expand your thinking. Look for the guidance within you and what feels right. If you look outward to gain guidance, with guidelines that have nothing to do with you, in a time different from yours, the guidance will be very different to the one you need. Saying that, nothing is wrong with the world's religions. Plenty of people are happy with them and have found what's works for them. Thus there is no need to have a crusade against anyone, as it pushes against your own happiness.

Instead, pick what works for you. Take aspects from religion and spirituality, which serve you. Evolve with it. Create your own inner religion. Not a sect or dogma, but your own values. Pick what is right for you now and let the next step come. You don't need to close the door to religion altogether. Some religions proclaim everything you are searching for is here. But everything that is created has to grow and expand. You are an eternal being; the Source you are reaching for is always accessible to you. Source does not reside within a religion. It resides within universal sources. Live your alignment without preaching to others, without telling them you found a better way. Let them be happy, and you be happy in your own inner knowing.

Think about all the bad that has come about from religion. Yes, of course, the faith and hope given to millions/billions is second to none. However, the incarnation of the likes of Jesus has created more war than anything. This was not the intention with which enlightened beings came. Humankind has twisted and used their ego to subjugate one another. Therefore the aim is not to create a new religion, new sect or new ideology. We are all in a new age of humanity; some call it the Age of Aquarius, the Age of Knowledge, the New World, the 5th Dimension, and some call it total chaos. Everyone in the Age of Aquarius, as we approach Sat yog (Age of Truth- Ancient Indian theology), need to become their own gurus. It is time to think what is best for you and to do that without harming others. Be kind, compassionate and loving, and forgive. (More details about eastern and western spirituality will be available in subsequent books. There is far too much content to put in one book ☺).

There is value in every religion. I do not condemn any of them. But reason and think for yourself. If you feel uncomfortable with something, you cannot fake it. You cannot say I will feel uncomfortable so that you feel comfortable. Deep down that vibration will resonate. Your inner guidance system always knows what feels right for you. The scanty guidance you get from one religious text compared to your infinite inner guidance is incomparable. Most texts were interpretations of the person who wrote them, whilst they were in alignment with Source (or not) according to their own life. You have your own unique interpretation. Activate the awareness of who you are and turn to who you want to be. Most religions don't want you to know how to guide your life. They decide that someone else has made the rules already. They become frustrated because of it. Life causes them to expand, and they don't go, and they condemn those who do.

Create your own private personal religion. A religion between you and your creator. A religion where you make the rules that can change according to your inner guidance system. Follow your gut instincts and listen to how you feel. What does Source mean for you? Love? How would you be treated by soul creation? What new beliefs would you like to add and which would you rapidly remove? The religion of the soul is one of peace, love and acceptance of all. I'm not saying gain a following; I'm merely saying gain a personal understanding with yourself and that which is God.

Show the world how you like to pray. Preach oneness, love and compassion for all. Get Facebooking, Tweeting, Pinning, Instagramming, and Emailing:

Bollywood Gay Message #5:
I create my own religion. A religion of love.
#BollywoodGay

Action Sheet 5: What's Your Belief?

What **religious beliefs** were you **brought** up in if any?

_____

_____

_____

Do you go to a religious place of worship? If so how do you **feel** once there?

_____

_____

_____

What beliefs would you like to **let go** of that no longer serve you?

_____

_____

_____

What beliefs about your religion do you **treasure** and would love to cultivate further?

_____

_____

_____

How can you incorporate these into your **day-to-day** life?

_____

_____

_____

What does your **inner guidance system** tell you about yourself and your sexuality?

_____

_____

_____

_____

If you could create your **own personal religion** what would it look like?

_____

_____

_____

_____

_____

'Choosing to date someone due to their sexual position in bed or mannerisms is both disrespectful to yourself and the other, but also limits the beauty of humankind itself. We are beyond this physical body, and we are always evolving. Open yourselves to the infinite possibilities of the Universe, and you shall reap the benefits.'

6) ARE YOU TOP, BOTTOM OR VERSATILE?

'We are spiritual beings and not just flesh defined by our sexual positions in bed.'

Many gay men define themselves very openly as either top, bottom or versatile. But what do these terms mean? A top is someone who plays the penetrative role in sexual activity and is generally considered masculine or the man in the relationship. A bottom is someone who receives penetration and is often considered feminine or the woman in the relationship (though there are masculine bottoms and feminine tops). Versatile men engage in both activities or are open to engaging in either activity and can play both masculine and feminine characteristics. There are also those men who prefer just to kiss, hug and engage in oral sex, rimming, mutual masturbation and rubbing on each other. These men enjoy other sexual practices apart from anal penetration of any kind. They might have experimented with it before deciding it was not for them. Some may even enjoy receiving or giving anal stimulation with a finger, but nothing beyond that.

Defining yourself as either top, bottom or versatile not only objectifies, falsifies and undermines your self-worth but also categorises you into a box. These categories then narrow your dating pool and stop you from challenging societal norms and prejudices. Added to this you are less likely to be open to prospective partners, experiences and growth. Imagine for a second, if the man of your dreams was a top or bottom just like you, would your narrow mindedness stop you from dating them? Furthermore, if you have never topped or bottomed how do you know you won't enjoy it? Is anal sex the be-all and end-all of a relationship or can you engage in other sexual activities with your partner instead? Finally, if you have never topped or bottomed how are you able to be good at it in the first place? A good top understands the pains and pleasures of being a bottom. A good bottom understands the tactfulness of a top. Bottoms take time and preparation to be ready for a top. They may have to make sure they are clean and fresh, be watchful of what they eat and sometimes douche. Tops have to be considerate to use enough lube, ease their way in and allow the bottom to relax. What I am saying is this; we should not be so rigid in our sexual preferences of what position we like to be in bed. Of course, you can decide whatever you like, but at least let's not ridicule those who are different from us.

On online dating platforms, one of the first things gay men do is to declare whether they are top, bottom or versatile. Men literally use a drop box to select the kind of man they want according to their sexual positioning in bed. But advertising yourself on sexual terms is not seeing yourself as a whole being. It's a reductive not an expansive view of oneself. Sex is evolutionary, and you are evolving each day. If we are too stuck in these stereotypes and box ourselves down, we will always fall down to discrimination. When we declare ourselves as top, bottom or versatile, we limit ourselves. Is this actually how we feel sexually? Or are we too afraid to be the diversified being we are meant to be? Does societal guilt and shame get you down? Or does the fear of one or two attempts to bottom stop you in your tracks? I understand if being a top is what you prefer. But a top cannot be a top without their being a bottom. Also most tops I meet, would love to bottom but due to societal shame with anal sex, and the difficulties in trying it they abandon it altogether.

INTERNALISED HOMOPHOBIA?

Studies show that tops are more likely than both bottoms and versatiles to reject a gay self-identity and to have had sex with a woman in the past three months. They also had higher rates of internalised homophobia, displaying self-loathing to their homosexual desires. Versatiles seem to enjoy better psychological health. This may be due to their greater sexual sensation seeking and greater comfort with a variety of roles and activities.

Being a top is generally revered in the gay scene.

Many tops and bottoms ridicule or put down other bottoms as though they are less than tops. Tops are seen as better as they are more masculine and fit well into gender norms of society. The feminine characteristics of bottoms are laughed at when someone acts out in a flamboyant manner declaring, 'He's such a bottom'. No fun of tops is however made. So many times I've heard bottoms complain about the lack of tops available declaring 'this town is just full of bottoms'. This is nonsense as studies show the distribution is pretty much equal. You attract what you are; you see what you want to, and you amplify what you put attention to. So if you search for bottoms, you will find them.

Just because someone is a twink or feminine, does not automatically mean they bottom. Likewise just because someone is a jock and masculine, does not mean they top. Open yourself up to the unlimited possibilities out there. When we go to bars, or clubs or even just out to a social group, when we are attracted to a guy we are attracted to him. We don't go up to him and put our hands down his pants to see how big he is or ask him straight up, 'hey are you a bottom?' Well, at least I do not. I think its offensive and de-humanising. Also when gay people ask one another 'who's the top and who's the bottom' it's almost as bad as when straight people ask so 'who's the woman in the relationship'. As LGBTI people we are beyond gender stereotypes, and we are here to open the mind of this planet's consciousness as to what is normal. We need to let go of limited heterosexual ideas of gender roles and instead create our own expansive expression of what sex and gender means to us.

I've met quite a few men, who call themselves muscle Mary's. They were feminine men who forced themselves to be masculine through steroids and gym addiction just to get laid, fit in or prove a point. I understand the difficulties being a feminine gay guy in the Western world poses. In a society where masculinity is revered feminine men may be forced to take measures to protect themselves from being beaten up at school or ridiculed in the street. I understand the need for self-defense. But let's accept who we are and be authentic, or at least be kind to those who are brave enough to be themselves, than being jealous and nasty to them. Let's support one another and change societal expectations and stereotypes of us.

The current hierarchy of revering tops and ridiculing bottoms exists due to our own self-loathing. In a community that idolises masculinity being a top is more macho, less feminine and thus less gay. The gay world seems to be obsessed with being masculine. Indeed on most sites, adverts from prospective partners explain that they are looking for muscular, masculine, straight acting guys. There is such shame in being feminine, which relates back to the supposed emasculation we felt as boys growing up gay. We felt like what was feminine was alien to us, and we should hide that and be more manly. The reason for such complexities within the gay scene is due to the obsession for men to be masculine. The commodification of gay men into stereotyping them is the root cause of shame.

It stems from childhood when our fathers would tell us 'boys don't cry'. We were repeatedly told by our mothers, teachers and friends, 'To man up, butch up and stop being a sissy'. We tried to fit in by playing manly sports like baseball, cricket or football and not hanging out with girls. There is undue pressure on boys to be masculine in our society today. Thankfully some fathers are doing away with these norms. I recently saw a video of a father allowing his son to buy a Barbie in a store because he wanted it or another father making a toy kitchen for his son to cook in. It is time to challenge and change these stereotypes for it is killing our society. The pressure to be a man, whatever that is, is insurmountable. We need to remove this insecurity about our masculinity and self-hatred of being gay. Real men and people celebrate who they are and accept the fullness of their sexuality.

STRAIGHT ACTING?

What does that even mean? That you're pretending to act straight, you are masculine, or you are in the closet? Saying you are straight acting online or in real life is not only disrespectful to yourself, and denies your homosexual characteristics but is also hateful towards feminine guys. Straight acting is not only homophobia it's misogyny devouring anything that is feminine. It's an unrealistic fetishisation. It also happens in South Asia where men who have sex with men as tops, proclaim they are straight, as they have not had receptive anal sex.

'If I wanted to date a girl, I would.'

All too many times I have heard guys talk discouragingly about dating feminine guys, proclaiming,

'If I wanted to date a girl, I would.' Again this is internalised homophobia at its worst, and I would advise feminine men not to waste their time and energy on men who don't want them. There are plenty of men who do want effeminate men, and I guarantee you effeminate men still have sex.

It is important not to get triggered by the fear of rejection. Out, gay and effeminate men may have been rejected early on by their family, classmates, and social groups. Now as adults, they have to deal with the rejection of another gay man not being attracted to them because they deem them too effeminate. However, we must remember that there are in fact plenty of men who love submissive or effeminate men. The key is to open your eyes to those men instead of wasting time and effort on the 'NO FEMS' men.

Indeed in the Stonewall riots, it was those LGBTI people (mainly of colour) who could not fit into societal stereotypes of being 'straight acting' that had to protest. 'Straight-acting' gay men and women could get away with institutionalised homophobia or rather the dislike of gender variance.

I take my hat off to any LGBTI folk who are outwardly seen as such. Those who carry the characteristics or mannerisms that sway away from gender norms have to endure much discrimination. We should applaud them, not ridicule them. Those who are not so obviously 'gay' generally get away with overt homophobia due to the gender-conforming way they walk, talk or behave. When 'straight acting' LGBTI folk discriminate their non-straight-acting counterparts, it is not only insulting, but it perpetuates the very thing we are fighting against. There is no glory in trying to mask or behave in a way to fit in with society. If you are that way, then fantastic, but don't force others to be the same.

I want to point out that I am not vilifying tops or masculine men. Bottoms or feminine men can be very attackful not only to one another but also to tops if they feel rejected or insecure. They can have their own criteria and may refuse to date masculine men due to the pain they have felt for being feminine. Again gender norms are to blame for this.

'Playing on both masculine and feminine characteristics can be playful and intriguing.'

We are all made up of male and female energies. It is the divine feminine energy we lack on this planet at this moment. We need to bring it back in all of us. The energies of love, unity, kindness and compassion need to overcome the overbearing masculine energies of fear, separation, hatred and anger.

In India, men do openly hold hands or show affection. It is also not a terrible thing to be feminine either. However, this is beginning to change. Due to Western media and mentality, middle-class men now try to behave in certain masculine ways. Going to the gym, no longer holding onto the pinky of their friend, and trying to be macho. Thankfully the poorer classes still show male affection regardless of their sexuality. This needs to remain, as the Western male is a lonely figure, without the real emotional affection of his fellow men.

WE NEED TO CHALLENGE GENDER NORMS

We need to stand up and declare our divine right to be who we are, as we are. The pressures of being masculine plague men in the West every day. Not being able to show their emotions, having to play masculine sports and having to bring home an income. All these nonsensical notions need to disappear. I mean only 100 years ago in England boys were dressed in pink and girls in blue. We should be allowed to play with Barbie's, Ken's, both or neither. It's time to put gender on its head and tell the world there is no fear in change. There is no fear in acceptance. There is no fear in a variety of expression. For it always existed and always will. Loosening the shackles on gender conformity will not only bring freedom to all those who suffocate under the guise of submission, but bring more authenticity and love to the world. Let's be proud of who we are and help one another to rise to do so.

Tell the world that you love your masculine and feminine self. Facebook, Tweet, Pin, Instagram, and Email the important message below:

Bollywood Gay Message #6:
I acknowledge and approve of my masculine and feminine traits.
#BollywoodGay

Action Sheet 6: How Do You Limit Yourself?

Do you **identify** yourself as **top**, **bottom**, **versatile** or **choose not** to label yourself this way?

_____
_____
_____
_____

Do you **ridicule** other LGBTI folk depending on their **sexual position** or **femininity**?

_____
_____
_____
_____

Why do you do this?

_____
_____
_____
_____
_____
_____
_____

What **feminine qualities** do you have?

_____
_____
_____
_____

Do you **embrace** and **rejoice** in them?

_____
_____
_____
_____
_____

What *masculine qualities* do you have?

_____
_____
_____
_____
_____

Do you *embrace* and *rejoice* in them?

_____
_____
_____
_____
_____
_____

How could you further *appreciate* your *masculine* and *feminine* qualities and cultivate them?

_____
_____
_____
_____
_____

How can you *support* other *feminine* guys in our culture?

_____
_____
_____
_____
_____

'I need to equip my people to shed their colonial perfume. I need to help my people stand up with dignity. I need to lead my people to the truth.'

7) NO FEMS, NO FATS, NO ASIANS!

'Muscular, Masculine, Straight Acting White guy seeks similar Muscular, Masculine, Straight Acting White guy. No Fems, No Fats, No Blacks, No Asians. Sorry, this is not racism, it's just my preference.'

This topic got on my nerves so much that I did an anthropology essay on it at university. I have thought long and hard about it, and I'm going to share how I experienced this myself and what I have learnt from it. When I was growing up, I thought the white culture was more liberal and accepting of gay people. Having been born in the UK and been bombarded with white ideals of beauty I wanted a white man. I remember fantasising about a muscular manly white man who would take me as his boyfriend.

When I went to University, I thought I would miraculously and automatically meet the man of my dreams. The typical good-looking, muscular archetypal man from porn movies and TV. This did not materialise.

During this time I had also made the unconscious decision not to hang out with South Asians. I thought they were homophobic, discriminatory, set in backwardness and would judge me. I wanted to hang out with white people, especially white gays. I thought they were my salvation. I fancied white guys, and I thought their culture was a lot more accepting and liberal. How wrong was I.

When I was 19 years old, someone told me to join a gay dating website called Gaydar as it was a great place for meeting men. It was one of the most traumatic experiences of my life. These were the days before smart phones and apps like Grindr. I was only on Gaydar for a couple of weeks. On reflection, I do remember searching the site typically for a white, muscular guy. Clearly, at that early age, I knew what I wanted. And it reflected the general masses. I grew frustrated at the lack of replies and the inherent racism and discrimination in the profiles themselves. Not knowing that I, myself was race profiling in my online searches and tastes for men. I too was doing the same, although, I was not blatantly writing on my profile that I was only looking to date white men. Though, I know some ethnic men do write this.

The more profiles I searched online, the more of them would confirm my own self-beliefs. 'Oh my!' I thought, as insecurity grew louder within me. All the men I wanted declared profile after profile: 'Muscular, Masculine, Straight Acting White Guy, seeks similar Muscular, Masculine, Straight

Acting White Guy. No Fems, No Fats, No Blacks, No Asians.' Jeez, how I was slapped in the face and kicked in the guts by all of this. I deleted my account swiftly. Never had I experienced race discrimination before. The very men I had fantasised about and the very men that were meant to be my saviours were proudly and directly telling me they were not interested in me.

I used to go to gay clubs with my white friends who used to hook up quite easily with other white gay men, but I would be left aside. I felt neglected and ashamed. I thought by going to university away from home to London I would find the man of my dreams straight away. A muscular hunk of a white man. This did not materialise. I started to realise muscular guys only went for muscular guys and that the gay scene (including myself) was very shallow indeed.

Now I know many of you feel the gay scene is inherently racist, sexist and discriminatory. Recently in an interview with my Vietnamese American friend I learnt of the racism he felt in the gay scene. He told me how according to him the white race is the preferred dating race. How he is usually the last on the list to be chosen, as white gay men prefer to date other white gay men. He told me there needs to be much more awareness for diversity. He said the gay dating scene was strictly superficial, and categorised people according to assumptions and prejudice.

I have heard the same story many times. I hear ethnic gay guys telling me repeatedly that there is no diversity in Western gay culture. That white men are preferred in the dating pool. My friend told me he believes this general consensus is based upon ego and not on essence. There is a need to recognise and bring in diversity and call people out on their racist paradigm. People should much rather articulate what they want as opposed to what they don't want. For the Universe makes no distinctions with negations. It simply hears the feeling behind the words you use and matches them up to you. So when someone writes, 'No Asians', the dominant word Asian is ignited within the person writing it, creating the vibrational energy that brings more Asians to them. Literally, more Asian guys will be attracted to that profile and message that individual. See we do ourselves no favour by listing our prejudices even if disguised as our preferences. Rather:

'Promote what you love not bash what you hate.'
Jordan Bach

Generalising an entire group of people as unattractive and thus not giving them a chance to date is considered racist. There could be an Asian or black guy out there who has your ideal personality, shares all of your interests, and is perfectly compatible with you, but just because of their race; they will never be given a chance. It's also an example of white privilege, where Eurocentric beauty standards take precedence over other definitions of beauty.

Also by typing 'No Asians/blacks' in one's profile, separation is created between different races within the gay community. Recently I have seen ethnic gay guys in frustration declaring 'Asians only'. Though I haven't seen them write 'No Whites' it does remind me of pre-apartheid South

Africa and pre-civil rights America. How we shy behind our ignorance online is shameful.

On dating sites and apps guys also write things like muscle only, hung for hung, or no oldies. People are not seen as whole beings but more like objects to use for personal gratification. We seem to be living in historical times. Even when only looking for friends, these men write NO ASIANS in capital letters. This needs to stop.

If you have 240 characters to share with the world, write about the wonderful human being you are. When we discriminate, not only does this turn those you discriminate away but it also turns away other people who disagree with your prejudice. A smart, intelligent person simply does not generalise and blatantly hurt people in this way.

It took me many years to realise that I had isolated myself from my own tribe, my own community: gay Asian men. I was judgmental thinking they would be homophobic. I was avoiding my Asian community, friends and avoiding dating gay Asian men. The very way, in which I judged myself, I judged my own tribe. I was running away from my own cultural heritage, loathing myself secretly inside and trying to cover it up. I felt very isolated.

I learnt I should not judge, but rather come from a place of love. That I needed to connect with South Asian LGBTI and even date South Asian men. I also learnt that as soon as I became comfortable with myself and my ethnicity, that I too started to attract men, of all races. This included white men who were also attracted to people of my race, or who saw beyond race as a means of love and connection. I preferred men who saw beyond my race as opposed to those who only dated people of my race, as I felt this fetishised me. I wanted to be seen for the true authentic soul within me.

Now I know not everyone is like this. Of course, if you live in the subcontinent you are surrounded by South Asian men. However, you may long for the light skinned, actor style men with bulging biceps and protruding packages. They may also not reply to your online messages. But I have never seen inherent racism in India on these apps because essentially we are all the same race.

South Asia, as well as Africa, is obsessed with being light skinned. As South Asian, growing up it is drilled into us that white skin is attractive. Lighter skin tones in our community are revered. Just watching a few Bollywood movies you will realise only lighter skinned actors are employed, many of them of Punjabi descent. We have so much prejudice because of this. I mean go to India and every 5 seconds there is an ad on how to bleach your skin white. Epidemic! I remember watching one advert where they had a dark skinned Indian woman in the advert using a whitening cream. Now it is clearly evident that this woman has had blackface, meaning her face has been purposely darkened using makeup. A clock tick tocks around her face as her skin is whitened. The end result is a new actress who is of Scandinavian descent smiling. This is clear false advertisement. We are beautiful no matter our colour. It's the colour of our heart, how loving and kind we are that matters the most. Skin is only a few millimetres thick.

WHY ARE WE BORN IN MINORITY RACES IN THE WEST OR IN LOWER SOCIAL STATUSES IN THE EAST?

You may ask the spiritual reason why we are born into minority races or lower social statuses in society. When you are part of an outsider group, you speed up your development. Great spiritual awareness and unity comes from separation and subjugation. When you experience the contrast of privilege and the lack of it you gain a new way of thinking. You experience compassion, are forced to love yourself and literally have to crack open your head to the idea that we are all one. Your ego dissolves when you see the world through separation. If you are born into a minority race or lower social class in society, it is simply because you wanted a head start into life to gain real meaning into what it means to be a spiritual being.

WHAT DOES THE LAW OF ATTRACTION SAY ABOUT ALL OF THIS?

What I have learnt from the Law of Attraction is this: focusing on the problem will never give you the solution. What you look for you will find. Whatever you are thinking, feeling, or are insecure about you will manifest. Thus if you are insecure about your race, you will attract people who pick that up and point it out to you.

We all need healing whether we are white, black or Asian. We all carry the dirty perfume of the colonial past. This recent colonial past was white, before that we had many colonisers of different races, religions and backgrounds. Who knows what other colonisers there will be in the future. Therefore finger pointing at one particular race and blaming it for its dominance or power does not help the situation. Let me explain, in the subcontinent the real reasons why we are told a white complexion is preferred is threefold. Firstly it is due to the colonisation of South Asia by the lighter-skinned Aryans who forced the darker-skinned Dravidians south thus discriminating them. Secondly, it is due to economical reasons, whereby people who worked the land, became darker skinned and thus were considered economically poorer than landlords who stayed indoors and remained lighter. Finally, it could be attributed to the colonial tactics of the British's divide and rule policy as well as the perception of the native population that being lighter skinned like their colonisers favoured them politically.

Personally, when I was attracting racist profiles or men, it was due to my own internalised pain about my race. Often when we are in pain, we are playing the victim, or we are not fully healed so we react in ways that create divisions between others and ourselves. I know many of you feel that there is a lot of racism in the gay scene, which I have heard many times. How white is the preferred race for dating. But we forget to realise that race is an illusion. There is only one race, the human race. All subdivisions are social constructs, which are used to subdivide, conquer and rule. They legitimise power through the use of various means, such as dictating ideal facial features, ideal skin colour and ideal behaviour. Spiritually we are one, all species, animals and plants are one. Spiritual author Marianne Williamson says if we have an illness in our body the whole body must work to cure it. The white blood cells, and antibodies must work together to heal the body. Therefore we can't say white people do this or Muslim people do that, or all Asian or black people are like this because essentially we are all one race. We need to work collaboratively and cohesively. If there is a problem somewhere we need to look why and find solutions. It is up to the privileged to help the suppressed to rise. White and higher caste people need to step up and atone for their privilege and ensure other marginalised groups are given the space and voice to be heard. (There is a powerful healing exercise that Marianne Williamson conducts on her YouTube Channel called 'Prayer of Apology for African Americans', which I recommend you have a look at).

Yes, you can blame society or colonialism, but that will never empower you. But instead, it will leave you victim to society's ills. If you are to rise you must come from a place of empowerment: self-love, acceptance and universal oneness. We must realise that deep down we discriminate against ourselves. The root cause of attracting these kinds of men, profiles or situations whereby we see 'no Asians' is because we see ourselves as second-class citizens.

We are well aware that the Internet and social media, just like everything else contains within it good and bad points. There are plenty of websites that are positively focused, as there are many that are hateful and negative. The Internet and social media allow people to feel safe to make nasty comments due to their ambiguity. To overcome this, we have to be sure not to empower their agendas by giving them more attention than they deserve.

Ask yourself why guys who are offended by 'Whites Only' on online or app profiles are Asian, Black or Latino men who are looking for 'Whites Only'? It's like you're saying you're upset that white men want the same thing that you want. Why invest so much time and emotional, mental energy into these profiles? Even if they look appealing, don't waste time challenging their preferences, racism, or shaming. There are plenty of other men to choose from. It's much better to view these dating profiles with preferences as a blessing. Men who write racist or anti-feminine statements on their profiles can be quickly written off as being unfit to date. Be grateful for the time they have saved you.

What other people think of me is none of my business.

Why would you want to surround yourself with people who are racist to you? Firstly let's identify if they are actually racist. The majority of societies in the straight world date, have sex with and marry those of the same race so why should it be any different in the gay world? Asian people have their own dating sites such as shaadi.com and Muslim dating. Then why does it hurt so much when you see No Asians? Why would the appearance of that text hurt so much?

Are you comfortable in your own race? Or are you in the vibrational set point of self-race hatred, hence you are attracting guys who dislike your race too? You may think your dating pool is lowered because so many of these guys don't want you because of your race. You may be frustrated as you keep seeing the same thing, 'No Asians No Asians'. But in your own head, you say the same thing about yourself, you see yourself as less than, and expect others to do the same. Why not love yourself and date people of all colours? Focus on those that do appreciate your qualities. There are plenty of men of all shapes, sizes and colours who do like Asian or feminine men. Open your eyes. Stop chasing those who are explicit in their nastiness towards you. Avoid the ones who are not attracted to you by firstly loving yourself and secondly focusing your attention on those who are attracted to you. You can't change the world. You can't control anyone. You can't force anyone to love you, want you and be with you. You can only love yourself and see your outer reality transform to reflect that.

Rejection does not mean that you are undesirable. There are plenty of men out there who would be happy to date you. Focusing your attention on men, who do want you, ensures energetically that they have access to you. There are tops, bottoms, and men of all shapes, sizes and colours who would be ecstatic to meet you. Racism exists, disguised as someone's personal preferences, but don't let that stop you from attracting the partner of your dreams.

HOW TO CHANGE THIS?

As we misunderstand why we attract things we don't want (such as racism), we look for reasons why this happens and keep reaffirming those reasons to others and our self. This, in turn, holds us in vibrational resistance to what we actually do want (inclusion and equality). Therefore if you want to improve something in a community, look for evidence of the outcome you do want and emphasise it with examples and words. In the gay community for example, instead of talking about racism, speaking about acceptance and diversity is a far better tool to bring positive social change.

Diversity is our strength and in our diversity, we can focus on the kind of life we each want. We are free to create as we practice our variety. The main thing is to figure out the life that you want and to be in perfect vibrational alignment to it. Thus speaking of the gay community in a positive, upbeat manner serves to carve out the vision of this community that you want to experience in your day-to-day life. We must remember that there are multitudinous parallel realities that occur around us. The one that we experience our self is related to the vibrational energy that we are emitting at that moment. Thus it is better to say: 'I love the LGBTI community. I can live my perfect world if I get my nose out of other people's business.'

There is injustice everywhere you look for it. The more you look for it, the more you will find it and the more it will be the basis of your perception. If you're noticing something unwanted, it means it's active in your vibration. No one mistreats anybody who is in alignment with who they are.

Looking to others for how they feel about you is always going to lead to disappointment. For if they are disconnected from Source they will never give you the interest and positive validation you seek. Racially abusive people are in need of soothing. No one is ever hateful, violent and mean if they are in alignment with who they really are. What we witness is the agony of their disconnection. Thus give compassion to the victim, but more compassion to the perpetrator. They are suffering the most. For the worse you feel, the worse you behave.

It is much better not to care what others think, and to focus on your own feeling, reassuring yourself that your inner being adores you. If you do this whilst disconnected to Source, and focus on the specific racist situation, you may experience great discomfort. In such a situation it is recommended to start appreciating all the good things in your life right now, without focusing on the racism you experience. It is a way of soothing your mind and allowing you to realise that your life is pretty damn good as it is. You can't change the way others feel about you; you are only in control of the way you feel about yourself. Thus meditate for that increases your vibration or take a nap as that stops all conscious thoughts. Then fewer of those people who make you feel bad have access to you, as you are no longer in their vibrational frequency. You will see less racism in your day-to-day life as you see in the eyes of Source, and if you do see it, you will not take it personally.

Let's end with a prayer:
'I release all limiting belief patterns about my race; that has kept me trapped in victimhood all these years. I love who I am. I focus my attention on those who love me back. I understand that the Law of Attraction brings to me that which I focus my attention on. Therefore I focus on loving, inclusive, men by being one first!'

Show solidarity to your brothers and sisters of different races. Facebook, Tweet, Pin, Instagram, and Email the message below:

Bollywood Gay Message #7:
I value my own race, gender and sexuality and stand up for others.
#BollywoodGay

Action Sheet 7: How Do You View Your Race?

What *colour* does or did your *ideal partner* look like?

_____
_____
_____
_____

Did this come from *rejecting* aspects of yourself?

_____
_____
_____
_____
_____

Have you experienced *discrimination*? Why do you think that was having read this chapter?

_____
_____
_____
_____
_____
_____

Do you love the *colour* of your own skin?

_____
_____
_____
_____
_____
_____
_____

Are you **supportive** of other guys of colour?

_____

_____

_____

_____

_____

_____

Do you **date** people from your **own race**?

_____

_____

_____

_____

_____

_____

Do you **date** guys of **other races**?

_____

_____

_____

_____

_____

What **colour** are your own **friends**?

_____

_____

_____

_____

_____

You are equal. Thus think yourself equal. Give off the vibration and energy of equality. Treat others as equal. Then no one will treat you unequally. Enough playing the victim. I want to see you rise and support others.

8) THE CURSE OF THE PRIVILEGED

'Hierarchy affects even those on the top of the ladder. By objectifying hierarchical roles, those on top are spiritually excluded from salvation.'

I used to think that those who were on top of the hierarchical ladder had it the best. That in my society in England, white, middle class, heterosexual men were enjoying unlimited privileges I was not. I was playing the victim. In the gay scene, I saw white, middle class, gay men enjoying all the attention, sex and validation that I wanted. I often felt beaten down by the comparison game. In the subcontinent, you may think that the ones who look like the TV serial men, models or actors are those who have it better. That light skinned, muscular men from high castes are living the high life. But let me tell you this, we have no idea what kind of life this person is leading. We cannot do the same, which has been done upon us, or rather, that which we have done to ourselves, and do it to others. We cannot generalise, assume or put large quantities of people in a box. We have no idea what their journey is all about. All we can do is stand in the glory of our own light and shine as bright as we can.

It took me quite some time to break free from my own mental restrictions. I understood that hierarchy indeed does little to empower the ones who feel they are on top. For they play into the ego manifestation of their outer being, trapped into behaving or acting in this way or the other, without treating themselves or others equally. To be frank, it is quite exhausting to play this game. Let me assure you, never think those on top have it better.

They may have the physical body and looks, but it does not mean they are spiritually evolved or are happy. Those at the top of the chain have to live in a way that conforms to the structure they are placed in. They are expected to behave in a certain way and treat people in a certain way. People judge them, favour them, dislike them or are hateful towards them. Their physical body may be adored, or they may be treated as mere objects. This then keeps them locked into the bondages of the ego, making it hard for them to break free.

Whilst living in Mumbai, I forget to count how many times my friends informed me of the insecurity of so and so actor, the substance abuse of so and so person, and the male model who is a prostitute on the side. The guys, who I thought had it all, were lonely and depressed instead. It was indeed a real eye opener.

I live in the UK so the examples I will use will reflect that. Feel free to insert what you think works best for your country. The conclusion is same for everyone: we are spiritual beings having a physical experience and ultimately there is no hierarchy.

The spirit is whole. The spirit is one. It is forever connected to Source, without any gender, colour, race or religion. We are all in our essence free and one. Never separated, never above or below. We are all the same. Indeed we are one of each other.

Let us assume that in the Western world white privilege is real. You are a straight, white, masculine, jock type, middle-class affluent, heterosexual man. You are generally believed to be at the top of the chain for privileges related to work, love and status.

However, if we objectify this person we are not being true to their soul or our own. Anyone living a spiritual life sees the universal internal light in all beings including their own. They realise we are all unique but equal. As energy sees it, we are all beings of light having a human experience.

You have to remember that as soon as you buy into the scarcity and separatist mentality you are already disconnected from Source, and your true self. Only when you are truly connected to who you are can you understand the futility in thinking in such a way.

It does great personal and social harm to think of yourself as lower then anyone. You are and always will be whole, full and imperfectly perfect as you are.

You may say, 'But they have got muscles, or 'they represent the ruling/elite class'. In the West it's the middle-class white man, in South Asia, those in the highest ranks are those with money, business and power. They may have servants in Asia; here they may not. They speak in a certain way, dress in a certain way and we presume they have got through life with privileges. Yes, they may have gone to boarding school; gone to great universities and acquired the best posts at work due to their family links, but are they truly happy? I have seen some of them off their faces on drugs, battling with alcohol abuse and bodily addictions. Not all are happy. So never assume. I've seen plenty of these types of men at clubs, high, partying away, dancing to the emptiness of their life. You have nothing to feel envious for.

You see them on Grindr, Gayromeo, Gaydar. Those guys who never reply. The ones with great bods, who are only looking for dates and mates with muscle dudes. Those who only look with shallow discerning eyes.

In India, sure I was the light-skinned foreigner- a catch. Here in the UK, white people are seen as the catch by some, but being on top of the hierarchy is a curse for your personal spiritual development for it locks you onto the ego. You hold onto your title, positions and physical exterior and act according to that. You may discriminate others or act unlawfully. A lack of compassion to others and attachment to ego means spiritual enlightenment moves further and further away from such people.

If you think someone is privileged, you separate yourself from the whole. You automatically tell the Universe that you are less than because this person is more than you. You seek out evidence to prove this and the Law of Attraction automatically makes it evident. The only way to release yourself from a limited mindset is by seeing everyone as equal. Focus your attention on evidence that proves this and don't get annoyed when in your disconnection to Source you see evidence to the contrary. See the privileged are only cursed because you make them so. You have made them privileged. Your thoughts, feelings and vibration, have placed them on pedestals. You can right this minute remove all inherited customs of race, caste, and class privilege by refusing to play that game. When you walk with your head held high, without contempt, ego or insecurity, you will match people who applaud you. You will assist others to stand in their glory by being a role model. Read more in Chapter 17.

Facebook, Tweet, Pin, Instagram, and Email the message below:

Bollywood Gay Message #8:
I no longer play the victim for I know I have the power in my own hands.
#BollywoodGay

Action Sheet 8: The Grass Is Not Always Greener

What **annoys** you about '**privileged**' people?

_____
_____
_____

How does this **affect you** when you believe this?

_____
_____
_____

Do you think **everyone** feels the **same** way about them?

_____
_____
_____

What **evidence** do you see that proves this to be **true**?

_____
_____
_____

How would you **prefer** they were like?

_____
_____

Do you believe your **negative perception** manifested your reality on this topic?

_____
_____
_____

If so, how have your **thoughts/feelings** made you see the **evidence** of this?

_____
_____
_____
_____

Do you think other people have **different realities** about the subject? Isn't truth **subjective**?

_____
_____
_____
_____

How could you **feel better** about the situation?

_____
_____
_____
_____

How can you look for **positive evidence** to back this up?

_____
_____
_____
_____

What can you do to **stop playing** the **victim** and blaming the other to **empower** yourself?

_____
_____
_____
_____

LIST 5 WAYS YOU CAN STOP NEGATIVELY MANIFESTING THIS SITUATION BY THINKING POSITIVELY ABOUT IT?

I.e.

Refrain from telling everyone that privileged people have it better than me.
Stop feeling like the victim by listening to fear (false evidence appearing real).

1. _____
2. _____
3. _____
4. _____
5. _____

'Hurt people, Hurt people.
Healed people, Heal people.'

9) DRUGS, PROSTITUTION & PORN

Growing up as South Asian, like most of you, I heard my parent's words vibrate inside of me.

'No drinking, no smoking, no drugs!'

Drinking was tolerated to some extent as my dad drank beer sometimes, even though my mum detested it, however smoking and drugs were and still are a total no-no. Normally when parents try to stop their children from doing something, they rebel and do that exact thing. Fortunately I did not rebel. I rarely drink, have never actually smoked, and drugs are not my thing. The only drug I prefer is meditation.

I do, however know many within the community who due to guilt and shame numb their pain with alcohol, drugs and sex. All self-harming addictions, which further cause depression and guilt rather than alleviate it. I remember going to clubs in London whilst at university and touts standing outside would sell ecstasy, coke or worse to youngsters. It is a known fact that LGBTI people are more likely to misuse alcohol and drugs and be more sexually promiscuous compared to their straight counterparts. This gets more complex when relating to ethnic minorities who feel further marginalised. The rates of mental and sexual health issues are higher for ethnic LGBTI and access to support much lower due to cultural issues in the West. In South Asia of course due to the illegality of homosexuality access to support services is near impossible.

ALCOHOL

Having a casual drink is something many people enjoy without any negative consequences. However, when alcohol becomes the prime method for feeling good or gaining confidence to socialise with other people, we have a problem. Using anything physical and external to release resistance to negative thought patterns or fears is a slippery road to addiction and self-abuse.

To know whether you are on the safe side of alcohol pay attention to how you feel before you have a drink. If you feel great and drink alcohol with friends to further feel good, your good intention will uplift and enhance your positive vibration. If you feel down, substances such as alcohol can slow your negative momentum (and thus your bad feeling state) as they slow your ability to focus on things that bother you. This, however, is impermanent, and when the effects of the drink wear off the negative momentum returns only stronger.

As a general rule, most people consume substances such as alcohol because they want to soothe themselves in some way. There is no right and wrong in this as the substance may well soothe you. Sometimes by soothing your sorrow, you allow yourself to surrender. Then from this place of surrender what you want to attract into your life may come easily as you allow it to. However, when you find alignment through a substance, you can become dependent on the substance itself. This is because you don't have the mental capacity to maintain the allowing state yourself when sober.

To use alcohol on an ongoing basis as opposed to working on your personal alignment to feel good is not healthy. It is far better to practice how to feel good by yourself. When you are in alignment with who you are, nothing is wrong, as you act from a balanced mind. Therefore get aligned, be happy and then choose the best course of action for yourself. Don't beat yourself up if you have an alcohol addiction, your motive to soothe yourself is not wrong. Realise that the root cause of your addiction is your misalignment to Source, which was causing you deep pain and suffering. Instead, next time you feel like having a drink, ask yourself what condition am I trying to soothe, and am I able to soothe it in a better way?

DRUGS

I have friends who do drugs, each to their own. I do not condemn them. Some people's minds are relaxed and easy going, they can handle drugs and enjoy it. However, there is a need to be vigilant. Can you have a meaningful conversation, a relationship or sex sober? Or are you addicted to drugs? (The feeling of addiction is when our body acclimates to the new substance and it feels to us like we want more). Is the addiction a way of coping and escaping? Is drug taking a conscious choice you are making or is your social circle swaying you to take them?

The state of oneness where you want to hug, kiss and make love with everyone you meet, that often comes from drugs like ecstasy or mephedrone is actually the returning to your original self: love. When you have not experienced such high levels of vibration before, either through your natural intelligence or vibration improving techniques such as meditation, the experience can be daunting and harrowing! We experience such levels of bliss never before obtained. That is why when lower vibrational beings, which include a lot of LGBTI individuals who take recreational drugs on a regular basis, experience such bliss they become addicted to that feeling of love they had longed for. This causes a desire to experience that same state repeatedly for prolonged times. However, once this contrast of love from fear is experienced, the sensation of it at a second or third drug-fuelled state lessens, and more and more drugs are needed to experience the nibanic bliss. What we must remember is this, if drugs are taken when we are in a low vibe state the effect it will have on us will be generally negative and addictive. But if taken whilst in our highest states of being whilst sober, the upliftment will be generally pleasant.

When we are in a negative vibration state, we hold a lot of resistance to being who we are, which is a love being that is in total oneness with Source. We worry, fear and get frustrated with our mind for causing us misery and suffering. We fail to realise that if we simply let go of the negative chitter chatter and trusted in the flow of life all that we want would simply follow. This is why if you take drugs when in a negative mind space you experience a release from this resistance.

However, we must realise we don't need the stimulant to release the depressant. Over time your body acclimates to the drug, so in order to release the resistance you have to keep increasing its quantity. With mind altering chemicals you cannot focus entirely on the experience to understand what is going on and maintain it thereafter. The use of substances can put you in a less resistance space, but your ability to focus, remember and sustain that vibration is just not there. Thus it is a temporary solution.

I do not condemn or condone drug use. I do, however, believe drugs should not be used as an escape from your problems. I understand some people use drugs for spiritual expansion as it helps them realise there is a lot more going vibrationally then just the world of reality. Thus if you must try drugs, it is better to try them in their purest form. Synthetic drugs should be avoided, and plant-based entheogens such as the Ayahuasca from the Banisteriopsis caapi plant are a better option. Only the purest form will give you the expansive experience that you desire. Have natural products instead and ask the Universe for the energy and clarity that many seek from drugs.

CHEMSEX

I know of guys who have ended up in hospital due to drug orgies, party and play (p&p) or chemsex as it is called. A closeted South Asian escort near me, was invited to a drugs orgy, collapsed and was rushed to hospital. Not only did his parents come to find out he had overdosed, that he was gay but also that he was prostituting himself! This must have been a triple shock and horror for them. Some guys think they are invincible if they have good looks, big cocks and muscly bodies. They get into this kind of stuff to make up for the shame of being gay. Someone offers them money on the night table after a one night stand confusing them for an escort or offers them money for sex on dating apps due to their hard to get attitude and attractiveness. Indeed it can be a curse to be attractive, especially if you are broken inside. You can become prey to hungry predators.

Chemsex is endemic in large cities around the world. From New York to New Delhi drug orgies are a growing practice amongst gay men. It is easily introduced over dating profiles or at parties to vulnerable young gay men who succumb to the pressure of trying it. Guilt and shame play a huge role in using drugs to have sex with multiple partners, for the thought of sober sex can be harrowing to those who have not accepted their sexuality. Please act with caution, because in such an induced state safe sex practices can go out of the window and overdoses are all too common. I know of many friends who have habituated into a lifestyle of weekend sex orgies only to feel worse after.

The orgies last anything up to 72 hours, with sex between multiple partners. The three main drugs used during chemsex parties are mephedrone, GHB, and crystal meth. They enable the user to inhibit ejaculation and thus be able to have sex for hours. When consumed in excessive amounts or mixed with alcohol they can lead to blackouts or fits and over stimulate the heart causing feelings of anxiety, paranoia or brain damage.

WHAT ABOUT WEED?

Cannabis is a psychoactive drug which alters your state of consciousness. It helps you to get out of your restricted limited perception and expand your consciousness beyond the 3rd dimension of reality. It also teaches the path of least resistance and oneness. Cannabis has been used as a spiritual drug since 2000 B.C. But the whole art of identifying plants for healing has been lost to us. Throughout history, people were able to see the structures of plants, know how they interacted with certain parts of the body and healed them. The medicinal benefits of cannabis in its purest form are not addictive or state altering, but merely pain reducing and healing. Many use cannabis for pain management; pain is a symptom of resistance. This is why cannabis helps relieve pain as it helps a person lose resistance by helping release negative thoughts and worry.

Being a high vibe plant its helix structure is made to bring a certain high vibration within a person. If you are a person with a lower vibration then by ingesting/inhaling the cannabis plant you are elevated and feel good and experience all sorts of relaxed and heightened states. But if like me you already vibrate at a higher frequency, by ingesting/inhaling the plant your vibration is brought lower making you paranoid. The actual point of cannabis is to make you realise that higher states of consciousness are available to you and be able to hold them without the addictive use of the plant. You need only use it a couple of times before being able to bring about those states mentally yourself. Cannabis is merely a guide.

The job of a teacher such as cannabis is to teach you how to feel and recognise a particular vibrational level, and once you get there to be able to generate that energy yourself. Continuing beyond the time needed for the teacher, it becomes a crutch. If you can experience that vibration, you have the ability to create that within yourself regardless of what you inhale. You can generate that energy, just by remembering what it feels like. The reason you need more and more stronger doses is because you have acclimated to the feeling and thus it is not as powerful each time. It is not a new experience for you and thus not such as shock or surprise.

Cannabis mellows you out and stops you from beating yourself up thus placing you in a process of allowing. But if it is illegal, or hard to get and that brings a feeling of fear within you, the process of allowing will not occur. You can feel powerlessness as you use this one method of losing resistance and connecting to higher states of consciousness and dimensions. Stress and resistance exist for a reason: to teach you about yourself. When stressed we need to examine ourselves and shift for something new to flourish. When we use drugs like cannabis to escape stress we avoid the root of the resistance and how to improve it ourselves. Cannabis thus prevents learning as you are right where you started when the effects wear off. It is far better to change the conditions that make you take drugs to escape your current stressful reality.

No one achieved enlightenment through marijuana compared to meditation. The same drug that helps you mellow out prevents you from focusing attentively to that what you do want. Meditation is a more specific focused action, compared to the passive allowing of marijuana. But once you come out of a 'high' state from either meditation or marijuana you are more likely to return to your negative thoughts. Therefore a more successful way of feeling good and maintaining it is to practice feeling good generally in our day-to-day conscious, awake lives. 10 or 15 minutes a day focusing on what makes you feel good is a better daily practice.

HIV & AIDS

With such unhealthy addictive practices going on due to guilt, shame and internalised homophobia it is no surprise that the rates of HIV are on the rise. Gay men in drug injected dazed states forget or choose not to use condoms whilst having sex. With group orgies, sex saunas and casual sex the norm, safe sex practices go out the window. Some believe HIV is inevitable and thus go ahead with the task of contracting the 'dis-ease' purposely. Such madness occurs when we forget to accept and love our self. On a spiritual level, HIV/AIDS is a physical manifestation of not liking oneself, or rather the lack of love for oneself. Indeed Louise Hay says:

'When you're talking about the 'dis-ease' called AIDS, I find you're really dealing with people who have a lot of self-hatred. They feel they're not good enough. There's a lot of resentment towards their families and very often there's been a lifestyle that's been very abusive for the body. They've not taken loving care of themselves and when this gets turned around, healings take place.' Louise Hay

The Law of Attraction goes a bit further in explaining this 'dis-ease'. There are some things in life that you attract by purpose and some by default. Are you at one with your sexuality? Or do you have discomfort with who you are? AIDS is not something that is thrust upon the sinner. Rather it is a 'dis-ease', which is attracted to those who struggle with themselves, those who have a good and bad struggle inside of themselves. Those who want to be good but feel inside they are not. There is tremendous struggle in this. I want to be good, but I might not be. There is a lot of guilt involved. It is a product of negative attraction, i.e. unintentional manifestation through focusing on the negative aspects one feels. Pretending to be happy or trying to accept yourself does not work. The way you feel is the point of attraction. You have to say and feel acceptance. (Action Sheet 9 will help).

GAY, ASIAN AND A PROSTITUTE?

Countless times I have seen adverts on Grindr with the dollar sign $ or any other money symbol incorporated in the headline name such as €$ast€rn. I never knew what it meant until recently. This is the typical sign for an escort, which basically is someone who is paid to have sex with. Other names could be a rent boy or prostitute. Yes in the straight world escorts tend to go for dinner with rich clients and then come home, like glorified paid dates. However, gay escorts generally if not always are paid to have sex with.

Initially when I found out that South Asians were doing this kind of stuff I was horrified. I always thought our people, especially in the West were brought up with the strict values against drugs, alcohol and sex abuse. I was wrong. Living in India, I realised how big a business it is there too. Lower income gay men; sell their bodies for money, affection, love and acceptance. However, middle class and rich established men do it also. In Bollywood some of the aspiring models and actors who are trying to make it sell themselves to get opportunities or make a living whilst trying.

This is quite a big business now and it is very scary. Some of the escorts I have spoken to have talked about the shame of being gay, being disowned or the fear of drug addiction and historical sexual abuse being some of the root causes of their escorting.

Some would say it's just sex, it doesn't mean anything and they get paid for it. The other person is paying for a service and they are just providing. Though I'm not to judge, it screams lack of self-esteem, wanting external validation, worthiness issues with love, insecurities and lack of self-respect. It objectifies the individual and thus separates them from the whole and their higher self. The ones who buy such services mirror the same feelings for they play the game. When spoken to, these clients inform me that it's just a service that fulfils their fantasies and that there is nothing wrong with it. For prostitution is the oldest job in the world.

Even during Buddha's time, there were cases of prostitutes whose veils of ego fell in the light of wisdom. Any profession can assist the spiritual evolvement of a person and prostitution is no less. Some people take birth to experience this kind of life, to expand and learn. Prostitution indeed can be a profession very similar to a counsellor. They work with and make clients happy. They can see the otherwise hidden aspects of the human psyche, sexual fantasies and tastes.

The hijra community (transgender) in India is forced to prostitute themselves. Originally revered and feared this group is now a marginalised and suppressed community. The police beat them, men rape them and finding work is very difficult. This is similar to trans youth in the West who also resort to prostitution as a means of financing themselves. This is all very sad and we need to understand it further.

CONVERSATION WITH INTERNATIONAL ITALIAN ESCORT:

Recently I had the privilege of speaking to an International Italian escort who also happens to be a friend of mine. This is what he had to say.

1) 'How can he be spiritual when he's an escort?'

Only judgemental people say this when they fear the sexual energy that resonates within them. Social conditioning dictates that prostitutes are bad, as is sex. We are all spiritual beings, whether we realise it or not, regardless of our profession.

2) Why do people escort?

It could be for a variety of reasons: desperation, laziness or to explore their own sexuality. Some use their good looks to get what they want. When sex, one of the most powerful energies is repressed some of us rebel against that.

3) Do you think it's a profession that should continue or end?

It's always been there. It should, therefore, be regulated by an approach by society for society. It should be a legalised profession with no shame in it. We should respect human beings according to sex. Sex is natural and it should not be repressed. We should take a middle path to it as stated by Buddha.

4) How can we embrace sex in society?

Humanity needs to evolve and drop the stigma about sexual energy. Repressed sexual fantasies are the origin of the matter. Sex should be an act of love. Currently, there exists a total confusion on sexual identity by society. The moment this is released, the need for escorts will stop. It will take a lot of work to get there. Until then escorts will continue to offer natural sexual energy to others.

IS PORN GOOD FOR YOU?

Porn is a controversial topic and given the availability and widespread use of it in our society the dangers of it can be profound. Most porn is void of love and equality. In heterosexual porn, gender roles are entrenched with females being subordinate to men. In gay porn we a have similar role-play between tops who dominate bottoms. Porn is about the biggest cock, tightest bottom, and roughest fuck. It's unrealistic, damaging and not always good for us. Most of us are addicted to it at some extent. We watch it daily or more and masturbate to it. It implants obscene and untrue ideas of what love should be like between two individuals. Instead of honouring and empowering ourselves, we reduce and objectify one another. In such contexts, the divinity of the person is not seen and indeed a wrong perception of what actual sexual union is meant to look like is portrayed. This happens due to the guilt, shame and fear society as a whole holds towards sex. Add this to the LGBTI spectrum and we have a recipe for disaster.

Most porn is directed by men and most of it is disrespectful both to the self and to the other person performing in it. For gay men, it can be even more brutal added with the shame and guilt we carry. There is some porn which is loving or more artistic, however, most is just about pure ego domination and subversion. Given how much porn we watch and how many years we have been watching it, the damaging effects on our subconscious mind is insurmountable. Don't get me wrong; I'm not here to put down your porn viewing habits or generalise, but the acknowledgement of this fact must not be taken lightly. Are you single? Do you cheat? Are you unsatisfied with the same partner? Does sex with them become stale for you? Do you reenact certain fantasies? Who do you think is to contribute for this?

Self-abuse to self-love

Be mindful of the porn you watch. The power and impact media can have on our unconscious mind is phenomenal. How is the porn industry conducted? Do actors do it willingly and from a place of love? Or are they doing it out of sheer desperation? Some may have experienced sexual abuse, have low self-esteem or are looking for external validation. They may objectify and reduce themselves to physical objects to be used and adored. Some may escort too. Drugs are a huge problem in the industry with many pornstars admitting to taking them. Thus by watching porn, we are feeding into and adding to the porn, drug and prostitution industries.

Porn is a multi-billion dollar industry that is out of alignment. Our out of alignment sexuality fuels out of alignment porn. Porn is the manifestation of sexual arousal and excitement, which is not a bad thing. However, chemicals in our brain release endorphins when watching porn, which can cause addiction. The most common feeling after watching porn is emptiness. It creates a new need as opposed to satisfaction and release. If you feel out of control with porn, especially if it creates negative consequences in your life, it has become an addiction. Like any addiction, it is an escape from pain by avoiding your feelings. It is self-medication and works by blunting your senses to make you forget your problems. Porn is sexual gratification through the objectification of both men and women. We are disconnected from the actors as they are on our screen so we are comfortable using them for our pleasure. However, if they were someone we loved, we would not objectify them. We have to be disconnected to someone to use them for physical arousal and relief which demonstrates our out of alignment. The minute we begin to objectify someone else we make our self a match to the vibration of objectification and thus lose our self-esteem and self-worth.

The world's religious leaders would go further and tell us that the human body itself is pornographic. This can cause self-loathing and war with our body and sexual desires rather than acceptance of them. We all know at our core, when we are aligned with sexuality, sex is more than just physical gratification. There are societies where sexuality is more natural, less restricted and less guarded. There are many people who are lined up with who they are and having sexual experiences with vibrational synchronicity. Pornography is about the distortion of sexual energies rather than the natural flow of it. Finally we must remind ourselves that alignment cannot come from religious, social or political viewpoints for it is a personal inside job.

WHAT DOES IT DO TO RELATIONSHIPS?

Whatever we put our attention to will be created in our life. When people watch porn, they often compartmentalise it, thinking that the Law of Attraction won't affect them. But it does affect their daily activities. You can go down the path of addiction moving from soft-core porn to much harder porn. The more you watch it, the more you become desensitised, meaning you need harder and harder porn to get that same release. You may search for perverse fantasies and even look to bondage, rape and incest, etc. We then want to practice these fantasies in our relationships. As we sleep with our partners, we think of the pornstars online and feel disconnected. Do you want to become your greatest version? Or do you want to do something that is not going to serve you in the long run? Because whatever you see with your eyes goes into your unconscious mind.

Porn focuses on being stimulated through the body. We are told over and over again that our sexuality depends on what we look like. We must be young, athletic, have big breasts or penises, otherwise, we can't be good lovers. This can cause self-worth issues in those who don't see themselves as matching these criteria. Even for the ones that do, they can still feel insecure for not having large enough breasts or penises. Ultimately, no one feels happy with themselves.

If you are in alignment and ok with using porn in sex, you will find a partner who is ok with it too. But if not in alignment you will attract a partner who disapproves of porn, which can create problems. Porn destroys intimacy. It is a sexual escape for people who have fear of intimacy as it helps them bond with someone without actually connecting. If we use porn to orgasm, we will seek it out again and again and may lose the ability to get turned on without it. But if we associate orgasm with our partner even the lightest kiss from them will turn us on. In porn, we don't see the full picture of sex. It's not real, it's fantasy. True love is through intimacy, not just penetration. It is connection and foreplay that brings you closer to the truth. Porn is I get off you get off, without any sharing, compassion or trust. It is quite simply mutual masturbation, using the others body to get off. Spending time getting off on porn is a waste of sexual or kundalini (vital force) energy which could be put to better use.

As it stands, the human race is using only a fraction of its sexual abilities with a partner. Rather we should see people for who they are: loving light beings, not objects to be used and abused. People are not our sexual gratification. See the love in them and yourself. Connect to their innocence, through connecting to your own and you will never want to just sleep with someone or allow yourself to be used. Sexual energy is similar to meditation if done whilst connected to Source. When both people are connected, a wonderful optimal sexual union is experienced. In this state, we feel loved and appreciated once it's over. It feels like we have one mind moving together. Think tantra. Aligned sex. The ego dissolves, chakras melt away, and divine energy 10x enters. It literally affects every cell and emotion field. We open up to the miracle of universal energy. A cleansing. So porn may not disappear but the addiction to it can. Once you experience the sexual experiences were meant to have, porn no longer has a hold on you. It simply won't come close to the genuine connection and love that comes from one that you love. More about tantra in Chapter 15.

WHY I STOPPED WATCHING PORN

I have been watching porn for over 15 years. Nearly half my life. Now removing that imagery from my mind is a big task I tell you. Yes, sex is normal, yes sex is healthy. But it is so from a healthy mind. Sleeping around, watching porn and masturbating to unreality will not bring in that healthy monogamous relationship you always envisioned. Sure if you want to be in an open relationship, go on ahead. I have tried it. But for me, it was about ego, self-worth issues and shame. I felt validated every time I slept with a new guy and let me tell you; no real love came of it. I felt empty and shallow afterwards. And let me not forget the addiction to apps like Grindr. The constant looking for love and the need for pleasure. My mind, to put it bluntly, was unbalanced, on edge and erratic. I was not the peaceful person I wanted to be. It's still a work in progress for me, so I cannot judge or direct. I simply want you to understand or put more thought into this and naturally evolve into the person you want to be, in the manner, you choose best. Life is a big experiment and you need to be your own boss. I can only offer you my story and suggestions. The rest is your choice.

MASTURBATION

Masturbation is the natural act of stimulating yourself to create sexual arousal. Society tells us it is wrong, and many spiritual teachers think it is detrimental to our enlightenment. We are told that it creates cravings and leads to suffering. However, from Source perspective, it can be both good and bad depending on the person.

When we are in pleasure, we are in alignment with Source and thus are open to Source energy. During orgasm our meridians, energetic bodies and chakras open. Our body starts to heal and releases oxytocin which relieves pain and bonds us with others. Our immune system improves as a result of cells receiving better respiration and fear and anxiety reduce. We can also use this build up of energy, excitement, plateau and climax and channel it into the body to manifest our desires. Through masturbation, you can learn a lot about yourself. By being aware of ourselves, it enhances self-intimacy and allows us to be intimate with others. During orgasm, your ego dissolves and you can realise oneness, such as through tantra. With a partner, you can then channel this primordial energy via meditation for greater union and connection (more in Chapter 15).

The downside of masturbation is that it can become an addiction. Addiction means that there is an underlying issue that needs an unconditional presence to heal it. If we use masturbation to escape pain by feeling relief in the form of release, it becomes self-medication. This does not relieve us of the thing that causes pain but covers it up. So we have to stop running away and deal with the root cause of the problem. Ask yourself what are you using masturbation to get away from? Are you using masturbation to avoid intimacy? Fear of intimacy means we condition our self to masturbation to avoid the pain and vulnerability of climaxing with another. Having non-intimate sex such as unemotional sex (very much like porn) is also mutual masturbation. There is no way to separate life force energy and sexual energy. When we use it for the sake of release, our energy is depleted, but when we use it for the sake of union, our energy is replenished. Thus sexual energy is better put to use towards the creation of life (not just offspring but desires, dreams, ideas and movement).

HOW TO RELEASE UNWANTED ADDICTIONS

Now that you have read all about the addictions that exist in the gay world you may be ready to release them from yourself. Firstly accept that you became addicted because you wanted to, and that it's not wrong, evil or bad. Take the shame and guilt aspect away from the addiction creating space to allow the healing. To heal yourself, your desire to release the addiction has to be stronger than your desire to want it. The fastest way to release yourself from addictions is to separate yourself from the substance and keep your focus on the life you actually want. There may be some physical discomfort, but it will be short-lived. It's the actual emotional desire of the substance that triggers that. Your body releases the substance much quicker than the mind. The craving for anything you introduce into your system will stop after separating yourself from it for three days. Only when you have a clear picture of something you want more, will you be able to leave it. A greater wanting must replace it. There are many ways to prepare yourself for this. Spend time before the separation from the substance, imagining yourself free from it and then that picture will come true for you. Remember that if it becomes too intense or uncomfortable, you can always go back to the habit. Then next time you try to get yourself off the habit, it will be easier. Keep working on the vision of you without it and then when the picture is clear enough you will be free of it. If you think it will be hard to rid yourself of the addiction, then it will be. All things you don't want to do are hard. But if something is what you really want to do it will be easy. You have to get to the stage where you want it enough for the Universe to assist you.

One helpful concept is to realise that time space reality all exists in the present moment. A timeline is, in fact, an illusion. In actuality, the past, present and future exist in the here and now. Linear time only exists in the physical reality; in non-physical you have access to everything. If you tell yourself now that you are no longer an addict to the thing that you were addicted to, it means that you never were. You create a new history for yourself, as the past is in the present moment. Therefore you were never an addict to the substance. This can help you when you are around others, alone or in the vicinity of the addictive substance. The mere knowledge that you have never had a problem with or addiction to a substance releases the power it holds over you. You are free in the knowledge that you are and always have been an addict free person. Then should you choose to occasionally smoke or drink you can do so without the fear of relapse because you never were addicted to it. The mind is the biggest tool we have to overcome all addictions if used wisely. But you have to believe that you can have that one cigarette without it affecting the balance of your mind.

Ask yourself if this addiction is adding something to your life or taking something away from it? Try not to justify it by saying everyone else is doing it. Rather try to think if it's affecting you negatively, as that is the only way you will want to change it. To do this you must become aware. Why do you have the urge to do it? What are your triggers? What causes the urge to occur? Is it stress and a need to release? Go in the direction of negative beliefs instead of avoiding them. Sink into that feeling and be unconditionally present with it. Integrate with it. Is it emptiness? If it's boredom, get busy. If it's stress, find out what is making you stressed and find healthier ways to remove stress from life. Addiction is the symptom your task is to find the cause. A good way of halting addiction is to imagine how you feel after using the substance. Do you feel low self-worth, shame, failure and lack of energy or depression afterwards? Knowing this normally helps you to be in a better frame of mind to make a judgement. You can harness this energy to more beneficial activities. Do things you enjoy, exercise, go outside, help others, laugh, meditate, practice yoga or listen to motivating music. You can't suppress your desires for it doesn't work. Look at Muslim countries where porn is banned; they make up some of the top 10 countries in the world that watch the most porn. If you think the addiction is bad, it won't feel good for you. Alcohol, drugs and porn themselves are not unhealthy; it is your attachment to them that is. You can happily watch or use them alone or with a partner as long as you are not using it to avoid real issues. Addiction, however, is about feeling disconnected and emotionally isolated. Human connection remedies this as well as increasing your self-esteem through self-care.

The meditation technique I have followed for many years now is called Vipassana. This is the very practice that helped Gautama The Buddha to gain enlightenment. It is a very difficult ten-day course, sitting for up to 12 hours a day cross-legged without dinner or talking to anyone, meditating on your bodily sensations. The aim of the course is to remove the unconscious mind of cravings and aversions. With doing so, it is believed suffering is ended, and nirvana gained. From this practice, I have learnt the deep reliance or addiction to substances and sex as a form of pleasing the ego. The sorrow from not obtaining what we think we want and the pain that results. By remaining equanimous (balanced) and observatory we rid ourselves of these dependencies thus removing deep complexes of the mind. In doing so, things like porn addiction do decrease. The eventual goal of Vipassana, enlightenment or nirvana (liberation from all suffering) comes with the side effect of celibacy. You literally are no longer into sexual actions. Now I am not saying we all become celibate. Nirvana takes lifetimes if not longer, thus do not expect that to happen now. But I am saying everything is a natural progression and with spiritual practice, you will become aware and release certain things, which do not support your inner and outer well-being. For what you do to others, you do onto yourself. Compassion is more important than passion. Thus treating ourselves and our bodies as well as partners with compassion is paramount.

The importance of this chapter needs to be taken seriously. Many new evolved souls that enter this planet feel isolated, alone and out of this world. They don't feel connected to earth or part of anything. Lost and fearful they may have had bad childhoods, or deviated towards unhealthy habits like drugs. They may be you, yes you reading right now. You have a purpose- read Chapter 16 to learn how. Chapter 13 goes into more depth about these new souls entering earth. You have a mission. Are you ready?

Drugs, Prostitution & Porn, takes over the lives of many LGBTI in our community. Stand in solidarity. Facebook, Tweet, Pin, Instagram, and Email the message below:

Bollywood Gay Message #9:
I choose to love myself above everything else.
#BollywoodGay

Action Sheet 9: How Much Do You Love Yourself?

From standing in front of the mirror and loving myself, to singing affirmations are just some of the ways I have become the confident person I am today! It wasn't easy at first as I couldn't even bare to look at myself in the mirror let alone appear or watch myself on camera. See being gay made me uncomfortable with my femininity, my voice, my walk, and my appearance. But then one day I said 'f' that and it all changed...

*I recommend you to try my **10 personal tricks**...*

1) Start taking loads of selfies of yourself and look at them from a non-judgemental place, focusing on all the good attributes you can find. It's ok, you may need to take 20, 30 or 50 shots before you get a couple of good ones, this is normal. You can also start filming yourself, start a YouTube channel or just a private video collection. The more you are comfortable with yourself on camera, the more you will be in real life. It's a trick that has really helped me. It can help you be bolder, and know your strengths. *Post these on your social media and hashtag #BollywoodGay so I can like them!*

2) Mirror trick. Look in the mirror at least once or twice a day and admire yourself. Often our negative self-talk ends up criticising every little thing about us and we fail to see the beauty we truly are. Everyone is beautiful inside and out; you just have to reprogramme your mind to look for the good characteristics. So look into your eyes and start appreciating yourself. I suggest doing a few gratitude sentences first, so when you do look at yourself in the mirror you are in your happy place!

3) Start appreciating other people's beauty, confidence and good traits. Instead of criticising others start complimenting them. How you treat others is a mirror of how you treat yourself. The Universe does not differentiate between you and I. So if you are critical of another, you are certainly critical of yourself. Remember criticism means a lack of confidence in oneself.

4) Stop comparing yourself to others. You are the light; you are on your own soul journey path, as long as you remain positive, connected and hopeful life will always give you more of what you want! Do some compassion meditation by sitting down and imagining love emanating from your whole being. You are love, and you choose words of love. Divine and sacred, perfect as you were made. This will give you a real confidence boost!

5) Start praising yourself for all the things you do right! For instance, 'I can draw very well', or 'I can sing melodically'. Whatever your gift, start blowing your own trumpet. We all have talents, whether it's cooking the most amazing exotic dinners or making people laugh. Find your gifts and praise yourself. Well done you!

6) Start doing affirmations with visualisations imagining the emotion of how you want to feel on a daily basis- such as:

'I am love. I accept and love myself completely. I am perfect the way I was made. I have a life purpose. I am important to the world.'

It is important to do these affirmations when you are feeling good. If you are feeling bad about yourself merely reciting these positive affirmations won't work. Indeed they may make you feel even worse about yourself. Another trick, therefore, is to focus thoughts of love towards a glass of water for two minutes and then to drink it. This tricks the ego, which thinks it's loving something external of itself. After sometime a vibrational shift takes place and the way you think about yourself will change.

7) A person who loves themselves prioritises the way they feel above everything else. A person who hates themselves works on shoulds. Here's a cool game to play: *Ask yourself what would someone who loved themselves do? Practice this for one year, when in a sticky situation or when you have free time. It is an easy downstream process. Follow your intuition, which is what the higher self knows. For example, you're at home and have a lot of things to do, and you ask what would someone who loves themselves do? Have a bath, nap, clean the house or work. Listen to your intuition and do what it says. You will find yourself over time feeling good when you act from a place of self-love.*

8) Love is often equated with pain and abuse. As a child, our parents often tell us off saying, 'I'm doing this because I love you'. As we get older and get into relationships if our partner treats us badly, we think it's love. We need to learn the warmth and softness that love actually is. Not abuse ourselves, thinking that's the only way to get love from the external world. If it feels like abuse, it is abuse. Get yourself out of the situation. Remove yourself from abuse rather than deal with it. Learn to gravitate towards things that feel good rather than bad.

9) Deal with negative self-talk by stepping outside the hating mind and loving it. Learn to love the self that hates the self. The purpose of self-hatred is the ego's way of re-enacting what our parents did to us believing by making us good we will get the love we crave. Our ego is simply trying to get love very much like a baby. So when you mind is eating itself, observe it. Remind yourself that your ego is trying to perfect itself so it can get love. Be compassionate to that. Then you are closer to self-love.

10) People who love themselves radiate joy, choose in the direction of what feels good, and treat others well. They don't start wars, they have peaceful auras, and allow others to be themselves without judging them. Try being like that today!

30-DAY SELF-LOVE EXERCISE: It takes 30 days to maintain a good habit. So why not repeat as often as possible for 30 days *'I love myself, I am worthy of love, I am love.'*

'Wrap yourself with love and what you attract will also be love. Love that overflows.'

10) GRINDR & FAKE PROFILES

You say you want it, but are you really ready for a relationship?

New technology brings with it newer, supposedly easier ways of meeting other people. Don't get me wrong; I've met past boyfriends on sites such as Gaydar, Gayromeo and Grindr. However, the brutalisation and objectification of men on gay dating apps is beyond what should be acceptable in a healthy functioning society. We need to say enough to the self-deprecation and superficial, meaningless validation that is sought after. Countless times rude, arrogant guys roam these sites looking for one thing in particular.

HOW SHOULD YOU CONDUCT YOURSELF IN THE DATING WORLD?

We have to accept that on apps like Grindr most people are primarily looking for sex. If you go on to the site even for 5 minutes, you will be bombarded with profiles looking for NSA (no strings attached sex) or topless torsos into certain types of sexual fetishes. Most, if not all gay dating sites are littered with porn advertisements, subconsciously making men lean towards sexual encounters rather than love. This makes it very distracting for someone to think about mutual friendship or dating. The whole dating scene is thus overtly sexualised. Unconsciously we end up looking for sex. This is worrying, especially if you are young and impressionable, for cock and ass pictures will be thrown at you, exposing and normalising you to them. It is dangerous. Such sites and apps do not have measures in place to check for age verification, such as with a credit card. I know of underage boys who have created accounts on such sites and had sex with much older men. Added to this there is codependency addiction to these apps where we constantly look for new messages on our phones each time we enter a new postcode.

Grindr is about muscular men parading their semi-naked pictures and non-muscular men lowering their self-esteem. People convince you to reciprocate and send nudes back, and you cave in. The constant rejection lowers your confidence forcing you into giving pictures to a hot guy to get his validation and love. Do these apps/sites really help anyway? Do they fulfil you or is it just a quick release? There is nothing wrong with 'fun' either. It really depends on what you are looking for. It can be a total waste of time and energy if you are after something meaningful as the app is very addictive. You can roam through it for hours every time you enter a new location or wait for people to reply. A lot of the time we are just asking to be acknowledged. Finally with it being the Internet people feel they can say, do and send anything they want to you. People end up doing or saying things that they would never do in real life. They can be overtly sexual, misogynistic, racist or rude because they feel they can get away with it.

That said, I have made friends time and time again on Grindr. Especially when I have been travelling I've met lovely guys to travel with, site see and also help me get a flat to live in, all without having sex with them! Shock horror! I believe it is all down to our intention. If you are clear and stick to your morals, you can easily date, find a boyfriend or make a social circle through gay dating sites. Anything is possible! Also apps like Grindr can help you firm up what you do want from a partner, whether you just want sex, or something more meaningful.

FAKE GRINDR PROFILES

The epidemic of fake profiles is startling. I used to think only in India fake or pictureless profiles existed, but by God I was wrong. In the UK, there are many faceless profiles on Grindr. The amount of torso pictures is frightening. Maybe these men are insecure about their physical features, are in the closet, or cheating on their partners. A lot of fake profiles are of course people trying to pretend to be someone else (usually some model or pornstar) in order to gain conversation, pictures and validation off others whom they deem attractive. This is not helped by the rudeness, discrimination and lack of response from many attractive guys on the app, which encourages such behaviour.

There are also guys who try to deceive you to get your nude pictures. You find guys who look like super hot models trying to get your credit card details. They get you to go on some site and enter your details saying you will never be charged so that you can see them in a nude cam show, only to extortionately take money from your account. Be aware. I have also seen the same guys picture in different parts of the world or country. Of pornstars or regular guys. Inviting guys for threesomes or orgies to their flats. Be weary of the fake profiles, especially in countries where the legal system does not support you.

ARE YOU READY FOR A RELATIONSHIP?

Do you seek a relationship to complete you, fulfil a certain aspect of yourself which you think is missing or to make you happy? These are all wrong intentions in which to seek a relationship. We have heard this time and time again, that the most important relationship is with ourselves. Yes, we have to love ourselves, cultivate harmony and acceptance. We need inner peace. As you are well aware, the gay community is very disenfranchised within itself. There are of course many positives such as meeting like-minded people, having a community to belong to and the confidence to be yourself. But there is also insecurity, bitchiness, self-loathing and hatred. That which you do upon yourself is what you do upon another and that which you do to another you are unconsciously doing to yourself.

How can you expect to have a loving, romantic, fulfilling relationship, if all you do is moan about everyone? The Universe does not make a distinction between the outside world and your internal one. We are all atoms of energy, and we are in fact one. So when we go to that wedding, birthday party or nightclub and judge, criticise or are two faced to people, we are doing that to ourselves. You will never be a happy, content, peaceful person who has the relationship of your dreams until you treat everyone with compassion. Even your enemies are there to teach you something. Forgiveness, compassion, self-love and knowledge that you are pure infinite Source energy. (Chapter 13 explains this in detail).

'Love your enemies.' Jesus

Ask yourself what do you actually want. Do you want a relationship? And if so are you acting like that. Though there are no hard and fast rules about getting into a relationship, it is a good idea to think about how you are conducting yourself in the pursuit of it, especially if you have been perpetually single for a long time. I mean if you want to date someone, I would recommend not sending nude pictures or talking about sex straight away. Rather, trust that the Universe will bring you the relationship you deserve.

Who are you dating or having sex with? Married men? What about karma? Are you selling yourself short? You have so much more worth then sleeping with men who cannot be authentic to themselves. Men who marry women, and cheat with you are not ideal partners for an authentic relationship. If you are ok with the fun aspect and lies, then cool. But if you want a meaningful relationship I would say avoid men who think like this. Who have their own internalised homophobia and are unable to be truly authentic.

All that matters is how you feel about yourself. What you feel will manifest. Thus if you think, feel and act like a good human being, those who also see the good in themselves will be attracted to you and mimic those qualities. The more positive, self-loving and forgiving you are, the better people's treatment, perception and interaction with you will become.

There are many steps to take to clean up your unconscious mind and your vibration to bring it to love and joy. When you emanate love and joy on a continual basis not only will you feel great, but you will attract all the desires you have wanted for a long while, including the man of your dreams. See happy people attract happy people. People who are secure, loving and compassionate attract the same. This is the Law of Attraction, and it's integral to understand. Read Chapter 15 to find out more.

SO HOW DO YOU ATTRACT A MATE?

We live in an attraction-based Universe. Thus you must feel as though you already have the man of your dreams! When we are happy and connected, we feel full as though we already have everything we want.

THESE ARE A FEW THINGS I DID TO MANIFEST MY RELATIONSHIP:

I didn't have sex for many months or go on any apps. I deleted them all. Waiting for my partner to come. I prepared myself, and met him at an event. There are many places to meet men. Go to your local LGBTI Centre. At the local South Asian LGBTI group. You can meet a partner anywhere. I would not recommend websites and apps as they are geared towards sex, porn, escorts and cocks size, etc. Unplug, delete and look within, cultivate and love yourself.

I would visualise and imagine having my partner already with me, 5 to 10 minutes a day. I would sit in my car and imagine him sitting next to me. I would feel the feelings of being in a relationship. I would feel happy and content with him being near me.

At night before going to bed, I would put a pillow near me vertically and turn my overthrow to one side to make the outline of a person and imagine it was him. You may think this is madness, but it mentally prepares you for the physical manifestation of your man. You can clear out some space in your closet for his clothes. Or as you cook imagine cooking for two.

As you imagine, so you behave. You will start acting like a person who is already in a relationship. Grindr will no longer have a hold on you. Naked pictures won't be exchanged, and you will speak to people with love. You have to become the man you want to date so that you mirror him into your life.

Now this whole process can take time. So don't just do it for a week, give up and go back to having random hookups. It could take several months or a year. The process is simple, as it removes all barriers and blockages that are in your mind stopping you from having the physical manifestation of your mate.

See he is waiting for you. In fact, there are an infinite amount of suitable mates waiting there for you. As you block yourself through misbelieving or acting out of alignment, a new mate that matches your vibration lines up to you. It's like a bus, if you miss one, that one goes, and another one is scheduled. Your job is to be at the bus stop long enough waiting; knowing it will come before boom it arrives.

Expectation is the surest way of bringing a miracle into your life.

I knew I would attract a man into my life. So I just waited for the good one to arrive. I turned down unsuitable suitors and made friends with men first. Your job is to be in alignment for as long as you can to allow the miracle to come to you. Of course, you may fall off the waggon, but you must get up and dust yourself by starting again. Make it a daily practice of feeling you have the partner of your dreams. Feel full and complete. When others ask you about how you are, reply and say, 'I am so happy and complete. I am excited and expecting my mate to appear any day now! It will be so fun when that day arrives. I have loads of cool ideas lined up for dates and adventures. I simply can't wait.'

PERPETUALLY SINGLE?

If you are perpetually single grab someone and date them! Don't be afraid to be vulnerable, or of getting hurt. If you were anything like me, searching for perfection, a perfect guy with the perfect body and perfect everything then stop. Because perfection does not exist. If you are perpetually single and tired of it then just date someone. Of course you have to be attracted to them to an extent, and of course, you have to find them interesting, but just because they are not the perfect image of the man you want does not mean you should not get experience. Go get relationship experience but also work on yourself objectively.

It's more than the big dick, the muscles and good looks. Having criteria's can create huge barriers for yourself. Even if your criteria's are not based on external physical characteristics and are about deeper inner values, it can still limit you. I used to be all about the physical, then changed to have these 5 criteria. I used to say the man I meet must tick most if not all of these characteristics. I must be attracted to him 1) physically 2) sexually 3) mentally 4) emotionally and 5) spiritually. Whilst it is good to know what you want, most of us forget that the Universe is a vibrational game. We attract what we are. We attract partners that match the deepest unhealed wounds within us that need healing. We play out the wounds of our parents, trying to heal their relationship in our heads through our partners. What is truly good for our healing and growth is not necessarily what our conscious mind can comprehend. We try with our ego to think our way into knowing what we want, but this is a very limited way of manifesting. Connect to Source, and trust the journey. Allow whoever comes to come. Your ascension is all that matters. Ascension on the dimension planes. You want to get from the third dimension of consciousness to fifth level Christ consciousness and beyond. Chapter 13 will explain more in detail.

WHAT IF I'M IN A NEGATIVE RELATIONSHIP?

Each person you meet is gearing you up to be with the person you were meant to be. Very much like a stairwell, as you experience one individual and learn you progress onto the next step. A step, which is more aligned to who you want to be, and with whom you want to be with. The trick is that you need to be aware. Awake. You need to automatically forgive the person you are with and realise the deeper lesson within it. For you have attracted this individual into your life in the first place. All the negative and irritating things they bring up are a shadow of the very things you dislike about yourself. Are they loud and obnoxious, rude and judgemental? Yep, you hold those qualities within yourself. This person simply reflects all that back at you. If you are aware you will learn, forgive, be detached in the realisation of the impermanence of everything and spiritual progress will follow quite fast.

Everyone has a vibration. If you experience violence growing up and unless you have healed from it, that vibration is within you. You will attract a guy who has a similar vibration within them. Perhaps they also experienced violence or are inherently violent. Until you learn to accept, acknowledge, release and heal from this violent experience, it will reappear time and time again in the other person. So identify what reoccurring patterns appear in your relationships or dating experiences and try to get to the root. If you are content with the vibration you hold about a situation then keep it, otherwise, understand it and then think of the thoughts/feelings of what you want, i.e. peace. Then the more you focus on peace, for instance, the more peaceful experiences will enter your life. Of course, if the relationship is destructive and violent, you need to assess your exit plans and learn your lessons whilst away from it.

Your work is the relationship between you and you. Focus on your connection with Source. When you are with a negative person, it means there is negativity within you too. This negative experience will help you to create your ideal relationship. If someone doesn't listen to you, it will help you create a relationship where you are heard. So don't be hard on the other person or yourself, because you can't get to where you want to by focusing and getting annoyed by all their bad points. It doesn't mean you have to leave this person either. This very person who helped you create this new vibration might indeed be the ideal mate for you. As your vibration increases, theirs may too, making them a better partner in the relationship.

WHAT KIND OF RELATIONSHIP IS RIGHT FOR YOU?

Guilt and shame force us to reject our sexuality. We don't accept it or feel others won't accept it either. Through shame we are unable to be open about who we are or live the life we want without fear. We are unable to have teenage romances, crushes or flings. We keep hidden our desire for men. We thus venture into saunas, online chat forums and apps looking for connection and validation in the form of sex. We want a deeper union but years of shaming have separated us from our soul. We cannot see another as whole and complete. We are unfulfilled by one man, and want open relationships or cheat. We make up excuses after excuses always avoiding the central issue. Societal guilt has caused us to cocoon within ourselves. We feel unlovable and alone but crave connection and union. Sex rules the roost. Slowly we lose our self. However, simply knowing this fact and then actively working on it can release us from the shame. It takes years of inner work and reconditioning to liberate yourself from shame. If you want a monogamous relationship, you need to emancipate yourself from this guilt. Look into your heart and discover what do I really want? Years spent on apps, sending naked pictures, venturing into soulless saunas, or a healthy loving relationship with one person? The choice is yours. And the choice is not limited to just these options. See what's best for you and go for it.

According to Abraham Hicks, the details of the kind of relationship we are in are not that important. Through life, we can come to different intentions and desires than other people.

There is nothing right or wrong. It's just a byproduct of what we have defined from our life experience. So it's not appropriate for society to say this is how you need to live to have a happy life. We should be more concerned about what we have put out into the Universe and what we would like to experience. Does more experience come from having many partners or just one? You may expand more with one person with whom you connect deeply then shallowly connecting with many. Equally having a variety of experiences may invigorate and liven you to experiences you come to love. The choice is yours, and it's always right. Indeed you can experiment and switch it up too.

Buddhist philosophy especially when following the route of Vipassana teaches the need to have a relationship with one person and to only experience sexual pleasures with them. The reason for this is that if we want to rid ourselves of all suffering, which is believed to come from craving or aversion, then by limiting ourselves from the sources that produce such desires we can overcome it. My Vipassana meditation teachers are always telling me not to sleep around and have multiple partners as it increases our craving for sex. Porn and masturbation are not seen as useful tools to enlightenment either as they enrage passion from within. They advise me that a monogamous relationship with a loving partner is best. Sex should occur in these circumstances ideally. Now, this may sound very strict and totalitarian. However, Buddhism does ultimately talk about the middle path and to allow things to naturally happen with time and practice. Thus by maintaining our spiritual path and working on ourselves regularly our desires for such things can diminish.

I would never prescribe anything. Or say by doing this your life will improve. That it is ultimately up to you to experiment and discover. For our bodies and minds interpret and react differently to varying circumstances. If you find the hours you spend on Grindr to be unhealthy and want to change that, then I urge you to try more positive ways of finding eligible men. I deleted my Grindr account because of the wasted hours I spent looking at naked torsos, the rejections and abuse!

I also think it important that we don't hate aspects of our psyche and selves. For by dismissing aspects of ourselves, we subjugate these to our unconscious, and they manifest in nasty ways. We need to accept and acknowledge them and decide ultimately whether they serve us or cause us harm.

OPEN RELATIONSHIPS VS. MONOGAMY

It is not wrong if through your experience you identify you want a variety of relationships, and you are in alignment with that. No one should make you feel bad about wanting to be free, expansive, and having relationships with multiple people. In pure vibration, without contradicting yourself, the Universe will bring others who align to that. Then you can have a satisfying experience with other people. However if you have an impure vibration, and contradict yourself you may have a problem. Sometimes in a relationship one person wants an open relationship and the other one wants monogamy. If someone has strong feelings about monogamy and a strong vibration of monogamy (what it would be like, how it feels), then they will attract it. But every subject is two things, the having of it and the absence of it. So if this very person who wants monogamy worries about not having it there focus of attraction is on not having monogamous relationships. They will then end up attracting people who want open relationships. So don't be surprised if you negatively manifest an open relationship. The Universe provides what you are vibrating, not what you are saying. By saying no I don't want that, vibrationally you are saying bring to me that thing I don't want. If two people want monogamy, then the Universe will bring them that. The same goes for those who want an open relationship. So be very clear with the message you are vibrating to the Universe.

Personally, I believe in a monogamous relationship love is beyond the ego. A monogamous relationship is about caring for an individual, being there for them and not just about your own needs. Yes, of course, it feels good to be around this one person, and much joy comes out of it. But to be truly successful in a relationship with them, you have to compromise and put your whole self aside.

Another reason why monogamy may be an option for you would be to do with spiritual energy exchange during intimacy. Every time you release your DNA during sex, you lose part of yourself. If you give that to someone you love you gain yourself at the same time as you absorb the love energy of your partner. In monogamous relationships we are attuned to our partner's energy, which easily assimilates into our auric field without much disturbance. This can be very healing and fulfilling especially if we are in a positive loving relationship. However, when in a negative relationship or when in relationships with multiple people who we don't attune with very well we can have a problem. We may need to be careful with who we allow to get intimate with us. If we sleep with negative people we carry that negative energy home with us. We deplete our spiritual energy by absorbing their negative, toxic energy. Therefore not only do you need to protect your body from STDs you also need to protect yourself from absorbing other people's energies.

However, if you cannot be with one guy for too long, do not despair. Either you are still figuring out the kind of man and relationship you want and thus are trying out different varieties or flavours of men, or you are just not meant to live that kind of life. There is nothing wrong with it. Some of us do get bored, and we want to gain many experiences to expand and grow as a being. Enjoy yourself, be safe and don't take life too seriously.

In open relationships, however if you are not careful the whole relationship between you and your partner can just become about getting other guys to hook up with. You may forget about your own intimate relationship and spend days surfing the web looking for sex with other guys on Grindr. Whilst out in a bar or club, instead of spending quality time gazing into each other's eyes discussing pressing topics, your gaze could be on the prowl for your next conquest. You need to balance what you do, and focus on the delicate relationship between you, else jealousy, ill will and distance will present itself quite quickly resulting in the failure of the relationship.

This jealousy can then cause problems especially when our partner appreciates someone else. When we are jealous, we are not in alignment with who we really are. Essentially we are depending on our partner's attention for our own well-being. We want their undivided attention because that is the only way we know how to feel good about ourselves. And if they do not give us that attention we feel as though they no longer love us. We depend on them for our happiness, which leaves us powerless. When ideally, we should look for happiness through our own connection to Source.

The sooner you make peace with allowing your partner to do what they want, the better your relationship will become. You cannot control them. Your happiness is not dependent on your partner's behaviour. Thus before getting into a relationship, get into alignment, and attract someone who is aligned too. When you feel bad, inform the person that you need to go and sort your thoughts so that you can come back when you feel better. You don't have to be joined at the hip to be in a healthy relationship. Try to stay in alignment and don't hold others responsible when you are not in alignment.

There is not a right or wrong way about anything. Understand what you want first. Focus on cleaning up your vibration. It's nice to have many partners, and it's also nice to have one person who is focused on their personal vibrational alignment. When you come together, you can have a wonderful experience when you make the relationship with Source paramount for you, as then everything becomes in alignment around you. If you are with someone who is also connected, it heightens your alignment. This does not mean you both have to be monogamous so that you can be connected to Source energy. It may be easier for you to focus when with one person. But never let what you are living be dependent on another. Choose what you choose and align to it. A good way of thinking about relationships is to go with the mindset; 'I like you pretty good, let's see how it goes.' And then focus on their positive aspects without criticising them. Then your relationship will flourish. (Read Chapter 15 to know more).

Affirm your readiness for a relationship. Facebook, Tweet, Pin, Instagram, and Email the message below:

Bollywood Gay Message #10:
I am ready to love.
#BollywoodGay

Action Sheet 10: Are You Ready For A Relationship?

Are you *looking* for a relationship?

_____

_____

_____

Where do you normally *meet* potential dates?

_____

_____

_____

_____

Do you use *dating apps* or sites?

_____

_____

_____

_____

How do you *conduct* yourself on them?

_____

_____

_____

_____

_____

_____

What is your *relationship pattern* so far?

_____

_____

_____

_____

_____

_____

_____

What *lessons* have you seen in each relationship you have been in?

_____
_____
_____
_____
_____
_____

If you've never had a relationship, write down what your own *relationship* is *with yourself*?

_____
_____
_____
_____

What do you *hope* to *bring* to a relationship?

_____
_____
_____
_____

Would you *date you* and *why*?

_____
_____
_____
_____
_____
_____

5 DATING TIPS:

1) Take it slow, get to know the real person. Your inner peace is first, so if this person does not contribute to that move on.

2) If the person is rushing it, asking you to be their partner straight away or telling you they love you or can't live without you within the first couple of dates, run for the hills, this person is neither stable nor knows how to be with themselves.

3) Do your inner work first. Everything is a direct reflection of you. Thus your partner will be a reflection of the deepest darkest wounds that need to be healed.

4) Only date those who have done a lot of their inner work already, are comfortable with themselves, secure, grounded and happy.

5) Enjoy and don't take it too seriously, but respect yourself and be honest.

PART 3:
COMING OUT

الكشف عن الميول الجنسية

ماذا يعني اختصار LGBTI؟

السحاقية (ليسبيان): الأنثى التي تنجذب جنسياً إلى الإناث الأخريات.

مثلي (غي): الذكر الذي ينجذب جنسياً إلى الذكور الآخرين.

ثنائي الميل (باي سيكشوال): شخص ينجذب جنسياً لكل من الذكور والإناث.

المتحول جنسياً (ترانس جيندر): شخصٌ لا ينسجم مع المعايير المقبولة اجتماعياً للجنس الذي ولد فيه. على سبيل المثال، من الممكن أن يكون قد ولد على أنه ذكر ولكنه يشعر بطبيعته أنه أنثى. ميوله الجنسية منفصلة عن هويته الجنسية، وبالتالي فإنه يمكن أن ينجذب جنسياً إلى أحدِ الجنسين فقط، أو يمكن أن ينجذب إلى كليهما على حد سواء أو قد لا ينجذب إلى أي منهما. قد يقرّر الشخص المتحول جنسيا أن يخضع لعملية إعادة تنظيم / تصحيح جنسي ليتحوّل جسدياً إلى الجنس الذي يشعر بالارتياح فيه. "الهجرة" هو المصطلح الأقرب لتلك العملية في جنوب آسيا.

أما المخنث، فهو الشخص الذي لا يمكن تصنيفه كذكر أو أنثى بشكلٍ كليّ. ويرجع ذلك إلى الاختلافات التي قد تكمن في خصائصه الجنسية بما في ذلك الصبغيات، أو الغدد التناسلية، أو الأعضاء التناسلية. غالبا ما يتم إجراء جراحات تغيير الجنس للأطفال المخنثين أثناء الولادة لجعلهم مقبولين أكثر لدى المجتمع ككل. وتعتبر هذه العملية اليوم إساءةً إلى حقوق الإنسان وتشويها للأعضاء التناسلية الخاصة بهؤلاء الأطفال لأنه لا يتم بموافقتهم وهو أمرٌ خطير. يمكن تعريف الأفراد المخنثين بدرجاتٍ متفاوتة من الذكورة والأنوثة أو الهويات الجنسية، والتي قد تتطور أثناء نموهم.

لماذا يحدث ذلك؟

ليس هناك دليل قاطع من المجتمع العلمي لماذا يحدث هذا. سواء كان السبب بيولوجياً، بيئياً، أو وراثياً، أو نفسياً لا زلنا لا نعرف. ما نعرفه هو أنه أمر طبيعي وموجود في كل الأنواع في العالم منذ بداية الزمان، وأنه لا يمكن تغييره.

كيف لنا أن نعرف إذا ما كان طفلنا واحداً من ألـ LGBTI؟

سيعلم طفلك لوحده ما إذا كان ينجذب جنسيا إلى شخص من نفس جنسه أو إذا كان يشعر بأنه ولد بالفعل في الجنس الخاطئ. ندعوك لكي تتحدث إلى طفلك بصراحة عن هذه القضايا في سن مبكرة، بحيث إذا كانو فعلاً أحد الـ LGBTI سيتمكنون من الانفتاح لكم حول هذا الموضوع لاحقاً.

ما الذي يمكن فعله حيال ذلك؟

انه ليس مرضاً، وبالتالي لا يجب القيام بشيء حيال ذلك. لستم بحاجة إلى أخذه للعلاج أو لرجالالدين، لأن هذا لن يؤدي إلا إلى جعل الأمور أسوأ. في محاولتك لعلاج طفلك سوف تؤثر سلباً فقط على صحته. ما عليك سوى أن تحب طفلك أكثر وأن تتفهم ما يمرّ به. ثقف نفسك وثقّف الآخرين. وحاول ألا تشعر بالعار بسبب ما سيظنونه المجتمع. علينا ببساطة أن نتقبل أنفسنا ونكون صادقين مع ما نحن عليه. فنحن لا يجب أن ندمر حياة الآخرين من خلال زواج زائف أو حياةٍ مصطنعة. لطالما كان الأشخاص المثليين موجودين دوماً في المجتمع. إنهم ليسوا قذرين ولا يشكّلون خطرا على المجتمع. بل في الواقع هم أحد العناصر الأساسية فيه. فهم موجودون لتعليمنا الحب غير المشروط وقبول الآخرين وأنفسنا. لقد جاءوا لتوسيع وجهات نظر المجتمعات بالنسبة للحب والاحتواء. وسوف يوفرون المزيد من الحقوق للإناث، والمعوقين، وأولئك المختلفون. الحكمة والمحبة، إنهم بمثابة هديةٍ لكم كأسرة.

أي نوعٍ من الحياة يمكن أن يحظى طفلي؟

طفلك عادي، وهو طبيعي تماماً وصحي. وهو قادرٌ على الحصول على أفضل حياةٍ ممكنة. بالطبع أنا أتفهم أنه قد تراودك مخاوف من أنهم سيتعرضون للترهيب أو للسخرية لكونهم مختلفون. ومع ذلك، إذا بقيت إيجابياً ومتصلاً وجدانياً بمصدر الإيمان خاصتك دوماً / الله / سوف تكون على ما يرام. حاول أن تتوقع أفضل النتائج، وغالباً سيحصل كلّ ما تتمناه، ولكن لا تقوم بإقصاء طفلك لمجرد أنه مختلف.

ماذا عن فيروس نقص المناعة البشرية / الإيدز؟

يحدث انتقال فيروس نقص المناعة البشرية / الإيدز عن طريق ممارسة الجنس الكامل دون استخدام حماية. طالما كان طفلك يمارس الجنس مستخدماً الواقي الذكري سيكون على ما يرام غالباً. حتى يمكن للشخص أن يعيش حياة صحية وسعيدة مع فيروس نقص المناعة البشرية مع خضوعه للعلاج.

أين يمكن لنا أن نحصل على الدعم؟

انت لست وحدك، وهناك الكثير من الناس الذين يشاركونك هذه التجربة. وخاصةً في المدن الكبيرة حيث يوجد العديد من مراكز المثليين، الذين يفسحون لك المجال للحصول على فحوصات طبية واجتماعية. وإذا كنت بعيداً عن المدن الكبيرة، توجد أيضاً إمكانية الاتصال على خطوط المساعدة المتوفرة في بلدك. من المؤسسات الموجودة في الهند هناك أمانة 'هوم سافار'، مؤسسة 'ناز' وغيرهما الكثير. كما يوجد في باكستان 'فيجن' وفي بنغلادش جمعية الرعاية الاجتماعية 'باندهو'. ويوجد في معظم الدول الكبرى في الغرب مراكز LGBT أو خطوط مساعدة ودعم يمكنك البحث عنها على محرّك البحث غوغل. اذا كنت بحاجة الى المزيد من المشورة أو الدعم يمكنك أيضاً أن تقوم بالاتصال بي على وسائل الاعلام الاجتماعية.

যৌন প্রবণতার প্রকাশ

LGBTI কি?

স্ত্রীসমকামীতা (লেসবিয়ান)-একজন নারী যিনি যৌনতা বিষয়ে অপর নারী প্রতি আকৃষ্ট হয়।

সমকামী (গে)-এমন একজন পুরুষ যিনি যৌনতা বিষয়ে অপর পুরুষের প্রতি আকৃষ্ট হয়।

উভয়লিঙ্গী (বাইসেক্সুয়াল)-এমন একজন ব্যক্তি যিনি যৌনতা বিষয়ে পুরুষ ও নারী উভয়ের প্রতি আকৃষ্ট হয়।

হিজড়া (ট্রান্সজেণ্ডার)-এমন একজন ব্যক্তি যিনি সামাজিকভাবে গ্রহণযোগ্য লিঙ্গ নিয়মের সাথে খাপ খায় না। উদাহরণ স্বরুপ, তারা হয়তো পুরুষ হয়ে জন্মায় কিন্তু ভেতরে ভেতরে নিজেকে নারীরূপে ভাবে। তাদের যৌন প্রবনতা, পরিচিত লিঙ্গের থেকে পৃথক হয়, এভাবেই তারা যৌন বিষয়ে যেকোন দিকের প্রতি আকৃষ্ট হয় অথবা উভয়ের প্রতি অথবা পুরুষ বা নারী কারোর প্রতিই আকৃষ্ট নাও হতে পারে। একজন হিজড়া যৌন পুর্ননির্ধারণ / সংশোধন অপারেশন করিয়ে স্বাচ্ছন্দ্য বোধ করে। হিজড়া শব্দটি দক্ষিণ এশিয়ায় বহুলভাবে প্রচলিত শব্দ।

উভলিঙ্গতা ব্যক্তিকে একজন স্বতন্ত্র পুরুষ কিংবা নারী হিসেবে চিহ্নিত করা হয় না। এটা ক্রোমোজম, জননগ্রন্থি, অথবা গুপ্তাঙ্গ সহ তাদের সেক্স বিশেষ্যের এক পরিবর্তিত কারণের দরুন হয়। মাঝে মধ্যেই, জন্মের সময়ে উভয়লিঙ্গ শিশুদের সামগ্রিকভাবে সমাজে তাদের গ্রহণযোগ্য করে তোলার জন্য সেক্স পুর্ননির্ধারণ অপারেশনসমূহ করে দেওয়া হয়। আজকাল শিশুদের এই ব্যবস্থাকে মানবধিকার লঙ্ঘন হিসাবে বিবেচনা করে প্রক্রিয়াটিকে অ-সন্মতিসূচক এবং বিপঞ্জনক হিসাবে আখ্যা দেওয়া হয়। উভলিঙ্গ ব্যক্তি হিসাবে তারা বেড়ে উঠতে হতে পারে, এবং লিঙ্গ অথবা যৌন পরিচয়ের ক্ষেত্রে সকলে সমান হিসাবে নিজেদের চিহ্নিত করতে পারে।

এমনটা কেন হয়?

এরকম কেন হয় তার বৈজ্ঞানিকভাবে কোন অকাট্য প্রমাণ নেই। এটা জৈবিক পরিবেশ, জিনগত বা মানসিক কিনা তা আমরা জানি না। আমরা যেটা জানি সেটা হল এটা প্রাকৃতিক এবং বিশ্বের সৃষ্টির সময় থেকেই যেকোন প্রানীর মধ্যেই বিদ্যমান এবং এটাকে পরিবর্তন করা যায় না।

আমাদের সন্তান LGBTI কিনা সেটা আমরা কিভাবে জানবো?

আপনার সন্তান নিজেই জানতে পারবে যে সে যৌনতা বিষয়ে নিজস্ব লিঙ্গের প্রতি আকৃষ্ট কিনা অথবা জেনে যাবে যে সে প্রকৃতঅর্থেই ভুল লিঙ্গ নিয়ে জন্মেছে কিনা। এক্ষেত্রে ছোট বয়স থেকেই বিষয়টি নিয়ে আপনার সন্তানের সাথে সরাসরি কথা বলুন, যাতে যদি সে LGBTI হয় তাহলে সেটা আপনার কাছে খোলাখুলি যেন বলে।

এই সম্পর্কে কি করা যায়?

এটা কোন রোগ নয় এবং তাই এক্ষেত্রে কিছুই করার নেই। বৈদ্য বা ধর্মীয় নেতাদের কাছেও যাওয়ার কোন প্রয়োজন নেই, কেননা পরিস্থিতিটা তাহলে আরো জটিল হয়ে উঠবে। আপনার সন্তানকে সুস্থ করার প্রচেষ্টার ফল ওর শারীরিক অবস্থা আরো সঙ্গীন হয়ে উঠবে। আপনার উচিত শুধু আপনার সন্তানকে আরো বেশী করে ভালোবেসে যাওয়া এবং বোঝা উচিত সে কিরকম অবস্থার মধ্যে দিয়ে পার হচ্ছে।নিজেকে শিক্ষিত করে তোলার সাথে সাথে অপরকেও শিক্ষিত করে তুলুন। সমাজ কি বলছে সেটা চিন্তা করে লজ্জা বোধ না করার চেষ্টা করুন। আমাদের সহজভাবে বিষয়টা মেনে নিতে হবে এবং আমরা কে সেটা সত্যিকরে জানতে হবে। লজ্জাজনক বিবাহ বন্ধনে বা অন্য উপায়ের মাধ্যমে আমরা অপরের জীবন ধ্বংস করতে পারি না। LGBT ব্যক্তি সর্বদাই সমাজে বিদ্যমান। এরা নোংরা নয় এবং এরা সমাজের পক্ষে হুমকিও নয়। এরা প্রকৃতপক্ষে সমাজের সম্পদ। এরা আমাদের নিঃশর্ত ভালোবাসা এবং গ্রহণযোগ্যতা শেখাতে এসেছে। এরা ভালোবাসার প্রতি সমাজের দৃষ্টিকোণ এবং অন্তর্ভুক্তি প্রসারিত করেছে। এরা নারীদের এবং অপরের থেকে পৃথক অক্ষম ব্যক্তিদের আরো অধিকার প্রদান করে। এরা বিজ্ঞ এবং প্রেমময়, এরা পরিবারের প্রতি উপহারস্বরূপ।

আমার সন্তানের জীবনটা কেমন হবে?

আপনার সন্তান স্বাভাবিক, প্রাকৃতিক এবং সুস্থ। সে জীবনের শ্রেষ্ঠতা লাভ করতে সক্ষম। হ্যাঁ, আমি বুঝতে পারছি যে ওর জন্য হয়তো আপনাকে উপহাস অথবা ঠাট্টা সহ্য করতে হতে পারে। তবে যাইহোক, যতক্ষণ আপনি সদর্থক থাকবেন, যতক্ষণ পর্যন্ত আপনি ওর সাথে নিজেকে যুক্ত করে রাখবেন ততক্ষণ পর্যন্ত উৎস / ঈশ্বর / প্রকৃতির সবকিছুই ভালো থাকবে। সম্ভাব্য সর্বোত্তম ফলাফল আশা করুন এবং এর চেয়ে আর আপনি বেশি কি আশা করতে পারেন। ওর পার্থক্যের জন্য ওকে ছেড়ে চলে যাবেন না।

এইচআইভি / এইডস –এর বিষয়ে কি হবে?

এইচআইভি / এইডস সংক্রমণ অরক্ষিত প্রবেশাত্মক যৌন সংসর্গের মাধ্যমে ঘটে। যতক্ষণ পর্যন্ত আপনার সন্তান কনডোম দ্বারা সুরক্ষিত যৌন সংসর্গ করবে ততক্ষণ পর্যন্ত সে নিরাপদে থাকবে। এমনকি একজন এইচআইভি ব্যক্তিও মেডিকেশনের দ্বারা সুস্থ স্বাভাবিক জীবন কাটাতে পারে।

আমরা কোথা থেকে সাহায্য পাব?

আপনি একা নন; আপনার মত আরো বহু মানুষ আছে। বিশেষকরে বড় বড় শহরগুলিতে অনেক LGBT সেন্টার আছে, যেখানে আপনি স্বাস্থ্য পরীক্ষা করে সামাজিকভাবে মেলামেশা করতে পারবেন। যদি আপনি বড় শহর থেকে দূরে থাকেন, তাহলে হেল্প লাইনের সাহায্যে আপনি আপনার নিজের দেশে তাঁদের ডেকে নিতে পারেন। ভারতবর্ষে হামসফর ট্রাস্ট, নাজ ফাউণ্ডেশনের মত আরো অনেক সংস্থা আছে। পাকিস্তানে আছে ভিশন এবং বাংলাদেশে আছে বন্ধু সোস্যাল ওয়েলফেয়ার সোসায়েটি। অধিকাংশ পশ্চিমী দেশগুলির বড় শহরে অনেক LGBT সেন্টার অথবা সাপোর্ট হেল্পলাইন আছে যার সম্পর্কে আপনি গুগলে জানতে পারবেন। যদি আপনি আরো অধিক জানতে চান তাহলে আপনি আমার সাথে সোস্যাল মিডিয়ায় যোগাযোগ করতে পারেন।

Disclosure Of Sexual Orientation

WHAT IS LGBTI?

Lesbian- a female who is sexually attracted to other females.

Gay- a male or female who is sexually attracted to someone of the same sex.

Bisexual- a person sexually attracted to both males and females.

Transgender- a person who does not fit into the socially accepted gender norm they were born in. For instance, they could be born male but feel inherently female. Their sexual orientation is separate from their gender identity; thus they could be sexually attracted to either, both or neither male and female individuals. A transgender person may or may not have decided to have a sexual realignment/correction operation to the gender they feel comfortable with. Hijra is the closest term in South Asia.

Intersex individuals are not distinctly identified as male or female. This is due to a variation in their sex characteristics including chromosomes, gonads, or genitals. Often during birth, intersex babies are given sex reassignment surgeries to make them more acceptable to society as a whole. This is now regarded as a human rights abuse and genital mutilation of these babies as it is nonconsensual and dangerous. Intersex individuals may identify with varying degrees of gender or sexual identities, which may evolve as they grow.

WHY DOES IT HAPPEN?

There is no conclusive evidence from the scientific community why this happens. Whether it is biological, environmental, genetic or psychological, we do not know. What we do know is that it is natural and exists in all species of the world since the beginning of time and that it cannot be changed.

HOW DO WE KNOW IF OUR CHILD IS LGBTI?

Your child itself will know if they are sexually attracted to someone of their own gender or if they feel that they are indeed born in the wrong gender. Speak to your child openly about these issues from an early age, so if they are LGBTI they can be open to you about it.

WHAT CAN BE DONE ABOUT IT?

It is not a 'dis-ease,' and therefore nothing needs to be done about it. There is no need in going to healers or religious leaders, as this will only make matters worse. Trying to cure your child will only adversely affect their health. You only need to love your child more and understand what they are going through. Educate yourself and educate others. Try not to fall into the shame of what society will think. We simply have to accept ourselves and be true to who we are. We cannot ruin other people's lives by having sham marriages or by being inauthentic. LGBTI people have always existed in society. They are not dirty, and are not a threat to society. Indeed they are an asset. They have come to teach unconditional love and acceptance. They have come to expand societies views on love and inclusion. They will bring more rights to females, disabled people and those who are different. Wise and loving, they are a gift to you family.

WHAT KIND OF LIFE CAN MY CHILD HAVE?

Your child is normal, natural and healthy. They can have the best life possible. Yes, I understand that you may have fears they will be bullied or ridiculed for being different. However, as long as you remain positive, in the present moment and connected to that which is Source/God/Nature you will be fine. Expect the best possible outcome and that is what will be more likely for you. Do not cast your child off due to their differences.

WHAT ABOUT HIV/AIDS?

HIV/AIDs transmission happens through unprotected insertive sex. As long as your child has protected sex with a condom, they are most likely safe. Even with HIV, a person can live a healthy, happy life whilst on medication.

WHERE CAN WE GET SUPPORT?

You are not alone; there are many people like you. Especially in big cities there are LGBT centres, where you can get health checks and socialise. If you are away from the big cities, there are helplines you can also call in your own country. In India, there is the Humsafar Trust, Naz Foundation and many more. Pakistan has Vision and Bangladesh has Bandhu Social Welfare Society. In the West most major cities have LGBT centres or support helplines which you can Google. If you need more advice or support, you can also contact me on my social media.

જાતીય વલણ અંગેની સમજ

એલજીબીટીઆઇ શું છે ?

સમલૈંગિક સ્ત્રી (લેસ્બિયન) એવી સ્ત્રી જે જાતીય રીતે અન્ય સ્ત્રીઓ તરફ આકર્ષાય છે

સમલૈંગિક પુરુષ (ગે) -એવો પુરુષ જે જાતીય રીતે અન્ય પુરુષો તરફ આકર્ષાય છે.

દ્વિજાતીય (બાયસેક્સ્યુઅલ) - એવી વ્યક્તિ જે જાતીય રીતે પુરુષો અને સ્ત્રીઓ, બંને તરફ આકર્ષાય છે.

કિન્નર (ટ્રાન્સજેન્ડર) - એવી વ્યક્તિ જે જન્મથી પોતાનું જ લિંગ હોય, તેને લગતાં સામાજિક ધોરણોમાં બંધબેસતી ન આવતી હોય. ઉદાહરણ તરીકે, પોતાનો જન્મ પુરુષ તરીકે થયો હોય, પરંતુ અંદરથી તેને સ્ત્રૈણભાવ અનુભવાતો હોય. જાતીયતા એટલે કે કામભાવ અંગેનું તેમનું જે વલણ હોય, તે વલણ તેમને (પોતાની મૂળ) લૈંગિક ઓળખથી અલગ પાડે છે, આમ તે વ્યક્તિ, બેમાંથી કોઇ એક તરફ આકર્ષણ અનુભવતી ન હોય. દક્ષિણ એશિયામાં આ માટે ઉપયોગમાં લેવાતો સૌથી નજીકનો શબ્દ છે કિન્નર (હિજડા).

ઇન્ટરસેક્સ - આવી વ્યક્તિઓ હોય તેઓને પુરુષો અથવા તો સ્ત્રી તરીકે સ્પષ્ટપણે, અલગ ઓળખ આપવામાં આવતી નથી. આનું કારણ એ છે કે તેમનાં રંગસૂત્ર (ક્રોમોઝોમ), જનનેન્દ્રિયો સહિતનાં તેમનાં લક્ષણો જુદાં જુદાં હોય છે. ઘણી વખત, જન્મ દરમ્યાન ઇન્ટરસેક્સ શિશુઓને ફરીથી લિંગ ઓળખ આપવા માટે તેમની શલ્યચિકિત્સા કરવામાં આવતી હોય છે, જેથી સમાજમાં તેઓ સમગ્રપણે સ્વીકાર્ય બને. હવે આ વાતને માનવ અધિકારના દુરુપયોગ તરીકે અને આવાં બાળકોની સાથે લૈંગિક છેડાં તરીકે ઓળખવામાં આવે છે, કારણ કે તેમાં સંમતિ લેવામાં આવતી નથી અને તે જોખમી છે. ઇન્ટરસેક્સ વ્યક્તિઓમાં જાતિ અંગેનાં જે લક્ષણો જોવા મળતાં હોય તેનું પ્રમાણ બદલાતું રહેતું હોય, જે શક્ય છે કે ઉંમર વધવાની સાથે કદાચ વિકાસ પામે.

આવું શા માટે થાય છે ?

વૈજ્ઞાનિક સમાજ પાસે પણ કોઇ પુરાવા નથી કે આવું શા માટે થાય છે. જૈવિક, પર્યાવરણીય, વંશાનુગત કે પછી માનસિક - ક્યાં કારણોસર આવું થાય છે તેની આપણને ખબર નથી. આપણે એટલું જ જાણીએ છીએ કે સમયના આરંભિક કાળથી, વિશ્વની દરેક પ્રજાતિઓમાં આવું જોવા મળે છે, તે પ્રાકૃતિક છે અને તેને બદલી શકાય નહીં.

કેવી રીતે જાણી શકીએ કે પોતાનું બાળક એલજીબીટીઆઇ પ્રકારનું છે ?

આપણાં બાળકને પોતાને જ ખબર પડી જશે કે તે કામુકતાનો ભાવ સમલૈંગિક માટે અનુભવે છે કે પછી તેને એવું લાગે છે કે પોતાનો જન્મ ખોટાં લિંગમાં થયો છે. નાનપણથી જ પોતાનાં બાળકની સાથે આ વિશે નિખાલસતાપૂર્વક વાત કરો, આથી જો તે એલજીબીટીઆઇ પ્રકારનું હોય, તો તે વિશે તમારી સાથે મુક્તપણે વાત કરી શકે.

આ માટે શું કરી શકાય ?

આ કોઇ રોગ નથી, આથી આને માટે કંઇ જ કરવાની જરૂર નથી. આ માટે કોઇ ઉપચારકો અથવા ધર્મગુરુઓ પાસે જવાની જરૂર નથી, આમ કરવાથી પરિસ્થિતિ વધારે વણસશે. આપનાં બાળકને ઠીક કરવાની કોશિશો, તેનાં આરોગ્ય ઉપર વિપરીત અસર કરશે. આપ ફક્ત પોતાનાં બાળકને વધારે વહાલ કરો, સમજો કે તે કયા પ્રકારની માનસિક પરિસ્થિતિમાંથી પસાર થાય છે. પોતાની જાતને (આ માટે) શિક્ષિત કરો અને અન્યોને પણ. સમાજ શું વિચારશે એવી ગ્લાનિ અનુભવવાથી બચવાનો પ્રયત્ન કરો. આપણે ફક્ત એટલું જ કરવાનું છે કે પોતાની જાતને સ્વીકારવી અને પોતે જ છીએ, તે જ બની રહેવું. (પોતાની સ્વાભાવિકતા જાળવી રાખવી.) દુખદાયક, શરમજનક લગ્નો અથવા તો અસ્વાભાવિક બનીને આપણે, લોકોનાં જીવનો બરબાદ કરી શકીએ નહીં. સમાજમાં એલજીબીટીઆઇ પ્રકારનાં લોકોનું અસ્તિત્વ હંમેશાંથી રહેતું આવ્યું છે. તેઓ ગંદાં નથી અને સમાજને માટે ખતરારૂપ પણ નથી. ખરેખર તો તેઓ એક સંપદા છે. તેઓ બિનશરતી પ્રેમ કરવાનું અને સ્વીકાર કરતાં શીખવવા આવ્યાં છે. પ્રેમ અને સમાવેશી વલણ (ઉદારતાભર્યું વલણ) એટલે શું, તે વિશે સમાજના જે વિચારો છે, તેને વિશાળતા આપવા માટે તેઓ આવ્યાં છે. આ પ્રકારના લોકો, સ્ત્રીઓ, દિવ્યાંગો (વિભિન્ન રીતે ક્ષમતાયુક્ત લોકો) અને જેઓ અલગ પ્રકારનાં છે, તેમને વધુ અધિકારી મેળવી આપનારાં બનશે. સમજુ અને પ્રેમાળ એવાં આ લોકો, આપના પરિવાર માટે એક ઉપહાર છે.

મારાં બાળકનું જીવન કેવા પ્રકારનું હોઇ શકે ?

આપનું બાળક સામાન્ય, સ્વાભાવિક અને તંદુરસ્ત છે. તેને માટે શક્ય હોય તેટલું શ્રેષ્ઠ જીવન જીવવા તે સક્ષમ છે. હા, હું સમજી શકું છું કે આપને કદાચ ડર હોય કે તે અલગ પ્રકારનું હોવાને કારણે, તેના પર ધાકધમકી કરવામાં આવશે અથવા તેની હાંસી ઉડાવવામાં આવશે. આમ છતાં, જ્યાં સુધી આપ પોતે હકારાત્મક અભિગમ ધરાવશો, વર્તમાનમાં રહેશો અને જેને ઉદ્ગમ/ ઇશ્વર/ કુદરત તરીકે ઓળખવામાં આવે છે તેની સાથે આપ પોતે હકારાત્મક અભિગમ ધરાવશો, ત્યાં સુધી બધું બરોબર હશે. આશા રાખો કે શક્ય શ્રેષ્ઠ પરિણામ આવશે અને શક્ય છે કે એવું જ બને. આપનું બાળક ભિન્ન હોવાને કારણે તેને અલગ ન પાડી નાખો.

એચઆઇવી / એઇડ્સ વિશે શું ?

એચઆઇવી/ એઇડ્સનું સંક્રમણ, અસુરક્ષિત જાતીય સંબંધોને કારણે થાય છે. જ્યાં સુધી આપનું સંતાન કોન્ડોમના ઉપયોગ દ્વારા સુરક્ષિત કામજીવન જીવે તો ત્યાં સુધી મહદ્અંશે તે સુરક્ષિત રહે. એચઆઇવી હોય તો પણ વ્યક્તિ દવાઓની મદદથી સ્વસ્થ અને સુખી જીવન ગાળી શકે છે.

અમને ક્યાંથી મદદ મળી શકે ?

આપ એકલા નથી, આપના જેવા અનેક લોકો છે. ખાસ કરીને મોટાં શહેરોમાં એલજીબીટી કેન્દ્રો આવેલાં હોય છે, જ્યાં આપ તબિયતની તપાસ કરાવી શકો અને હળીભળી શકો. જો આપ મોટા શહેરથી દૂર હો તો ઘણી હેલ્પલાઇન છે, જેની મદદ લઇ શકો. ભારતમાં હમસફર ટ્રસ્ટ, નાઝ ફાઉન્ડેશન અને અન્ય ઘણાં છે. પાકિસ્તાનમાં વિઝન છે, બાંગ્લાદેશમાં બંધુ સોશિયલ વેલ્ફેર સોસાયટી છે. પશ્ચિમમાં. મોટા ભાગનાં મુખ્ય શહેરોમાં એલજીબીટી કેન્દ્રો છે અથવા મદદ મેળવવા માટે અનેક હેલ્પલાઇન છે, ગુગલ દ્વારા આની માહિતી મેળવી શકો છો. જો આપને વધુ સલાહ અથવા મદદની જરૂર હોય તો આપ મારા સોશિયલ મીડિયા ઉપર પણ મારો સંપર્ક કરી શકો છો.

यौन उन्मुखीकरण की घोषणा

एलजीबीटीआई (LGBTI) क्या है?

समलैंगिक स्त्री(लेस्बियन) - एक महिला जो दूसरी महिलाओं के प्रति यौन आकर्षण रखती है।

समलैंगिक पुरुष(गे) - एक पुरुष जो दूसरे पुरुषों के प्रति यौन आकर्षण रखता है।

उभयलिंगी(बाईसेक्सुअल) - एक व्यक्ति जो पुरुषों व महिलाओं दोनो के प्रति यौन आकर्षण रखता(ती) हो।

किन्नर (ट्रांसजेन्डर) - एक व्यक्ति जो अपने जन्म वाले समाज में सामाजिक रूप से स्वीकृत लैंगिक नियमों में फिट नहीं होता है। उदाहरण के लिए वे पुरुष रूप में जन्म लेने के बावजूद महिला जैसा महसूस कर सकते हैं। उनका यौन उन्मुखीकरण उनकी लैंगिक पहचान से पृथक होता है, इस प्रकार से वे किसी एक, दोनो लिंगों या न तो पुरुष न ही महिला से यौन रूप से आकर्षण रख सकते हैं। एक किन्नर व्यक्ति अपनी सहजता वाले लिंग के लिए यौन पुनःसंरेखण/संशोधन का ऑपरेशन करने का निर्णय ले सकता(ती) है या नहीं ले सकता(ती)। दक्षिण एशिया में इनके लिए अधिकांशतः हिंजड़ा शब्द का उपयोग किया जाता है।

मध्यलिंगी (इंटरसेक्स) व्यक्ति पुरुष या महिलाओं की तरह स्पष्ट रूप से पहचाने नहीं जाते हैं। इसका कारण उनके यौन गुणों में विविधता होती है, जिसमें गुणसूत्र, जनन ग्रंथियां या जननांग शामिल होते हैं। अक्सर जन्म के समय मध्यलिंगी बच्चों के साथ यौन पुनःसंरेखण शल्य क्रियाएं की जाती हैं जिससे कि वे समाज में समग्र स्वीकार्यता हासिल कर सकें। इसे अब इन शिशुओं के मानव अधिकारों का दुरुपयोग तथा इनके लिंगों का खतना माना जाता है, क्योंकि यह बिना सहमति के व खतरनाक होता है। मध्यलिंगी (इंटरसेक्स) व्यक्ति लिंग के भिन्न रूपों या यौन पहचानों से खुद को जोड़ सकते हैं, जो उनके बढ़ने के साथ विकसित हो सकता है।

ऐसा क्यों होता है?

ऐसा होने के कारण के संबंध में वैज्ञानिक समुदाय के पास कोई निर्णायक सबूत नहीं है। यह जीव वैज्ञानिक, पर्यावरणीय, लैंगिक या मनोवैज्ञानिक में से क्या है इस बारे में हमारे पास जानकारी नहीं है। हमें यह अवश्य पता है कि यह सामान्य सी बात है तथा समय की शुरुआत से ही दुनिया की सभी प्रजातियों में ऐसा हो रहा है और इसे बदला नहीं जा सकता है।

हम कैसे जाने कि हमारा बच्चा एलजीबीटीआई (LGBTI) है?

आपका(की) बच्चा(ची) खुद ही इस बात को जान जाएगा(गी) कि क्या वह समान लिंगी व्यक्ति के प्रति आकर्षण रखता(ती) है या वह गलत लिंग में पैदा हुआ(ई) है। कम उम्र से ही, अपने बच्चे से इन मामलों पर खुल कर बात करें, जिससे कि अगर वे एलजीबीटीआई (LGBTI) हैं तो वे इसके बारे में आपसे खुल सकें।

इसके बारे में क्या किया जा सकता है?

यह एक रोग नहीं है और इसलिए इसके बारे में कुछ भी करने की जरूरत नहीं है। आरोग्य करने वालों या धार्मिक लीडरों के पास जाने की कोई जरूरत नहीं है, क्योंकि इससे बात और बिगड़ जाएगी। अपने बच्चे को ठीक करने के प्रयास केवल उसके स्वास्थ्य पर बुरा प्रभाव डालेगा। आपको बस अपने बच्चे को और प्यार देने की व उस परिस्थिति को समझने की जरूरत है जिससे वह गुजर रहा(ही) है। खुद व दूसरों को शिक्षित करें। कोशिश करें कि समाज क्या सोचेगा, इस शर्म में न फंसे। बस हमें सहज रूप से खुद को तथा अपनी हकीकत को स्वीकारना होगा। दिखावे वाले विवाह करके या अप्रमाणित तमाशा करके हम दूसरों के जीवन को बरबाद नहीं कर सकते हैं। एलजीबीटीआई (LGBTI) हमेशा से समाज में मौजूद रहे हैं। वे गंदे नहीं हैं और वे समाज के लिए खतरा नहीं हैं। वास्तव में वे एक संपत्ति हैं। वे शर्तरहित प्रेम व स्वीकार्यता सिखाने के लिए आए हैं। वे प्रेम तथा समावेशन पर समाज के दृष्टिकोण को व्यापक करने आए हैं। वे महिलाओं, अक्षम लोगों तथा भिन्न लोगों के लिए अधिक अधिकार लाने आएं हैं। समझदार व प्रेम भरे ये लोग, आपके परिवार के लिए एक उपहार हैं।

मेरे बच्चे का जीवन कैसा हो सकता है?

आपका बच्चा सामान्य, प्राकृतिक तथा स्वस्थ है। वे सर्वश्रेष्ठ संभव जीवन जीने में सक्षम हैं। हाँ, मैं समझता(ती) हूँ आपको यह भय हो सकता है कि उनके भिन्न होने के कारण उनको धमकाया जा सकता है या उनका उपहास उड़ाया जा सकता है। हालांकि, जब तक आप वर्तमान पल में सकारात्मक बने रहते(ती) हैं और स्रोत/ईश्वर/प्रकृति से जुड़े(डी) रहते(ती) है आप ठीक रहेंगे(गी)। सर्वश्रेष्ठ परिणाम की अपेक्षा रखें और वैसा ही होने की सबसे अधिक संभावना होगी। अपने बच्चे की भिन्नता के कारण उससे भेदभाव न करें।

एचआईवी/एड्स (HIV/AIDs) का क्या?

एचआईवी/एड्स (HIV/AIDs) का ट्रांसमिशन असुरक्षित प्रवेशी यौन संबंधों द्वारा होता है। जब तक आपका(की) बच्चा(च्ची) निरोध के साथ सुरक्षित यौन संबंध रखता(ती) है वह काफी हद तक सुरक्षित है। एचआईवी(HIV) से पीड़ित व्यक्ति भी दवाओं के साथ स्वस्थ व खुश जीवन जी सकता है।

हमें कहां से समर्थन मिल सकता है?

आप अकेले(ली) नहीं हैं; आप जैसे अनेक लोग हैं। विशेष रूप से बड़े शहरों में एलजीबीटी(LGBT) केन्द्र होते हैं, जहां से आप स्वास्थ्य जांच तथा सामाजिक मेलजोल हासिल कर सकते(ती) हैं। यदि आप बड़े शहरों से दूर हैं तो आप अपने देश में उपलब्ध हेल्पलाइनों से संपर्क कर सकते(ती) हैं। भारत में हमसफर ट्रस्ट, नाज़ फाइंडेशन तथा अन्य संगठन हैं। पाकिस्तान में विज़न तथा बांग्लादेश में बंधु सोशल वेलफेयर सोसाइटी है। पश्चिम में अधिकांश बड़े शहरों में एलजीबीटी (LGBT) केन्द्र या समर्थन हेल्प लाइनें है जिनको आप गूगल पर खोज सकते(ती) हैं। यदि आपको अधिक सलाह या समर्थन की जरूरत हो तो आप मुझसे सोशल मीडिया पर संपर्क कर सकते(ती) हैं।

ಲೈಂಗಿಕ ಆದ್ಯತೆಯನ್ನು ಬಹಿರಂಗಪಡಿಸುವಿಕೆ

ಎಲ್‌ಜಿಬಿಟಿಐ ಎಂದರೇನು?

ಸ್ತ್ರೀಸಲಿಂಗಕಾಮಿ(ಲಸ್ಬಿಯನ್) – ಇತರ ಮಹಿಳೆಯರತ್ತ ಲೈಂಗಿಕ ಆಕರ್ಷಣೆ ಹೊಂದುವ ಓರ್ವ ಮಹಿಳೆ.

ಸಲಿಂಗಕಾಮಿ (ಗೇ) - ಇತರ ಗಂಡಸರತ್ತ ಲೈಂಗಿಕ ಆಕರ್ಷನೆ ಹೊಂದುವ ಓರ್ವ ಪುರುಷ.

ಉಭಯಲಿಂಗಕಾಮಿ (ಬೈಸೆಕ್ಸ್‌ಯುಯಲ್) - ಪುರುಷರು ಮತ್ತು ಮಹಿಳೆಯರತ್ತ ಲೈಂಗಿಕವಾಗಿ ಆಕರ್ಷಣೆ ಹೊಂದುವ ವ್ಯಕ್ತಿ.

ಲಿಂಗಮಧ್ಯಂತರಿ/ಅಂತರಲಿಂಗ (ಟ್ರಾನ್ಸ್‌ಜೆಂಡರ್) – ಅವರು ಜನಿಸಿರುವ ಸಾಮಾಜಿಕವಾಗಿ ಅಂಗೀಕಾರ್ಹ ಲಿಂಗದ ಮಾನದಂಡದಲ್ಲಿ ಹೊಂದಾಣಿಕೆ ಆಗದ ವ್ಯಕ್ತಿ. ಉದಾಹರಣೆಗೆ ಅವರು ಗಂಡಾಗಿ ಜನಿಸಿರಬಹುದು ಆದರೆ ಅಂತರಿಕವಾಗಿ ಅವರು ಹೆಣ್ಣು ಎಂದು ಭಾವಿಸಿಕೊಳ್ಳಬಹುದು. ಅವರ ಲೈಂಗಿಕ ಆಸಕ್ತಿಯು ಅವರ ಲಿಂಗದ ಗುರುತಿಗಿಂತ ಭಿನ್ನವಾಗಿರಬಹುದು, ಅದರಿಂದಾಗಿ ಅವರು ಇಬ್ಬರಲ್ಲಿ, ಒಬ್ಬರತ್ತ, ಇಬ್ಬರತ್ತಲೂ ಆಕರ್ಷಿತರಾಗಬಹುದು ಅಥವಾ ಪುರುಷ ಮತ್ತು ಮಹಿಳಾ ವ್ಯಕ್ತಿಗಳತ್ತ ಆಕರ್ಷಣೆ ಹೊಂದಿರಬಹುದು. ಲಿಂಗಮಧ್ಯಂತರಿ ವ್ಯಕ್ತಿಯು ತಾವು ಆರಾಮಕರ ಎಂದು ಭಾವಿಸುವ ಲಿಂಗದತ್ತ ಸಾಗಲು ಲೈಂಗಿಕ ಮರುಹೊಂದಾಣಿಕೆ/ಸರಿಪಡಿಸುವಿಕೆ ಶಸ್ತ್ರಚಿಕಿತ್ಸೆಗೆ ಒಳಗಾಗಲು ನಿರ್ಧರಿಸಬಹುದು ಅಥವಾ ನಿರ್ಧರಿಸದೇ ಇರಬಹುದು.. ದಕ್ಷಿಣ ಏಷ್ಯಾದಲ್ಲಿ ಈ ಸ್ಥಿತಿಗೆ ಹಿಜ್ರಾ (ಹಿಜಡಾ) ಅತ್ಯಂತ ಸನಿಹವಾದ ಪದವಾಗಿದೆ.

ಅಂತರಲಿಂಗ ವ್ಯಕ್ತಿಗಳನ್ನು ಗಂಡು ಅಥವಾ ಹೆಣ್ಣು ಎಂದು ನಿರ್ದಿಷ್ಟವಾಗಿ ಗುರುತಿಸಲು ಸಾಧ್ಯವಿರುವುದಿಲ್ಲ. ಇದು ಕ್ರೋಮೋಸೋಮ್‌ಗಳ, ಗೊನಾಡ್‌ಗಳ ಅಥವಾ ಲೈಂಗಿಕ ಅಂಗಾಂಗಗಳನ್ನು ಒಳಗೊಂಡಂತೆ ಅವರ ಲೈಂಗಿಕ ಗುಣಲಕ್ಷಣಗಳ ವೈವಿಧ್ಯತೆಯಿಂದಾಗಿ ಇರುತ್ತದೆ. ಬಹುತೇಕ ಸಮಯಗಳಲ್ಲಿ ಜನನದ ಸಮಯದಲ್ಲಿ ಅಂತರಲಿಂಗ ಶಿಶುಗಳಿಗೆ ಅವರು ಒಟ್ಟಾರೆಯಾಗಿ ಸಮಾಜಕ್ಕೆ ಹೆಚ್ಚು ಅಂಗೀಕಾರ್ಹವಾಗುವಂತೆ ಅವರಿಗೆ ಲೈಂಗಿಕ ಮರುಹೊಂದಾಣಿಕೆ ಶಸ್ತ್ರಚಿಕಿತ್ಸೆಯನ್ನು ಮಾಡಲಾಗುತ್ತದೆ. ಇದನ್ನು ಈಗ ಮಾನವ ಹಕ್ಕುಗಳ ದುರ್ಬಳಕೆ ಮತ್ತು ಲೈಂಗಿಕ ಅಂಗದ ವಿರೂಪಗೊಳಿಸುವಿಕೆ ಎಂದು ಪರಿಗಣಿಸಲಾಗುತ್ತದೆ ಏಕೆಂದರೆ ಅದಕ್ಕೆ ಸಮ್ಮತಿ ಇರುವುದಿಲ್ಲ ಮತ್ತು ಅದು ಅಪಾಯಕರ ಎನ್ನುವ ಭಾವನೆ ಇದೆ. ಅಂಗರಲಿಂಗ ವ್ಯಕ್ತಿಗಳ ಅವರು ಬೆಳೆಯುತ್ತಿರುವಂತೆ, ಲಿಂಗ ಅಥವಾ ಲೈಂಗಿಕ ಗುರುತುಗಳ ವಿಭಿನ್ನ ಮಟ್ಟಗಳೊಡನೆ ತಮ್ಮನ್ನು ಗುರುತಿಸಿಕೊಳ್ಳಬಹುದು.

ಆದು ಏಕೆ ಆಗುತ್ತದೆ?

ಇದು ಏಕೆ ಸಂಭವಿಸುತ್ತದೆ ಎನ್ನುವುದಕ್ಕೆ ವೈಜ್ಞಾನಿಕ ಸಮುದಾಯದಿಂದ ನಿರ್ಣಯಾತ್ಮಕ ಸಾಕ್ಷ್ಯಾಧಾರಗಳು ಇರುವುದಿಲ್ಲ. ಅದು ಜೈವಿಕವೇ, ಪರಿಸರಾತ್ಮಕವೇ, ಅನುವಂಶಿಕವೇ ಅಥವಾ ಮಾನಸಿಕವೇ ಎನ್ನುವುದು ನಮಗೆ ತಿಳಿದಿಲ್ಲ. ನಮಗೆ ತಿಳಿದಿರುವುದೇನೆಂದರೆ ಅದು ಸ್ವಾಭಾವಿಕವಾದುದು ಮತ್ತು ಸಮಯದ ಪ್ರಾರಂಭದಿಂದ ಅದು ಪಿಶ್ಚದ ಎಲ್ಲಾ ಜೀವ ಪ್ರಭೇದಗಳಲ್ಲಿ ಜರುಗುತ್ತಿದೆ ಮತ್ತು ಅದನ್ನು ಬದಲಾಯಿಸಲು ಸಾಧ್ಯವಿಲ್ಲ.

ನಮ್ಮ ಮಗು ಎಲ್‌ಜಿಬಿಟಿಐ ಎನ್ನುವುದು ನಮಗೆ ಹೇಗೆ ತಿಳಿಯುತ್ತದೆ?

ನಿಮ್ಮ ಮಗು ತನ್ನದೇ ಲಿಂಗಕ್ಕೆ ಸೇರಿದ ಯಾರನ್ನು ಕುರಿತಾದರೂ ಲೈಂಗಿಕ ಆಕರ್ಷಣೆ ಹೊಂದಿದೆಯೇ ಅಥವಾ ಅವರು ತಪ್ಪಾದ ಲಿಂಗದಲ್ಲಿ ಜನಿಸಿದ್ದಾರೆ ಎನ್ನುವುದನ್ನು ಸಂವೇದಿಸುತ್ತಾರೆ. ಎಳೆಯ ವಯಸ್ಸಿನಿಂದಲೇ ಈ ಸಮಸ್ಯೆಗಳನ್ನು ಕುರಿತು ನಿಮ್ಮ ಮಗುವಿನೊಡನೆ ಬಿಚ್ಚುಮನಸ್ಸಿನಿಂದ ಮಾತನಾಡಿರಿ, ಅವರು ಎಲ್‌ಜಿಬಿಟಿಐ ಆಗಿದ್ದರೆ ಅವರು ನಿಮ್ಮ ಬಳಿ ಅದರ ಬಗ್ಗೆ ಮುಕ್ತವಾಗಿ ಮಾತನಾಡಬಹುದು.

ಅದರ ಬಗ್ಗೆ ಏನು ಮಾಡಬಹುದು?

ಅದು ರೋಗವಲ್ಲ, ಮತ್ತು ಅದರಿಂದಾಗಿ ಅದನ್ನು ಕುರಿತು ಏನೂ ಮಾಡಬೇಕಾಗಿಲ್ಲ. ಅದಕ್ಕಾಗಿ ಗುಣಪಡಿಸುವ ವ್ಯಕ್ತಿಗಳು ಅಥವ ಧಾರ್ಮಿಕ ಮುಖಂಡರ ಬಳಿ ಹೋಗುವ ಅಗತ್ಯವಿರುವುದಿಲ್ಲ, ಅದು ವಿಷಯವನ್ನು ಇನ್ನೂ ಬಿಗಡಾಯಿಸುತ್ತದೆ. ನಿಮ್ಮ ಮಗುವನ್ನು ಗುಣಪಡಿಸಲು ಪ್ರಯತ್ನಿಸುವುದು, ಅವರ ಆರೋಗ್ಯವನ್ನು ಬಾಧಿಸುತ್ತದೆ. ನೀವು ನಿಮ್ಮ ಮಗುವನ್ನು ಇನ್ನೂ ಹೆಚ್ಚಾಗಿ ಪ್ರೀತಿಸಬೇಕು ಮತ್ತು ಅವರು ಏನು ಅನುಭವಿಸುತ್ತಾರೆ ಎನ್ನುವುದನ್ನು ಅರ್ಥ ಮಾಡಿಕೊಳ್ಳಬೇಕು. ನಿಮಗೆ ಮತ್ತು ಇತರರಿಗೆ ತಿಳಿವಳಿಕೆ ಪಡೆದುಕೊಳ್ಳಿ. ಸಮಾಜವು ಏನು ಆಲೋಚಿಸುತ್ತದೆ ಎನ್ನುವ ನಾಚಿಕೆಯಲ್ಲಿ ಬೀಳದಿರಲು ಪ್ರಯತ್ನಿಸಿ. ನಾವು ನಮ್ಮನ್ನು ಅಂಗೀಕರಿಸಿಕೊಳ್ಳಬೇಕು ಮತ್ತು ನಾವು ಏನಾಗಿದ್ದೇವೆಯೋ ಅದನ್ನು ಕುರಿತು ಸತ್ಯಸಂಧರಾಗಿರಬೇಕು. ಹುಸಿ ಮದುವೆಗಳನ್ನು ಮಾಡುವ ಮೂಲಕ ಅಥವಾ ಅನಧಿಕೃತವಾಗಿ ಇರುವ ಮೂಲಕ ಇತರ ಜನರ ಜೀವನವನ್ನು ಹಾಳು ಮಾಡಲು ಸಾಧ್ಯಪಿರುವುದಿಲ್ಲ. ಎಲ್ಜಿಬಿಟಿಐ ಜನರು ಸಮಾಜದಲ್ಲಿ ಯಾವಾಗಲೂ ಇರುತ್ತ ಬಂದಿದ್ದಾರೆ. ಅವರು ಕೊಳೆಯಾದವರಲ್ಲ, ಮತ್ತು ಸಮಾಜಕ್ಕೆ ಬೆದರಿಕೆಯಲ್ಲ. ಅವರು ನೈಜವಾಗಿ ಸಮಾಜಕ್ಕೆ ಸ್ವತ್ತಾಗುತ್ತಾರೆ. ಅವರು ಪರತ್ತುರಹಿತ ಪ್ರೀತಿ ಮತ್ತು ಅಂಗೀಕಾರವನ್ನು ಕಲಿಸುವ ಸಲುವಾಗಿ ಬಂದಿದ್ದಾರೆ. ಅವರು ಪ್ರೀತಿ ಮತ್ತು ಒಳಸೇರಿಸುಪಿಕೆಯನ್ನು ಕುರಿತಂತೆ ಸಮಾಜದ ದೃಷ್ಟಿಕೋನವನ್ನು ಪಿಸ್ತರಿಸುವ ಸಲುವಾಗಿ ಬಂದಿದ್ದಾರೆ. ಅವರು ಮಹಿಳೆಯರಿಗೆ, ಪಿಕಲಾಂಗ ಜನರಿಗೆ ಮತ್ತು ಪಿಭಿನ್ನವಾಗಿರುವ ಜನರಿಗೆ ಹೆಚ್ಚು ಹಕ್ಕನ್ನು ತರುತ್ತಾರೆ. ಬುದ್ಧಿವಂತಿಕೆ ಮತ್ತು ಪ್ರೀತಿಪಾತ್ರತೆ ಹೊಂದಿರುವ ಅವರು ನಿಮ್ಮ ಕುಟುಂಬಕ್ಕೆ ಉಡುಗೊರೆಯಾಗಿದ್ದಾರೆ.

ನನ್ನ ಮಗು ಯಾವ ವಿಧವಾದ ಜೀವನವನ್ನು ಹೊಂದಬಹುದು?

ನಿಮ್ಮ ಮಗು ಸಾಮಾನ್ಯವಾಗಿದೆ, ನೈಸರ್ಗಿಕವಾಗಿದೆ ಮತ್ತು ಆರೋಗ್ಯಕರವಾಗಿದೆ. ಅವರು ಸಾಧ್ಯಪಿರುವಷ್ಟು ಅತ್ಯುತ್ತಮ ಜೀವನವನ್ನು ಹೊಂದುವ ಸಾಮರ್ಥ್ಯ ಹೊಂದಿರುತ್ತಾರೆ. ಹೌದು, ಅವರು ಪಿಭಿನ್ನರಾಗಿ ಇರುವ ಕಾರಣದಿಂದಾಗಿ ಅವರನ್ನು ಹೆದರಿಸಲಾಗುತ್ತದೆ ಅಥವಾ ಗೇಲಿ ಮಾಡಲಾಗುತ್ತದೆ ಎನ್ನುವ ಭಯಗಳನ್ನು ನೀವು ಹೊಂದಿರಬಹುದು ಎಂದು ನಾನು ಅರ್ಥ ಮಾಡಿಕೊಂಡಿದ್ದೇನೆ. ಆದರೆ, ನೀವು ಸಕಾರತ್ಮಕವಾಗಿ ಇರುವ ವರೆಗೆ, ಪ್ರಸಕ್ತ ಫಳಿಗೆಯಲ್ಲಿ ಮತ್ತು ಅದರ ಮೂಲ/ದೇವರು/ಪ್ರಕೃತಿಯೊಡನೆ ಸಂಪರ್ಕ ಹೊಂದಿರುವ ವರೆಗೆ, ನೀವು ಚೆನ್ನಾಗಿ ಇರುತ್ತೀರಿ. ಸಾಧ್ಯತೆ ಇರುವ ಅತ್ಯುತ್ತಮ ಫಳಿತಾಂಶವನ್ನು ನಿರೀಕ್ಷಿಸಿರಿ ಮತ್ತು ಅದು ನಿಮಗೆ ಹೆಚ್ಚಿನ ಸಾಧ್ಯತೆ ನೀಡುತ್ತದೆ. ಅವರ ವಿಭಿನ್ನತೆಯಿಂದಾಗಿ ನಿಮ್ಮ ಮಗುವನ್ನು ತ್ಯಜಿಸಬೇಡಿ.

ಹೆಚ್ಐಪಿ/ಏಡ್ಸ್ ಬಗ್ಗೆ ಏನು?

ಹೆಚ್ಐಪಿ/ಏಡ್ಸ್ ಪ್ರಸರಣವು ಅಸುರಕ್ಷಿತ ಒಳಸೇರಿಸುವ ಲೈಂಗಿಕ ಸಂಪರ್ಕದ ಮೂಲಕ ಉಂಟಾಗುತ್ತದೆ. ನಿಮ್ಮ ಮಗು ಕಾಂಡೋಮ್ ಜೊತೆಯಲ್ಲಿ ಸುರಕ್ಷಿತ ಲೈಂಗಿಕ ಸಂಪರ್ಕ ಮಾಡುವುದರಿಂದ, ಅವರು ಬಹುತೇಕವಾಗಿ ಸುರಕ್ಷಿತವಾಗಿ ಇರುತ್ತದೆ. ಹೆಚ್ಐಪಿ ಇರುವ ವ್ಯಕ್ತಿ ಸಹ ಔಷಧೋಪಚಾರ ತೆಗೆದುಕೊಳ್ಳುತ್ತಿರುವ ಸಮಯದಲ್ಲಿ ಆರೋಗ್ಯಕರ, ಸಂತೋಷಕರ ಜೀವನವನ್ನು ಬಾಳಬಹುದು.

ನಾವು ಎಲ್ಲಿ ಬೆಂಬಲ ಪಡೆಯಬಹುದು?

ನೀವು ಒಂಟಿಯಲ್ಲ; ನಿಮ್ಮಂತಹ ಅನೇಕ ಜನರು ಇದ್ದಾರೆ. ಪಿಶೇಷತಃ ದೊಡ್ಡ ನಗರಗಳಲ್ಲಿ ಎಲ್ಜಿಬಿಟಿ ಕೇಂದ್ರಗಳಿವೆ, ಅಲ್ಲಿ ನೀವು ಆರೋಗ್ಯ ತಪಾಸಣೆ ಮಾಡಿಸಿಕೊಳ್ಳಬಹುದು ಮತ್ತು ಸಾಮಾಜಿಕ ಸಂಬಂಧಗಳನ್ನು ಪಡೆಯಬಹುದು. ನೀವು ದೊಡ್ಡ ನಗರಗಳಿಂದ ದೂರವಿದ್ದರೆ, ನಿಮ್ಮ ದೇಶದಲ್ಲಿ ನೀವು ಕರೆ ಮಾಡಬಹುದಾದ ಸಹಾಯವಾಣಿಗಳಿವೆ. ಭಾರತದಲ್ಲಿ ಹಂಸಫರ್ ಟ್ರಸ್ಟ್, ನಾರ್ಫ್ ಫೌಂಡೇಶನ್ ಮತ್ತು ಇನ್ನೂ ಅನೇಕ ಕೇಂದ್ರಗಳಿವೆ. ಪಾಕಿಸ್ತಾನದಲ್ಲಿ ಪಿಹೆಸನ್ ಮತ್ತು ಬಾಂಗ್ಲಾದೇಶದಲ್ಲಿ ಬಂಧು ಸೋಶಿಯಲ್ ವೆಲ್ಫೇರ್ ಸೊಸೈಟಿಗಳಿವೆ. ಪಶ್ಚಿಮದಲ್ಲಿ ಬಹುತೇಕ ದೊಡ್ಡ ನಗರಗಳು ಎಲ್ಜಿಬಿಟಿಕೇಂದ್ರಗಳ ಅಥವಾ ಬೆಂಬಲ ಸಹಾಯವಾಣಿಗಳಿದ್ದು ನೀವು ಅವುಗಳನ್ನು ಗೂಗಲ್ ಮಾಡಬಹುದು. ನಿಮಗೆ ಹೆಚ್ಚಿನ ಸಲಹೆ ಅಥವಾ ಬೆಂಬಲ ಬೇಕಾಗಿದ್ದರೆ, ನೀವು ನನ್ನನ್ನು ನನ್ನ ಸಾಮಾಜಿಕ ಮಾಧ್ಯಮದಲ್ಲಿ ಸಹ ಸಂಪರ್ಕಿಸಬಹುದು.

സെക്ഷ്വൽ ഓറിയന്റേഷൻ വെളിപ്പെടുത്തൽ

എൽ ജി ബിടിഐ എന്നാൽ എന്താണ്?

സ്ത്രീ സ്വർഗ്ഗാനുരാഗി (ലെസ്ബിയൻ) - മറ്റ് സ്ത്രീകളോട് മാത്രം ലൈംഗിക ആകർഷണം തോന്നുന്ന സ്ത്രീ

പുരുഷ സ്വർഗ്ഗാനുരാഗി(ഗേ) - മറ്റ് ആണുങ്ങളോട് മാത്രം ലൈംഗിക ആകർഷണം തോന്നുന്ന പുരുഷൻ

ഉഭയ വർഗ്ഗാനുരാഗി (ബൈസെക്ഷ്വൽ) പുരുഷൻമാരോടും സ്ത്രീകളോടും ലൈംഗിക ആകർഷണം തോന്നുന്ന വ്യക്തി

ലിംഗമാറ്റം വരുത്തിയയാൾ(ട്രാൻസ്ജെന്റർ)- ഒരാൾ ജനിച്ച സാമൂഹികമായി അംഗീകരിക്കപ്പെട്ടിട്ടുള്ള ലിംഗഭേദ ചട്ടങ്ങളുമായി യോജിക്കാത്ത വ്യക്തി. ഉദാഹരണത്തിന്, അവർ ആൺകുട്ടി ആയാണ് ജനിച്ചതെങ്കിൽ, വളരുന്നത് തങ്ങൾ ഒരു സ്ത്രീ ആണെന്ന ചിന്തയിലും ബോധത്തിലുമായിരിക്കും. അവരുടെ സെക്ഷ്വൽ ഓറിയന്റേഷൻ അവരുടെ ലൈംഗിക വ്യക്തിത്വത്തിൽ നിന്നും വിഭിന്നമായിരിക്കും, അതിനാൽ, അവർ ലൈംഗികമായി പരസ്പരം ആകർഷിക്കപ്പെടുകയും ചെയ്യും. ചിലപ്പോൾ സ്ത്രീകളെയും പുരുഷൻമാരെയും ഒരുപോലെ ഇഷ്ടപ്പെടുകയോ, ഒരുപോലെ ഇഷ്ടപ്പെടാതിരിക്കുകയോ ചെയ്യാം. ഇത്തരത്തിൽ ഭിന്ന ലൈംഗികതയുള്ള ഒരു വ്യക്തി, തങ്ങൾക്ക് ഏറ്റവും ആശ്വാസപ്രദമായി തോന്നുന്ന ഒരു ലിംഗഭേദത്തിലേക്ക് ലൈംഗിക പുനക്രമീകരണം/ തിരുത്തൽ ശസ്ത്രക്രിയ നടത്തുവാനോ അല്ലെങ്കിൽ നടത്താതിരിക്കുവാനോ തീരുമാനിച്ചേക്കാം. ഹിജഡ എന്നാണ് തെക്കേ ഏഷ്യയിൽ ഇവരെ പൊതുവായി വിശേഷിപ്പിക്കുന്ന പദം.

ഭിന്നലൈംഗിത കാണിക്കുന്ന വ്യക്തികൾ സ്ത്രീയോ പുരുഷനോ എന്ന് വ്യക്തമായി തിരിച്ചറിഞ്ഞിട്ടുണ്ടാകില്ല. ക്രോമസോമുകൾ, ബീജഗ്രന്ഥികൾ, ജനനേന്ദ്രിയം എന്നിവ ഉൾപ്പെടെ അവരുടെ ലൈംഗിക സ്വഭാവസവിശേഷതകളിലുള്ള വ്യത്യാസങ്ങളാണ് ഇതിന് കാരണം. പലപ്പോഴും ഇത്തരത്തിൽ ജനിക്കുന്ന ശിശുക്കളെ ജനനസമയത്ത്, സമൂഹത്തിൽ കൂടുതൽ സ്വീകര്യത ഉണ്ടാക്കുവാൻ ലൈംഗിക പുനഃക്രമീകരണ ശസ്ത്രക്രിയക്ക് വിധേയമാക്കാറുണ്ട്. എന്നാൽ, ഇപ്പോൾ ഇത് ഒരു മനുഷ്യാവകാശ ദുരുപയോഗം ആയി കണക്കാക്കപ്പെടുകയും ഈ കുഞ്ഞുങ്ങളുടെ ജനനേന്ദ്രിയ ഛേദം അപകടകരവും സമ്മതം ഇല്ലാതെയുള്ള പ്രവൃത്തിയായും കണക്കാക്കുന്നു. ഭിന്ന ലൈംഗികതയുള്ള കുഞ്ഞുങ്ങളിൽ അവരുടെ ലൈംഗികതയുടെ ചായ്‌വ് എങ്ങോട്ടാണെന്നും അതിന്റെ അളവ് അല്ലെങ്കിൽ ലൈംഗിക വ്യക്തിത്വം എത്രത്തോളമുണ്ടെന്നും അവർ വളർന്നു വരുമ്പോൾ മാത്രമാണ് പൂർണ്ണമായി തിരിച്ചറിയാൻ സാധിക്കുക.

എന്തുകൊണ്ട് ഇതു സംഭവിക്കുന്നു?

ഇത് എങ്ങനെ സംഭവിക്കുന്നു എന്നതിന് ശാസ്ത്ര സമൂഹത്തിന്റെ പക്കൽ തെളിവുകൾ ഒന്നും ഇല്ല. അത്, ജീവശാസ്ത്രപരമോ, പരിസ്ഥിതി, ജനിതക, മാനസിക പ്രശ്നങ്ങളാണോ എന്നും നമുക്കറിയില്ല. നമ്മൾക്ക് അറിയാവുന്ന ഒരു കാര്യം ഇത് തികച്ചും സ്വാഭാവികവും ലോകാരംഭം മുതൽ എല്ലാ ജീവജാലങ്ങളിലും ഉള്ളതാണെന്നും അതു മാറ്റാൻ കഴിയുന്നതല്ലെന്നുമാണ്.

നമ്മുടെ കുട്ടി എൽജിബിടിഐ ആണോ എന്ന് എങ്ങനെ അറിയാം?

ലൈംഗികമായി തങ്ങളുടെ സ്വന്തം ലിംഗഭേദത്തിലുള്ളവരോടാണോ ആകർഷണം തോന്നുന്നത്, അല്ലെങ്കിൽ താൻ ഈ ലിംഗ വിഭാഗത്തിലല്ല ജനിക്കേണ്ടിയിരുന്നതെന്ന് ആ കുട്ടിക്കു മാത്രമേ അറിയാൻ സാധിക്കൂ. ഇത്തരം കാര്യങ്ങൾ കുട്ടിയോട് അവരുടെ ചെറുപ്പത്തിലേ തന്നെ തുറന്നു സംസാരിക്കുക. ഇതിലൂടെ അവർ എൽ ജി ബിടിഐ ആണെങ്കിൽ, അവർക്ക് അക്കാര്യം നിങ്ങളോടു തുറന്നു പറയാനാകും.

ഇക്കാര്യത്തിൽ എന്തു ചെയ്യാൻ കഴിയും?

ഇത് ഒരു രോഗം അല്ല, ആയതിനാൽ ഇക്കാര്യത്തിൽ ഒന്നും ചെയ്യാനുമില്ല. രോഗ ശാന്തി നൽകുന്നവരുടെ അടുത്തോ മത നേതാക്കളുടെ അടുത്തോ പോകുകയും ചെയ്യരുത്. ഇത് കാര്യങ്ങൾ മോശമാക്കുകയേ ചെയ്യൂ. നിങ്ങളുടെ കുട്ടിയെ ചികിത്സിക്കാൻ ശ്രമിക്കുന്നത് അവരുടെ ആരോഗ്യത്തെ പ്രതികൂലമായി ബാധിക്കുകയേ ഉള്ളൂ. നിങ്ങളുടെ കുട്ടിയെ കൂടുതൽ സ്നേഹിക്കുകയും അവരെ മനസ്സിലാക്കുകയും മാത്രമേ നിങ്ങൾക്കു ചെയ്യാനാകൂ. നിങ്ങളെത്തന്നെ അവബോധമുള്ളവരാക്കുകയും മറ്റുള്ളവർക്ക് ബോധവൽക്കരണം നൽകുകയും ചെയ്യുക. സമൂഹം എന്തു വിചാരിക്കും എന്ന ചിന്തകൾ ഒഴിവാക്കുക. നമ്മൾ സത്യത്തെ അംഗീകരിക്കുകയും അതിനോട് നീതി പുലർത്തുകയും ചെയ്യുക. ഇക്കാര്യങ്ങൾ മറച്ചു വച്ച് വിവാഹം നടത്തി മറ്റുള്ളവരുടെ ജീവിതം നശിപ്പിക്കുവാനിം പാടില്ല. എൽ ജി ബിടിഐ ആളുകൾ എപ്പോഴും സമൂഹത്തിൽ നിലനിന്നിരുന്നു. അവർ വൃത്തികെട്ടവർ അല്ല, അവർ സമൂഹത്തിന് ഒരു ഭീഷണിയും അല്ല. തീർച്ചയായും അവർ ഒരു മുതൽക്കൂട്ട് തന്നെയാണ്. അവർ നിരുപാധികമായ സ്നേഹവും സ്വീകാര്യതയും പഠിപ്പിക്കാൻ വന്നവരാണ്. അവർ സ്നേഹത്തെയും ഉൾക്കൊള്ളലിനെയും കുറിച്ചുള്ള സമൂഹത്തിന്റെ കാഴ്ചപ്പാടുകൾ വിപുലീകരിക്കാൻ വന്നിരിക്കുന്നവരാണ്. അവർ സ്ത്രീകൾക്കും, അംഗവൈകല്യമുള്ള ആളുകൾക്കും വ്യത്യസ്തരായ ആളുകൾക്കും കൂടുതൽ അവകാശങ്ങൾ നേടിത്തരും. ബുദ്ധിയുള്ളവരും സ്നേഹമുള്ളവരും ആണവർ, നിങ്ങളുടെ കുടുംബത്തിന് ഒരു സമ്മാനമാണവർ.

എന്റെ കുട്ടിക്ക് ഏതു തരത്തിലുള്ള ജീവിതമാകും ഉണ്ടാകുക?

നിങ്ങളുടെ കുട്ടി, നോർമൽ ആണ്, നാച്ചുറൽ ആണ് ആരോഗ്യമുള്ളയാളാണ്. അവർക്ക് ഏറ്റവും മികച്ച ജീവിതം തന്നെ ലഭിക്കും. അവർ വ്യത്യസ്തരായതിനാൽ അവരെ കളിയാക്കുകയും പരിഹസിക്കുകയും ചെയ്യുമോ എന്നുള്ള നിങ്ങളുടെ ഭയാശങ്കകൾ ഞാൻ മനസിലാക്കുന്നു. എന്നാൽ, നിങ്ങൾ ഇക്കാര്യത്തിൽ എത്രത്തോളം അനുകൂല നിലപാടും പിന്തുണയും നൽകുന്നോ, ഇപ്പോഴത്തെ നിമിഷവുമായി ബന്ധപ്പെട്ട സ്രോതസ്സ് / ദൈവം / പ്രകൃതം എല്ലാം മികച്ചതായിരിക്കും. ഏറ്റവും മികച്ച അനന്തരഫലം തന്നെ പ്രതീക്ഷിക്കുക. അതുതന്നെ ആയിരിക്കും സംഭവിക്കുക. ഈ വ്യത്യാസങ്ങൾ കാരണം നിങ്ങളുടെ കുട്ടിയെ തള്ളിക്കളയരുതേ.

എച്ച്.ഐ.വി / എയ്ഡ്സിന്റെ കാര്യമോ?

എച്ച്ഐവി / എയ്ഡ്സ് പകരുന്നത് സുരക്ഷിതമല്ലാത്ത ലൈംഗിക ബന്ധത്തിലൂടെയാണ്. നിങ്ങളുടെ കുട്ടി സുരക്ഷിതമായ രീതിയിൽ ഒരു കോണ്ടം ഉപയോഗിച്ച് ലൈംഗിക ബന്ധത്തിലേർപ്പെട്ടാൽ സുരക്ഷിതരായിരിക്കും. എച്ച്.ഐ.വി ബാധിതനായാൽ പോലും ഒരു വ്യക്തിക്ക് കൃത്യമായ മരുന്നുകൾ കൊണ്ട് ആരോഗ്യകരമായ സന്തുഷ്ട ജീവിതം നയിക്കാൻ കഴിയും.

എവിടെ നിന്ന് നമുക്ക് പിന്തുണ ലഭിക്കും?

നിങ്ങൾ ഒറ്റക്കല്ല; നിങ്ങളെ പോലുള്ള ധാരാളം ആളുകൾ നമുക്കു ചുറ്റും ഉണ്ട്. പ്രത്യേകിച്ച് വലിയ പട്ടണങ്ങളിൽ. അവിടെ എൽ ജി ബിടി സെന്ററുകൾ ഉണ്ട്. നിങ്ങൾക്ക് ആരോഗ്യ പരിശോധനകൾ നടത്താനും കൂടിച്ചേരലുകൾ നടത്താനും സാധിക്കും. നിങ്ങൾ നഗരങ്ങളിൽ നിന്ന് അകലെയാണെങ്കിൽ നിങ്ങൾക്ക് സഹായം നൽകുന്ന ഹെൽപ്പ്ലൈനുകൾ ഉണ്ട്. ഇന്ത്യയിൽ ഹംസഫർ ട്രസ്റ്റ്, നാസ് ഫൗണ്ടേഷൻ തുടങ്ങിയ നിരവധി സംഘടനകൾ പ്രവർത്തിക്കുന്നുണ്ട്. പാകിസ്ഥാനിൽ വിഷൻ, ബംഗ്ലാദേശിൽ ബന്ധു സോഷ്യൽ വെൽഫെയർ സൊസൈറ്റി എന്നിവയും പ്രവർത്തിക്കുന്നുണ്ട്. പാശ്ചാത്യ രാജ്യങ്ങളിൽ, പ്രധാന നഗരങ്ങളിൽ എൽജിബിടി കേന്ദ്രങ്ങൾ ഉണ്ട്. ഗൂഗിളിൽ നിങ്ങൾക്ക് വിശദാംശങ്ങൾ ലഭിക്കും. നിങ്ങൾക്ക് കൂടുതൽ ഉപദേശമോ പിന്തുണയോ ആവശ്യമാണെങ്കിൽ നിങ്ങൾക്ക് എന്റെ സോഷ്യൽ മീഡിയയിൽ എന്നെ ബന്ധപ്പെടാൻ കഴിയും.

लैंगिक ओढ व्यक्त करणे/लैंगिक कल उघड करणे

एलजीबीटीआय म्हणजे काय?

समलैंगिक स्त्री(लेस्बियन)- जिला इतर स्त्रियांविषयी लैंगिक आकर्षण वाटते, अशी स्त्री.

समलैंगिक पुरुष(गे)- ज्याला इतर पुरुषांविषयी लैंगिक आकर्षण वाटते, असा पुरुष.

उभयलिंगी(बायसेक्स्युअल)- जिला पुरुष आणि स्त्रिया अशा दोहोंविषयी लैंगिक आकर्षण वाटते, अशी व्यक्ती.

किन्नर(ट्रान्सजेंडर)- अशी व्यक्ती जी, ज्या लिंगासहित जन्माला येते आणि ज्याला समाजाने मान्यता दिलेली आहे, त्या निकषांमध्ये बसत नाही. उदाहरणार्थ, अशा व्यक्ती पुरुष म्हणून जन्माला येऊ शकतात, पण त्यांना ते मूळची स्त्री असल्यासारखे वाटते. त्यांची लैंगिक ओढ त्यांच्या लैंगिक ओळखीपेक्षा वेगळी असते, म्हणून त्यांना स्त्री आणि पुरुषांपैकी कोणत्यातरी एका किंवा दोन्हींविषयी लैंगिक आकर्षण असू शकते किंवा दोघांपैकी कुणाहीविषयी ते नसू शकते. ट्रान्सजेंडर व्यक्ती त्यांना ज्याविषयी सुखकारक वाटेल अशा लिंगाबरोबर जोडले जाण्याची/लैंगिक दुरुस्तीची शस्त्रक्रिया करून घेण्याचा निर्णय घेऊ शकतात किंवा घेऊ शकत नाहीत. या शब्दाच्या अर्थाच्या जवळपास जाणारा दक्षिण आशियातील शब्द म्हणजे हिजडा.

इंटरसेक्स व्यक्तींना स्त्री किंवा पुरुष असे वेगवेगळे ओळखता येत नाही. त्यांच्यातील लैंगिक गुणधर्मांतील बदल, ज्यात गुणसूत्रे, जननग्रंथी किंवा जननेंद्रिये यांचा समावेशही असतो, त्यांच्यातील वेगवेगळेपणामुळे हे घडते. समाजाने एकूणच स्वीकार करावा म्हणून बऱ्याचदा जन्माच्या वेळी इंटरसेक्स बालकांवर लिंगनिश्चिती (सेक्स रिअसाईनमेंट) शस्त्रक्रिया केल्या जातात. हल्ली ह्याला मानवी हक्कांचे उल्लंघन आणि या बालकांचे शारीरिक विद्रुपीकरण समजले जाते, कारण हे त्यांच्या संमतीशिवाय केलेले आणि धोकादायक कृत्य असते. इंटरसेक्स व्यक्ती लिंगाच्या बाबतीत किंवा लैंगिक ओळखीच्या बाबतीत वेगवेगळ्या पातळ्यांमध्ये ओळखल्या जाऊ शकतात, जी त्यांच्या वाढीबरोबरच उत्क्रांत होऊ शकते.

असे का घडते?

हे असे का घडते याविषयी शास्त्रज्ञांकडून कोणताही ठाम पुरावा देण्यात आलेला नाही. यामागे जैविक, पर्यावरणाशी संबंधित, आनुवंशिक किंवा मानसिक कारणे आहेत किंवा काय हे आपल्याला माहीत नाही. आपल्याला फक्त एवढेच माहीत आहे की, हे नैसर्गिक आहे आणि जगातील सर्व प्राणिमात्रांमध्ये अगदी अनादी कालापासून सुरू आहे आणि हे बदलता येऊ शकत नाही.

आपले मूल एलजीबीटीआय आहे किंवा काय, हे आपल्याला कसे समजेल?

तुमच्या मुलाला स्वतःलाच समजेल की, त्याला त्यांच्यासारख्याच व्यक्तीविषयी लैंगिक आकर्षण वाटते किंवा ते चुकीच्या लिंगासहित जन्माला आलेले आहे असे वाटते किंवा काय. ह्या बाबींविषयी तुमच्या मुलाशी त्यांच्या लहान वयातच मोकळेपणी बोला, ज्यामुळे ते जर एलजीबीटीआयपैकी असेल, तर तुमच्याशी मन मोकळे करू शकेल.

ह्याविषयी काय करता येईल?

हा काही रोग नाहीए आणि म्हणून त्याविषयी काहीही करण्याची आवश्यकता नाही. त्यासाठी रोग बरे करणाऱ्यांकडे किंवा धार्मिक नेत्यांकडे जाण्याची आवश्यकता नाही, कारण त्यामुळे परिस्थिती अधिकच चिघळेल. तुमच्या मुलाला यातून बरे करण्याचा प्रयत्न केल्यास त्याच्या आरोग्यावर विपरित परिणाम होईल. तुम्हाला फक्त तुमच्या मुलाला अधिक प्रेम देण्याची आणि ते कोणत्या स्थितीतून जात आहे हे समजून घेण्याची गरज आहे. स्वतःला आणि इतरांनाही शिक्षित करा. समाज काय म्हणेल याची लाज वाटणार नाही असा प्रयत्न करा. आपण फक्त स्वतःचा स्वीकार करायला हवा आणि आपण जसे आहोत त्याच्याशी प्रामाणिक रहायला हवे. आपण फसवून लग्न लावून आणि काहीतरी अनधिकृत करून इतरांचे जीवन उध्वस्त करू शकत नाही. एलजीबीटीआय लोक समाजात पूर्वीपासून होते आणि यापुढेही राहणार आहेत. ते घाणेरडे नसतात किंवा समाजासाठी धोकादायकही नसतात. ते खरे म्हणजे जमेची बाजू (असेट) आहेत. ते निरपेक्ष प्रेम आणि स्वीकार करणे शिकविण्यासाठी जन्माला आलेले असतात. समाजाचा प्रेमाविषयीचा आणि समावेशकतेचा दृष्टिकोन व्यापक करण्यासाठी ते जन्माला आलेले असतात. त्यांच्यामुळे स्त्रिया, अपंग लोक आणि जे इतरांपेक्षा वेगळे आहेत, त्यांच्यासाठी अधिक हक्क मिळवून देण्यासाठी ते आलेले आहेत. ते शहाणे आणि प्रेमळ असतात आणि तुमच्या कुटुंबासाठी वरदान असतात.

माझ्या मुलाचे आयुष्य कसे असू शकते?

तुमचे मूल सर्वसाधारण, नैसर्गिक आणि निरोगी आहे. ते जीवनात सर्वोत्तम ते प्राप्त करू शकतात. हो, मला हे समजते की, त्यांना कुणीतरी फसवील किंवा त्यांच्याशी कुणी दांडगाई करील किंवा त्यांची थट्टा करील अशी भीती तुम्हाला वाटू शकते. परंतु जोपर्यंत तुम्ही सकारात्मक रहाल आणि जे निर्मात्याने/देवाने/निसर्गाने त्या क्षणापर्यंत निर्माण केलेले आहे त्याच्याशी जोडलेले रहाल तोपर्यंत तुम्ही निश्चिंत राहू शकता. सर्वकाही छान होईल अशी अपेक्षा ठेवा, आणि हेच तुमच्यासाठी चांगले आहे. तुमच्या मुलाच्या वेगळेपणामुळे त्याला वेगळे पाडू नका.

एचआयव्ही/एडस्बद्दल काय?

असुरक्षित लैंगिक संबंधांमुळे एचआयव्ही/एडस्चे संक्रमण होते. जोपर्यंत तुमचे मूल कॉंडोमच्या सहाय्याने सुरक्षित लैंगिक संबंध ठेवील, तोपर्यंत ते सुरक्षित राहू शकते. एचआयव्ही असलेली व्यक्तीसुद्धा औषधोपचार घेत आरोग्यपूर्ण, आनंदी जीवन जगू शकते.

आपल्याला पाठिंबा कुठून मिळू शकतो?

तुम्ही एकटे नाहीएत; तुमच्यासारखे अनेक लोक आहेत. विशेषतः मोठ्या शहरांमध्ये एलजीबीटीआय सेंटर्स असतात, जेथे तुम्ही तुमची शारीरिक तपासणी करून घेऊ शकता आणि समाजात मिसळू शकता. तुम्ही जर मोठ्या शहरांपासून दूर असलात, तर तुमच्या स्वतःच्या देशातील हेल्पलाईनवरही तुम्ही कॉल करू शकता. भारतात हमसफर ट्रस्ट, नाझ फाऊंडेशन आणि अशा अनेक संस्था आहेत. पाकिस्तानमध्ये व्हिजन आणि बांगलादेशात बंधू सोशल वेल्फेअर सोसायटी आहे. पाश्चिमात्य देशांतील बहुतेक मोठ्या शहरांमध्ये एलजीबीटी सेंटर्स किंवा सपोर्ट हेल्पलाईन असतात, जे तुम्ही गूगल करू शकता. जर तुम्हाला अधिक सल्ल्याची किंवा पाठिंब्याची आवश्यकता असेल, तर तुम्ही मला माझ्या सोशल मेडियावरही संपर्क करू शकता.

यौन अभिमुखीकरणबारे खुलासा

LGBTI भनेको के हो?

समलिङ्गी महिला(लेस्बियन) - अन्य महिलाहरूसँग यौन आकर्षण हुने महिला।

समलिङ्गी पुरुष (गे) - अन्य पुरुषहरूसँग यौन आकर्षण हुने पुरुष।

द्विलिङ्गी(बाइसेक्सुअल) - महिला तथा पुरुषहरू दुवैसँग यौन आकर्षण हुने व्यक्ति।

तेस्रो-लिङ्गी(ट्रान्सजेन्डर) - यस्तो व्यक्ति जो आफू जन्मेको लिङ्गका आधारमा सामाजिक रूपमा स्वीकृत लैङ्गिक मापदण्ड भित्र पर्दैनन्। उदाहरणको लागि, उनीहरू पुरुष भएर जन्मेका हुन्छन् तर निहित रूपमा महिला भएको महसुस गर्न सक्छन्। उनीहरूको यौन अभिमुखीकरण उनीहरूको लैङ्गिक पहिचान भन्दा बेग्लै हुन्छ, तसर्थ उनीहरू कुनै एकमा वा दुवैमा आकर्षित हुन्छन् अथवा पुरुष वा महिला कसैमा पनि आकर्षित हुँदैनन्। कुनै तेस्रो लिङ्गी व्यक्तिले आफूलाई सहज लाग्ने लिङ्गमा परिवर्तन हुन सेक्सुअल रिअलाइनमेन्ट/सुधारात्मक शल्यक्रिया गर्ने निर्णय गर्न वा नगर्न पनि सक्छन्। दक्षिण एसियामा यसको लागि सबभन्दा मिल्ने शब्द हिजडा हो।

तेस्रो लिङ्गी व्यक्तिहरूको पुरुष वा महिलाका रूपमा प्रस्ट पहिचान हुँदैन। यो क्रोमोजम, यौन कोष सम्बन्धी ग्रन्थि, वा जननेन्द्रिय लगायतका उनीहरूको यौन विशेषताहरूमा पार्थक्य भएको कारण हुन्छ। प्राय तेस्रो लिङ्गी शिशुहरूलाई समाजमा बढ्ता स्वीकारयोग्य बनाउन जन्मेको बेला सेक्स रिअसाइनमेन्ट शल्यक्रिया गराइन्छ। हाल यसलाई सहमत बेगर भएको र खतरनाक हुने कारणमा मानव अधिकारको दुरुपयोग भएको र शिशुहरूको जननेन्द्रिय भङ्ग गरेको मानिन्छ। तेस्रो लिङ्गी व्यक्तिहरूमा लिङ्ग वा लैङ्गिक पहिचानहरू फरक स्तरको हुन सक्छ, जुन उनीहरूको विकाससँगै विकसित हुन सक्छ।

यस्तो किन हुन्छ?

यस्तो किन भएको हो भनेर वैज्ञानिक समुदायबाट कुनै निर्णायक पुष्टि छैन। यसको कारण जैविक, वातावरणीय, वंशाणुगत वा मनोवैज्ञानिक हो भन्ने हामीलाई थाहा छैन। हामी के जान्दछौं भने यो प्राकृतिक कुरा हो र सुरु देखिनै संसारको सबै प्राणीमा हुन्छ र यसलाई परिवर्तन गर्न सकिँदैन।

हाम्रो बच्चा LGBTI हो कि भनेर हामीले कसरी थाहा पाउनु?

यदि उनीहरू आफ्नै लिङ्गको कसैसँग यौन आकर्षित छन् भने अथवा उनीहरू वास्तवमै गलत लिङ्गमा जन्मेका रहेछन् भन्ने अनुभव भएमा तपाईंको बच्चालाई आफैं थाहा हुनेछ। उक्त विषयहरूमा आफ्नो बच्चासँग सानै उमेर देखि नै प्रस्ट रूपमा कुरा गर्नुहोस्, ता कि यदि उनीहरू LGBTI हुन् भने यसबारे तपाईंलाई बताउन सकुन्।

यसबारे के गर्न सकिन्छ?

यो कुनै रोग होइन र त्यस कारण यसबारे केही पनि गर्न आवश्यक छैन। धामी झाँक्री वा धार्मिक गुरुकहाँ जाने जरुरत छैन, किनभने यसले गर्दा कुरा बिग्रेर मात्र जानेछ। तपाईंको बच्चाको उपचार गर्ने प्रयासले उनीहरूको स्वास्थ्यमा नकारात्मक असर मात्र पार्नेछ। तपाईंले आफ्नो बच्चालाई बढ्ता माया दिने र उनीहरू कुन अवस्थाबाट पार हुँदैछन् त्यसबारे बुझ्ने मात्र गर्नुपर्छ। तपाईं आफू र अरूलाई पनि सचेत बनाउनुहोस्। समाजले के भन्छ होला भनेर शरम नमान्ने प्रयास गर्नुहोस्। हामीले हामी आफैंलाई स्वीकार मात्र गर्नु पर्छ र हामी को हौं भनेर साँचो हुनुपर्छ। हामीले नक्कली विवाहहरू गरेर अथवा असत्य भएर अरूको जीवन बरबाद गर्न सक्दैनौं। LGBTI मानिसहरूको अस्तित्व समाजमा सदा कायम थियो।   उनीहरू फोहोर होइनन् र समाजको लागि खतरा होइनन्। वास्तवमा उनीहरू त सम्पत्ति हुन्। उनीहरू निःस्वार्थ प्रेम र स्वीकृतिबारे सिकाउन आएका हुन्। उनीहरू माया र समावेशबारे समाजको दृष्टिकोण विस्तार गर्न आएका हुन्। उनीहरूले महिलाहरू, अपाङ्ग मानिसहरू तथा फरक मानिसहरूका लागि अझै अधिकारहरू दिलाउनेछन्। ज्ञानी र स्नेही, उनीहरू तपाईंको परिवारमा उपहार हुन्।

मेरो बच्चाको जीवन कस्तो हुन सक्छ?

तपाईंको बच्चा सामान्य, प्राकृतिक र स्वस्थ छ। उनीहरू सम्भव हुने सबभन्दा असल जीवन यापन गर्न समर्थ छन्। हो मलाई थाहा छ बेग्लै भएको कारण उनीहरूमाथि थिचोमिचो हुन्छ वा हाँसोको पात्र हुन सक्छन् भन्ने तपाईंलाई केही डर लागेको हुन सक्छ। तथापि, तपाईं सकारात्मक भएर, वर्तमान समयमा साथै स्रोत/ईश्वर/प्रकृतिसँग गाँसिएर रहेमा तपाईंको सबैकुरा राम्रै हुनेछ। सर्वोत्तम नतिजाको आशा गर्नुहोस्, र यो नै तपाईंको लागि सबभन्दा सम्भव कुरा हो। उनीहरू फरक भएको कारण तपाईंको बच्चालाई त्याग नगर्नुहोस्।

HIV/AIDs को बारे चैं?

असुरक्षित यौन सम्पर्कको माध्यमबाट HIV/AIDs सर्छ। तपाईंको बच्चाले कन्डमको प्रयोग गरि सुरक्षित यौन सम्पर्क गरेमा उनीहरू सुरक्षित नै हुन्छन्। HIV सँग पनि औषधिको सहायताले कुनै व्यक्ति स्वस्थ, सुखी जीवन बाँच्न सक्छ।

हामीले कहाँबाट सहयोग पाउन सक्छौं?

तपाईं एक्लो हुनु हुँदैन; तपाईं जस्ता धेरै छन्। विशेष गरि ठूला सहरहरूमा LGBT केन्द्रहरू हुन्छन्, जहाँ तपाईंले स्वास्थ्य जाँच गर्न र समाजमा हेलमेल गर्न पाउनु हुन्छ। यदि तपाईं ठूला सहरदेखि टाढा हुनुहुन्छ भने तपाईंको आफ्नो देशमा तपाईंले फोन गर्न सक्ने हेल्पलाइनहरू पनि हुन्छन्। भारतमा हमसफर ट्रस्ट, नाज फाउन्डेशन र अरू पनि धेरै छन्। पाकिस्तानमा भिजन र बङ्गलादेशमा बन्धु सोसल वेल्फेयर सोसाइटी भन्ने संस्था छ। पश्चिमका देशहरूमा प्राय प्रमुख सहरहरूमा LGBT केन्द्रहरू वा सहयोग हेल्पलाइनहरू हुन्छन् जसबारे तपाईंले गुगलबाट खोज्न सक्नुहुन्छ। यदि तपाईंलाई अझै सुझाव वा सहयोग चाहिएमा तपाईंले मलाई मेरो सोसल मिडियामा सम्पर्क गर्न सक्नुहुन्छ।

ਜਿਨਸੀ ਝੁਕਾਅ ਦਾ ਖ਼ੁਲਾਸਾ

ਐਲ.ਜੀ.ਬੀ.ਟੀ.ਆਈ. ਕੀ ਹੈ?

ਸਮਲਿੰਗੀ ਔਰਤ (ਲੈਸਬੀਅਨ) – ਇੱਕ ਔਰਤ ਜੋ ਯੌਨ ਪੱਖੋਂ ਦੂਜੀਆਂ ਔਰਤਾਂ ਵੱਲ ਆਕਰਸ਼ਿਤ ਹੁੰਦੀ ਹੈ।

ਸਮਲਿੰਗੀ ਪੁਰਸ਼ (ਗੇਅ) - ਇੱਕ ਉਹ ਪੁਰਸ਼ ਜੋ ਯੌਨ ਪੱਖੋਂ ਦੂਜੇ ਪੁਰਸ਼ਾਂ ਵੱਲ ਆਕਰਸ਼ਿਤ ਹੁੰਦਾ ਹੈ।

ਦੋ-ਲਿੰਗੀ (ਬਾਇਸੈਕਸੁਅਲ) –ਇੱਕ ਉਹ ਵਿਅਕਤੀ ਜੋ ਯੌਨ ਪੱਖੋਂ ਪੁਰਸ਼ ਅਤੇ ਔਰਤਾਂ ਦੋਹਾਂ ਵੱਲ ਆਕਰਸ਼ਿਤ ਹੁੰਦਾ ਹੈ।

ਹਿਜੜਾ (ਟ੍ਰਾਂਸਜੈਂਡਰ) - ਇੱਕ ਉਹ ਵਿਅਕਤੀ ਜੋ ਲਿੰਗ ਦੇ ਉਸ ਮਾਪਦੰਡ ਪੱਖੋਂ ਸਮਾਜਿਕ ਤੌਰ ਤੇ ਸਵੀਕਾਰ ਨਹੀਂ ਹੁੰਦਾ ਜਿਸ ਵਿੱਚ ਉਹ ਪੈਦਾ ਹੋਇਆ ਸੀ। ਉਦਾਹਰਣ ਵਜੋਂ, ਉਹ ਪੁਰਸ਼ ਦੇ ਰੂਪ ਵਿੱਚ ਪੈਦਾ ਹੋ ਸਕਦਾ ਹੈ ਪਰ ਸੁਭਾਵਿਕ ਰੂਪ ਵਿੱਚ ਔਰਤ ਮਹਿਸੂਸ ਕਰਦਾ ਹੈ। ਉਨ੍ਹਾਂ ਦਾ ਜਿਨਸੀ ਝੁਕਾਅ ਉਨ੍ਹਾਂ ਦੇ ਲਿੰਗ ਦੀ ਪਹਿਚਾਣ ਤੋਂ ਅਲੱਗ ਹੁੰਦਾ ਹੈ, ਇਸ ਲਈ ਉਹ ਜਿਨਸੀ ਰੂਪ ਵਿੱਚ ਕਿਸੇ ਇੱਕ ਵੱਲ, ਦੋਹਾਂ ਵੱਲ ਆਕਰਸ਼ਿਤ ਹੋ ਸਕਦੇ ਹਨ ਜਾਂ ਨਾ ਤਾਂ ਪੁਰਸ਼ ਵੱਲ ਅਤੇ ਨਾ ਹੀ ਔਰਤ ਵੱਲ ਆਕਰਸ਼ਿਤ ਨਹੀਂ ਹੋ ਸਕਦੇ। ਇੱਕ ਹਿਜੜਾ ਵਿਅਕਤੀ ਉਸ ਲਿੰਗ ਲਈ ਇੱਕ ਯੌਨ ਰੀਅਲਾਇਨਮੈਂਟ/ਸੋਧ ਅਪਰੇਸ਼ਨ ਕਰਵਾਉਣ ਦਾ ਫੈਸਲਾ ਕਰ ਵੀ ਕਰ ਸਕਦਾ ਹੈ ਅਤੇ ਨਹੀਂ ਵੀ ਨਹੀਂ ਵੀ ਕਰ ਸਕਦਾ ਹੈ ਜਿਸ ਨਾਲ ਉਹ ਸੰਤੁਸ਼ਟ ਮਹਿਸੂਸ ਕਰਨ। ਹਿਜੜਾ ਦੱਖਣੀ ਏਸ਼ੀਆ ਵਿੱਚ ਇਸ ਦਾ ਨੇੜਲਾ ਸ਼ਬਦ ਹੈ।

ਅੰਤਰਲਿੰਗੀ ਵਿਅਕਤੀਆਂ ਦੀ ਪਹਿਚਾਣ ਸਪੱਸ਼ਟ ਰੂਪ ਵਿੱਚ ਨਰ ਜਾਂ ਮਾਦਾ ਵਜੋਂ ਨਹੀਂ ਹੁੰਦੀ। ਇਹ ਗੁਣਸੂਤਰਾਂ, ਜਨਨ ਗ੍ਰੰਥੀਆਂ, ਜਾਂ ਗੁਪਤ ਅੰਗਾਂ ਸਮੇਤ ਉਨ੍ਹਾਂ ਦੀਆਂ ਯੌਨ ਵਿਸ਼ੇਸ਼ਤਾਵਾਂ ਵਿੱਚ ਬਦਲਾਵ ਦੇ ਕਾਰਨ ਹੁੰਦਾ ਹੈ। ਅੰਤਰਲਿੰਗੀ ਬੱਚਿਆਂ ਦੇ ਜਨਮ ਵੇਲੇ ਉਨ੍ਹਾਂ ਨੂੰ ਸੰਪੂਰਨ ਰੂਪ ਵਿੱਚ ਸਮਾਜ ਲਈ ਵਧੇਰੇ ਸਵੀਕਾਰ ਕਰਨਯੋਗ ਬਣਾਉਣ ਲਈ ਜਿਆਦਾਤਰ ਉਨ੍ਹਾਂ ਦੀਆਂ ਲਿੰਗ ਪੁਨਰ-ਨਿਰਧਾਰਨ ਸਰਜਰੀਆਂ ਕੀਤੀਆਂ ਜਾਂਦੀਆਂ ਹਨ। ਹੁਣ ਇਸ ਨੂੰ ਇੰਨਾਂ ਬੱਚਿਆਂ ਲਈ ਮਨੁੱਖੀ ਅਧਿਕਾਰਾਂ ਨਾਲ ਬਦਸਲੂਕੀ ਅਤੇ ਜਨਨ ਅੰਗਾਂ ਦਾ ਨਿਸ਼ਕਾਰਜੀਕਰਨ ਸਮਝਿਆ ਜਾਂਦਾ ਹੈ ਕਿਉਂਕਿ ਇਹ ਸਹਿਮਤੀਰਹਿਤ ਅਤੇ ਖਤਰਨਾਕ ਹੁੰਦਾ ਹੈ। ਅੰਤਰਲਿੰਗੀ ਵਿਅਕਤੀਆਂ ਦੀ ਪਹਿਚਾਣ ਲਿੰਗ ਜਾਂ ਯੌਨ ਪਹਿਚਾਣਾਂ ਦੀ ਬਦਲਦੀ ਡਿਗਰੀ ਰਾਹੀਂ ਕੀਤੀ ਜਾ ਸਕਦੀ ਹੈ, ਜਿਹੜੀ ਵਿਕਸਿਤ ਹੋ ਸਕਦੀ ਹੈ ਜਿਵੇਂ ਜਿਵੇਂ ਉਨ੍ਹਾਂ ਦਾ ਵਿਕਾਸ ਹੁੰਦਾ ਹੈ।

ਇਹ ਕਿਉਂ ਵਾਪਰਦਾ ਹੈ?

ਵਿਗਿਆਨਕ ਸਮੁਦਾਇ ਵਜੋਂ ਇਸ ਦਾ ਕੋਈ ਵੀ ਨਿਰਣਾਇਕ ਸਬੂਤ ਨਹੀਂ ਹੈ ਕਿ ਇਹ ਕਿਉਂ ਵਾਪਰਦਾ ਹੈ। ਕਿ ਕੀ ਇਹ ਜੈਵਿਕ, ਵਾਤਾਵਰਣਕ, ਜਨਨ ਅੰਗੀ ਜਾਂ ਮਨੋਵਿਗਿਆਨਕ ਹੁੰਦਾ ਹੈ ਇਹ ਅਸੀਂ ਨਹੀਂ ਜਾਣਦੇ ਹਾਂ। ਅਸੀਂ ਸਿਰਫ ਇਹ ਜਾਣਦੇ ਹਾਂ ਕਿ ਇਹ ਪ੍ਰਾਕਿਰਤਕ ਹੁੰਦਾ ਹੈ ਅਤੇ ਆਰੰਭ ਤੋਂ ਹੀ ਵਿਸ਼ਵ ਦੀਆਂ ਸਾਰੀ ਪ੍ਰਜਾਤੀਆਂ ਵਿੱਚ ਮੌਜੂਦ ਹੁੰਦਾ ਹੈ ਅਤੇ ਇਹ ਕਿ ਇਸ ਨੂੰ ਬਦਲਿਆ ਨਹੀਂ ਜਾ ਸਕਦਾ।

ਅਸੀਂ ਕਿਵੇਂ ਪਤਾ ਲਗਾਈਏ ਕਿ ਕੀ ਸਾਡਾ ਬੱਚਾ ਐਲ.ਜੀ.ਬੀ.ਟੀ.ਆਈ. ਹੈ?

ਤੁਹਾਡੇ ਬੱਚੇ ਨੂੰ ਖੁਦ ਹੀ ਪਤਾ ਲੱਗੇਗਾ ਕਿ ਕੀ ਉਹ ਯੌਨ ਪੱਖੋਂ ਆਪਣੇ ਹੀ ਲਿੰਗ ਵੱਲ ਆਕਰਸ਼ਿਤ ਹੁੰਦਾ ਹੈ ਜਾਂ ਕੀ ਉਹ ਮਹਿਸੂਸ ਕਰਦੇ ਹਨ ਕਿ ਕੀ ਉਹ ਸੱਚਮੁੱਚ ਗਲਤ ਲਿੰਗ ਵਿੱਚ ਪੈਦਾ ਹੋ ਗਏ ਹਨ। ਇੱਕ ਮੁਢਲੀ ਉਮਰ ਤੋਂ ਹੀ ਇੰਨਾਂ ਮੁੱਦਿਆਂ ਬਾਰੇ ਆਪਣੇ ਬੱਚੇ ਨਾਲ ਖੁੱਲੀ ਗੱਲਬਾਤ ਕਰੋ, ਤਾਂ ਕਿ ਜੇਕਰ ਉਹ ਐਲ.ਜੀ.ਬੀ.ਟੀ.ਆਈ. ਹੋਣ ਤਾਂ ਉਹ ਇਸ ਬਾਰੇ ਤੁਹਾਡੇ ਨਾਲ ਖੁੱਲੀ ਗੱਲਬਾਤ ਕਰ ਸਕਣ।

ਅਸੀਂ ਇਸ ਬਾਰੇ ਕੀ ਕਰ ਸਕਦੇ ਹਾਂ?

ਇਹ ਇੱਕ ਬਿਮਾਰੀ ਨਹੀਂ ਹੈ ਅਤੇ ਇਸ ਲਈ ਇਸ ਬਾਰੇ ਕੁਝ ਵੀ ਕਰਨ ਦੀ ਲੋੜ ਨਹੀਂ ਹੁੰਦੀ। ਚਿਕਿਤਸਕ ਜਾਂ ਧਾਰਮਿਕ ਆਗੂਆਂ ਕੋਲ ਜਾਣ ਦੀ ਲੋੜ ਨਹੀਂ ਹੁੰਦੀ, ਕਿਉਂਕਿ ਇਹ ਚੀਜ਼ਾਂ ਨੂੰ ਹੋਰ ਭੈੜਾ ਬਣਾਏਗਾ। ਆਪਣੇ ਬੱਚੇ ਦਾ ਇਲਾਜ ਕਰਵਾਉਣ ਦੀ ਕੋਸ਼ਿਸ਼ ਉਨ੍ਹਾਂ ਦੀ ਸਿਹਤ ਤੇ ਪ੍ਰਤਿਕੂਲ ਪ੍ਰਭਾਵ ਪਾਏਗੀ। ਤੁਹਾਨੂੰ ਕੇਵਲ ਆਪਣੇ ਬੱਚੇ ਨੂੰ ਵਧੇਰੇ ਪਿਆਰ ਕਰਨ ਅਤੇ ਇਹ ਸਮਝਣ ਦੀ ਲੋੜ ਹੁੰਦੀ ਹੈ ਕਿ ਉਹ ਕੀ ਕਰ ਰਹੇ ਹਨ। ਆਪਣੇ ਆਪ ਜਾਣਕਾਰੀ ਪ੍ਰਾਪਤ ਕਰੋ ਅਤੇ ਦੂਜਿਆਂ ਨੂੰ ਸਿਖਾਓ। ਸਮਾਜ ਕੀ ਸੋਚੇਗਾ ਇਸ ਸ਼ਰਮਿੰਦਗੀ ਵਿੱਚ ਫਸਣ ਦੀ ਕੋਸ਼ਿਸ਼ ਨਾ ਕਰੋ। ਸਾਨੂੰ ਸਿਰਫ਼ ਆਪਣੇ ਆਪ ਨੂੰ ਸਵੀਕਾਰ ਕਰਨਾ ਪੈਣਾ ਹੈ ਅਤੇ ਅਸੀਂ ਕੀ ਹਾਂ ਉਸ ਨੂੰ ਸਹੀ ਮੰਨਣਾ ਪੈਣਾ ਹੈ। ਅਸੀਂ ਦਿਖਾਵੇ ਵਾਲਾ ਜਾਂ ਅਪ੍ਰਮਾਣਿਤ ਵਿਆਹ ਕਰਵਾਉਣ ਦੁਆਰਾ ਦੂਜੇ ਲੋਕਾਂ ਦੇ ਜੀਵਨ ਤਬਾਹ ਨਹੀਂ ਕਰ ਸਕਦੇ। ਐਲ.ਜੀ.ਬੀ.ਟੀ.ਆਈ. ਲੋਕ ਹਮੇਸ਼ਾਂ ਸਮਾਜ ਵਿੱਚ ਮੌਜੂਦ ਹੁੰਦੇ ਹਨ। ਉਹ ਗੰਦੇ ਨਹੀਂ ਹੁੰਦੇ ਅਤੇ ਉਹ ਸਮਾਜ ਲਈ ਇੱਕ ਖਤਰਾ ਨਹੀਂ ਹੁੰਦੇ। ਵਾਸਤਵ ਵਿੱਚ ਉਹ ਇੱਕ ਸੰਪਤੀ ਹੁੰਦੇ ਹਨ। ਉਹ ਸ਼ਰਤਰਹਿਤ ਪਿਆਰ ਅਤੇ ਸਵੀਕ੍ਰਿਤੀ ਸਿਖਾਉਣ ਲਈ ਆਉਂਦੇ ਹਨ। ਉਹ ਪਿਆਰ ਅਤੇ ਸਮਾਵੇਸ਼ ਤੇ ਸਮਾਜਾਂ ਦੇ ਦ੍ਰਿਸ਼ਟੀਕੋਣਾਂ ਦਾ ਵਿਸਤਾਰ ਕਰਨ ਲਈ ਆਉਂਦੇ ਹਨ। ਉਹ ਔਰਤਾਂ, ਵਿਕਲਾਂਗ ਲੋਕਾਂ ਅਤੇ ਭਿੰਨ ਲੋਕਾਂ ਲਈ ਵਧੇਰੇ ਅਧਿਕਾਰ ਲਿਆਉਣਗੇ। ਸਮਝਦਾਰ ਅਤੇ ਪਿਆਰੇ, ਉਹ ਤੁਹਾਡੇ ਪਰਿਵਾਰ ਲਈ ਇੱਕ ਤੋਹਫਾ ਹੈ।

ਮੇਰੇ ਬੱਚੇ ਦਾ ਜੀਵਨ ਕਿਸ ਕਿਸਮ ਦਾ ਹੋ ਸਕਦਾ ਹੈ?

ਤੁਹਾਡਾ ਬੱਚਾ ਸਧਾਰਨ, ਪ੍ਰਾਕਿਰਤਕ ਅਤੇ ਸਿਹਤਮੰਦ ਹੁੰਦਾ ਹੈ। ਉਹ ਸੰਭਵ ਵਧੀਆ ਜੀਵਨ ਪ੍ਰਾਪਤ ਕਰਨ ਦੇ ਯੋਗ ਹੁੰਦੇ ਹਨ। ਹਾਂ ਮੈਂ ਸਮਝਦਾ ਹਾਂ ਕਿ ਤੁਹਾਨੂੰ ਡਰ ਹੋ ਸਕਦਾ ਹੈ ਕਿ ਭਿੰਨ ਹੋਣ ਕਾਰਨ ਉਨ੍ਹਾਂ ਨਾਲ ਪੱਖਪਾਤੀ ਹੋਵੇਗੀ ਜਾਂ ਉਨ੍ਹਾਂ ਦਾ ਮਜ਼ਾਕ ਉਡਾਇਆ ਜਾਏਗਾ। ਹਾਲਾਂਕਿ, ਜਿਨੇ ਸਮੇਂ ਤੱਕ ਤੁਸੀ ਵਰਤਮਾਨ ਸਮੇਂ ਵਿੱਚ ਸਾਕਾਰਾਤਮਕ ਰਹਿੰਦੇ ਹੋ ਅਤੇ ਉਸ ਨਾਲ ਜੁੜੇ ਰਹਿੰਦੇ ਹੋ ਜਿਹੜਾ ਸ੍ਰੋਤ/ਰੱਬ/ਪ੍ਰਕਿਰਤੀ ਹੈ ਤੁਸੀ ਠੀਕ ਰਹੋਗੇ। ਬੇਹਤਰ ਸੰਭਾਵਿਤ ਨਤੀਜੇ ਦੀ ਅਤੇ ਜੋ ਤੁਹਾਡੇ ਲਈ ਵਧੀਆ ਹੋਵੇਗਾ ਉਸ ਦੀ ਆਸ ਕਰੋ। ਉਨ੍ਹਾਂ ਦੇ ਫਰਕਾਂ ਕਰਕੇ ਆਪਣੇ ਬੱਚੇ ਨੂੰ ਦੂਰ ਨਾ ਕਰੋ।

ਐਚਆਈਵੀ/ਏਡਜ਼ ਬਾਰੇ ਕੀ ਜਾਣਦੇ ਹੋ?

ਐਚਆਈਵੀ/ਏਡਜ਼ ਸੰਚਾਰ ਅਸੁਰੱਖਿਅਤ ਪ੍ਰਵੇਸ਼ਾਤਮਕ ਸੰਭੋਗ ਦੁਆਰਾ ਵਾਪਰਦਾ ਹੈ। ਜਿਨੇ ਸਮੇਂ ਤੱਕ ਤੁਹਾਡਾ ਬੱਚਾ ਇੱਕ ਨਿਰੋਧ ਨਾਲ ਸੁਰੱਖਿਅਤ ਸੰਭੋਗ ਕਰਦਾ ਹੈ ਉਨ੍ਹਾਂ ਦੇ ਸੁਰੱਖਿਅਤ ਰਹਿਣ ਦੀ ਸੰਭਾਵਨਾ ਹੁੰਦੀ ਹੈ। ਐਚਆਈਵੀ ਨਾਲ ਪੀੜਿਤ ਇੱਕ ਵਿਅਕਤੀ ਪ੍ਰਸਤਾਵਿਤ ਦਵਾਈਆਂ ਦੀ ਵਰਤੋਂ ਕਰਨ ਦੁਆਰਾ ਇੱਕ ਸਿਹਤਮੰਦ, ਖੁਸ਼ੀ ਭਰਿਆ ਜੀਵਨ ਜੀਅ ਸਕਦਾ ਹੈ।

ਅਸੀਂ ਸਹਾਇਤਾ ਕਿੱਥੋਂ ਪ੍ਰਾਪਤ ਕਰ ਸਕਦੇ ਹਾਂ?

ਤੁਸੀ ਇਕੱਲੇ ਨਹੀਂ ਹੋ; ਤੁਹਾਡੇ ਵਰਗੇ ਹੋਰ ਬਹੁਤ ਸਾਰੇ ਲੋਕ ਹਨ। ਖਾਸ ਤੌਰ ਤੇ ਵੱਡੇ ਸ਼ਹਿਰਾਂ ਵਿੱਚ ਐਲ.ਜੀ.ਬੀ.ਟੀ. ਸੈਂਟਰ ਹਨ, ਜਿੱਥੇ ਤੁਸੀ ਸਿਹਤ ਦੀਆਂ ਜਾਂਚਾਂ ਕਰਵਾ ਸਕਦੇ ਹੋ ਅਤੇ ਸਮਾਜਿਕ ਬਣ ਸਕਦੇ ਹੋ। ਜੇਕਰ ਤੁਸੀ ਵੱਡੇ ਸ਼ਹਿਰਾਂ ਤੋਂ ਦੂਰ ਰਹਿੰਦੇ ਹੋ ਤਾਂ ਉੱਥੇ ਹੈਲਪਲਾਈਨਾਂ ਹਨ ਤੁਸੀ ਆਪਣੇ ਹੀ ਦੇਸ਼ ਵਿੱਚੋਂ ਵੀ ਕਾਲ ਕਰ ਸਕਦੇ ਹੋ। ਭਾਰਤ ਵਿੱਚ ਹਮਸਫਰ ਟ੍ਰਸਟ, ਨਾਜ਼ ਫਾਊਂਡੇਸ਼ਨ ਅਤੇ ਹੋਰ ਬਹੁਤ ਸਾਰੇ ਹਨ। ਪਾਕਿਸਤਾਨ ਵਿੱਚ ਵਿਜ਼ਨ ਅਤੇ ਬੰਗਲਾਦੇਸ਼ ਵਿੱਚ ਬੰਧੂ ਸੋਸ਼ਲ ਵੈਲਫੇਅਰ ਸੁਸਾਇਟੀ ਹੈ। ਪੱਛਮ ਵਿੱਚ ਬਹੁਤ ਸਾਰੇ ਵੱਡੇ ਸ਼ਹਿਰਾਂ ਵਿੱਚ ਐਲ.ਜੀ.ਬੀ.ਟੀ. ਸੈਂਟਰ ਜਾਂ ਸਹਾਇਤਾ ਹੈਲਪਲਾਈਨਾਂ ਹਨ ਜਿਨ੍ਹਾਂ ਨੂੰ ਤੁਸੀ ਗੁਗਲ ਤੋਂ ਲੱਭ ਸਕਦੇ ਹੋ। ਜੇਕਰ ਤੁਹਾਨੂੰ ਹੋਰ ਸੁਝਾਅ ਜਾਂ ਸਹਾਇਤਾ ਲੈਣ ਦੀ ਲੋੜ ਹੋਵੇ ਤਾਂ ਤੁਸੀ ਮੇਰੇ ਨਾਲ ਸੋਸ਼ਲ ਮੀਡੀਆ ਤੇ ਵੀ ਸੰਪਰਕ ਕਰ ਸਕਦੇ ਹੋ।

பாலினத்தை வெளிப்படுத்துதல்

LGBTI என்றால் என்ன?

பெண்விழையாள் (லெஸ்பியன்) – ஒரு பெண் மற்ற பெண்களுடன் ஒருபாற்புணர்ச்சி ஆர்வம் கொண்டிருத்தல்.

ஆண்விழையாள் (கே) – ஆண் ஒருவர் மற்ற ஆண்களுடன் ஒருபாற்புணர்ச்சி ஆர்வம் கொண்டிருத்தல்.

திருநங்கைகள் (டிரான்ஸ்ஜெண்டர்) - ஆண் பெண் இருவர்களுடனும் புணர்ச்சி ஆர்வம் கொண்டிருத்தல்.

இடையிலிங்கம் (இன்டர்செக்ஸ்) - சமூக ரீதியாக ஆண் பெண் என்று வகைப்படுத்தப்பட்ட பாலினத்தில் சேராதவர். உதாரணத்திற்கு, ஆண் மகனாகப் பிறந்திருந்தாலும் மனதளவில் தன்னை ஒரு பெண்ணாக பாவித்து உணர்பவர். பாலின அடையாளங்கள் ஒரு புறமிருக்க, பாலியல் விழைவு இவர்களிடம் மாறுபட்டிருக்கும், அதாவது ஆண் பெண் இருவரிடமும் ஆர்வம், ஆண் அல்லது பெண்ணிடம் மட்டும் ஆர்வம் அல்லது ஆண் அல்லது பெண் இருவரிடமும் ஆர்வம் இல்லாமை காணப்படும். திருநங்கை எனப்படும் ஒருவர் தனக்கு விருப்பமான பாலியல் ஆர்வத்தை, ஒரு பெண்ணாகவோ அல்லது ஆணாகவோ, முறைபடுத்திக்கொள்ள / திருத்திக்கொள்ள அறுவை சிகிச்சை செய்துகொள்ள முடிவெடுக்கலாம். தென் ஆசியப் பகுதிகளில் இவர்கள் ஹிர்ஜா (தமிழில் அலி அல்லது திருநங்கை) என்று பொதுவாக அழைக்கப்படுகிறார்கள்.

இன்டர்செக்ஸ் (இடையிலிங்கம்) நபர்கள் ஆண் அல்லது பெண் என்று திட்டவட்டமாக அறியப்படுவதில்லை. குரோமசோம்ஸ், பாலுறுப்புகள் உட்பட பாலியல் பண்புகள் இவர்களிடம் வித்தியாசப்படும் என்பதே காரணம். பல சமயங்களில், இது போன்ற (இடையிலிங்கம்) குழந்தைகள் பிறக்கும் சமயங்களில் அவர்கள் எந்த பாலினத்தைச் சேர்ந்தவராக இருக்க வேண்டும் என்ற விருப்பத்திற்கிணங்க பாலின அறுவை சிகிச்சை செய்யப்படுவதும் ஒரு பொதுவான சிகிச்சையாக உள்ளது. சம்பந்தப்பட்ட குழந்தையின் ஒப்புதல் இல்லாமல் செய்யப்படுவதாலும், ஆபத்தானது என்பதாலும் இன்றைய சூழலில், இந்த மருத்துவ சிகிச்சை மனித உரிமை மீறல் செயல்பாடாகக் கருதப்படுகிறது. இடையிலிங்க நபர்கள் வளர்ந்து பெரியவர்கள் ஆகும் சமயத்தில் தங்கள் பாலின உணர்வுகளை அல்லது பாலின பழக்க வழக்கங்களை பல்வேறு அளவுகளில் பின்பற்றுவார்கள்.

இந்த நிகழ்வுகளுக்கு என்ன காரணம்?

இந்த நிகழ்வுகளுக்கு என்ன காரணம் என்று அறிவியல் சமூகத்திலிருந்து முடிவான விடைகள் எதும் இன்றுவரை கிடைக்கவில்லை. உயிரியல் ரீதியான, சுற்றுச்சூழல், மரபணு அல்லது உளவியல் காரணங்கள் இதற்கு மூலமா என்று தெரியவில்லை. ஆனால் ஒன்று மட்டும் நிச்சயம்; உயிரினம் தோன்றிய நாள் முதற்கொண்டு இந்த வகையினர் ஒவ்வொரு இனத்திலும் இயற்கையாகத் தோன்றிக் கொண்டிருக்கிறார்கள், இதை மாற்ற இயலாது என்பது தான் அது.

ஒரு குழந்தை LGBTI வகையினதா என்பதை எவ்வாறு தெரிந்துகொள்வது?

ஒரே பாலினத்தைச் சேர்ந்தவர்களிடம் தங்களுக்கு ஆர்வம் ஏற்படுகிறதா என்பதை உங்கள் குழந்தை தெரிந்து கொள்ளும், அல்லது ஆண் என்றோ அல்லது பெண் என்றோ தாம் தவறாகப் பிறந்திருக்கிறோம் என்பதை உங்கள் குழந்தை புரிந்துகொள்ளும். சிறு வயதிலிருந்தே உங்கள் குழந்தையுடன் இதைக் குறித்து வெளிப்படையாகப் பேச வேண்டும், ஒரு வேளை குழந்தை LGBTI என்றால், அவர்கள் இதை உங்களுக்குத் தெரிவிப்பார்கள்.

தெரிந்து கொண்ட பிறகு என்ன செய்ய வேண்டும்?

இது ஒன்றும் வியாதி இல்லை, ஆகையால் நீங்கள் ஒன்றும் செய்யத் தேவையில்லை. மந்திரவாதிகள் அல்லது ஆன்மீக தலைவர்களைத் தேடிச் செல்லவும் கூடாது, ஏனென்றால் இது பிரச்சனையை மோசமாக்குமே தவிர பிரயோஜனம் எதுவும் கிடைக்காது. குழந்தைக்கு சிகிச்சை அளிக்க எடுக்கப்படும் நடவடிக்கைகள் அதன் ஆரோக்கியத்தைப் பாழாக்கிவிடும். உங்கள் குழந்தையின் மனநிலையைப் புரிந்துகொண்டு அதற்கு ஆதரவாக அன்பு செலுத்துங்கள். உங்களை நீங்கள் புரிந்து கொள்ளுங்கள், மற்றவர்களையும் புரிய வைக்க முயலுங்கள். சமூகத்தில் அவமானமாக இருக்குமே என்று ஒருபோதும் கவலைப் படாதீர்கள். நம் நிலைமையை நன்றாகப் புரிந்துகொண்டு அதற்கேற்ப நம் நடவடிக்கைகளை அமைத்துக்கொள்ள வேண்டும். மற்றவர்களுடைய வாழ்க்கையையும் சுதந்திரத்தையும் பாழ்படுத்தும் விதத்தில் திருமண ஏற்பாடுகளில் ஈடுபடாதீர்கள். பொய்மையாக வாழக் கூடாது. LGBTI நபர்கள் மனித சமூகத்தில் தொன்றுதொட்டு வாழ்ந்திருக்கிறார்கள். அவர்கள் தூய்மைக் கேடுள்ளவர்கள் இல்லை, சமூக நியதிகளுக்கு ஊறுவிளைவிப்பவர்களும் இல்லை. ஒரு வகையில் அவர்கள் சமூக மதிப்புகளுக்கு உரியவர்கள் என்பது தான் உண்மை. இவர்கள் நிபந்தனையற்ற, வரம்பில்லாத அன்பு செலுத்துவதில் ஒப்பற்றவர்கள். சமூக வாழ்வியலில் அன்புக்கும் அரவணைப்புக்கும் எடுத்துக்காட்டாக விளங்குபவர்களுக்கு இவர்கள் உதாரண புருஷர்களாக அடையாளம் காணப்படுபவர்கள். பெண்கள், மாற்றுத் திறனாளிகள் மற்றும் மாறுபட்டவர்கள் உரிமைகளை சமூகத்தில் நிலைநாட்டும் பொறுப்பை ஏற்றுக்கொள்ள தயங்காதவர்கள். புத்திசாலித்தனத்துடன் நிறைந்த அன்புள்ளம் கொண்ட இவர்கள் உங்கள் குடும்பத்திற்கு வரப்பிரசாதமாக இருப்பார்கள்.

என் குழந்தையின் வாழ்க்கை எப்படிப்பட்டதாக இருக்கும்?

உங்கள் குழந்தை சாதாரணமானது, இயற்கையானது, ஆரோக்கியமுள்ளது. வாழ்க்கையை அதன் உன்னத அனுபவங்களுடன் வாழ முடியும். பொது சமூக ரீதியாக அவர்கள் வித்தியாசமானவர்கள் என்பதால் கிண்டல்களுக்கும் ஏளனங்களுக்கும் உட்படுவார்கள் என்பது எனக்குப் புரிகிறது. இருந்தாலும், நீங்கள் உங்கள் நிலைமைப் புரிந்துகொண்டு உங்கள் கடவுள் / இயற்கை / விதி அளித்த பிரசாதம் என்பதை உணர்ந்து பக்குவமாக நடந்துகொள்ள வேண்டும். இந்த நிலைமையை உங்களுக்குச் சாதகமாக மாற்ற உங்களால் முடிந்த அனைத்தையும் செய்வது தான் உங்களுக்கும் குழந்தைக்கும் நன்மை பயக்கும். குழந்தை வித்தியாசமானது என்பதால் அதை நீங்கள் வெறுத்துவிடக் கூடாது.

HIV / AIDs தொல்லைகள் அண்டுமா?

பாதுகாப்பில்லாத உட்செருகல் பாலியல் நடவடிக்கைகளால் HIV/AIDs நோய் பரவும். பாதுகாப்புடன் (காண்டம் பயன்படுத்தி) உடலுறவில் ஈடுபடும் போது உங்கள் குழந்தைக்கு ஒரு தீங்கும் விளையாமல் பாதுகாப்புடன் இருக்கும். HIV பாதிப்புள்ள நபர் கூட, மருந்து எடுத்துக்கொண்டு ஆரோக்கியத்துடன் சந்தோஷமாக வாழ்ந்து கொண்டிருக்கிறார்.

எங்களுக்கு ஆதரவளிக்கும் அமைப்புகள் உள்ளனவா?

இதில் நீங்கள் தனிமையாக உணரத் தேவையில்லை, உங்களைப் போலவே பலர் இருக்கிறார்கள். பெரு நகரங்களில் LGBT மையங்கள் உள்ளன, அவர்களுடன் தொடர்பு கொண்டு உடல்நலப் பரிசோதனைகளைச் செய்துகொள்ளலாம், சமூக சூழ்நிலையும் கிடைக்கும். நீங்கள் பெரு நகரங்களிலிருந்து ஒதுங்கி வாழ்பவர் என்றால், ஹெல்ப்லைன் மூலமாக நீங்கள் அவர்களுடன் தொடர்பு கொள்ள முடியும். ஹம்சஃபர் டிரஸ்ட், நாஜ் ஃபவுண்டேஷன் போன்ற பல அமைப்புகள் இந்தியாவில் செயல்பட்டுக் கொண்டிருக்கின்றன. பாகிஸ்தானில் விஷன் என்ற அமைப்பும், பங்களா தேஷில் பந்து சோசியல் வெல்ஃபேர் சொசைட்டி அமைப்புகளும் உள்ளன. மேலை நாடுகளில் LGBT மையங்களும், ஆதரவளிக்கும் ஹெல்ப்லைன் அமைப்புகளும் உள்ளன. கூகுல் பக்கத்தில் இதை நீங்கள் தேடி தெரிந்துகொள்ளலாம். உங்களுக்கு மேலும் அதிக விபரங்கள் தேவைப்பட்டால் நீங்கள் என்னுடன் என் சமூக வலைத்தளத்தில் தொடர்பு கொள்ளுங்கள்.

లైంగిక సంబంధిత వివరాలని తెలియజేయుట

ఎల్ జి బిటిఐ అంటే ఏమిటి?

లెస్బియన్ : ఒక మహిళ మరో మహిళ పట్ల ఆకర్షితం కావడం

గే : మగవాడు మరో మగవాడి పట్ల ఆకర్షితం కావడం

బైసెక్స్యువల్ : ఒక వ్యక్తి మగ మరియు ఆడ ఇద్దరి పట్ల ఆకర్షితం కావడం

ట్రాన్స్ జెండర్ : ఒకవ్యక్తి జన్మ సామాజికంగా అంగీకరించలేని విధంగా ఉండటం. ఉదాహరణకు, వారు మగవారిలా పుట్టి ఉండచ్చు, కాని స్వభావం అంతర్గతంగా ఆడవారిలా ఉంటారు. వారి లైంగిక ప్రవర్తన వారి లింగానికి భిన్నంగా ఉంటుంది. కనుక వారు మగవారు మరియు ఆడవారు ఇద్దరి పట్ల ఆకర్షితులు కావచ్చు. ఒక ట్రాన్స్ జెండర్ వ్యక్తి లైంగిక పునరేకీకరణకు /దిద్దుబాటు ఆపరేషన్ కోసం వారికి నచ్చిన జెండర్ ని ఎంచుకోవడంలో నిర్ధారించుకోవచ్చు లేదా లేకపోవచ్చు. దక్షిణ ఆసియాలో కోజ్జా/ హిజ్రా అని వీరిని అంటారు.

ఉభయ లింగ వ్యక్తులు మగ లేదా ఆడ వారిలా గుర్తించబడరు. దీనికి కారణం క్రోమోజోమ్స్, బీజకోశాలు లేదా జననాంగాలతో సహ లైంగిక లక్షణాల వైవిధ్యం. తరచుగా కొన్ని సార్లు ఉభయ లింగ శరీరంతో పుట్టిన పిల్లలకు సమాజం ఆమోదించే విధంగా సర్జరీలను చేస్తారు. ఇప్పుడు ఇది మానవ హక్కులని దుర్వినియోగం చేయడం మరియు జననాంగాల విరూపణకు సంబంధించి ఉంటుంది, దీనికి పిల్లల అంగీకారం ఉండదు మరియు ప్రమాదకరమైనది కూడా. ఉభయ లింగ వ్యక్తులని వారి లింగ లేదా వివిధ రకాల లైంగిక గుర్తింపులని బట్టి వారు పెరిగి పెద్ద వారయ్యాక గుర్తించబడతారు.

ఇలా ఎందుకు జరుగుతుంది?

ఇలా ఎందుకు జరుగుతుంది అనడానికి సెంటిఫిక్ పరంగా ఎలాంటి ఆధారం లేదు. బయోలోజికల్, పర్యావరణం, జన్యు లేదా మానసిక లోపమా అన్నది మనకు తెలీదు. మనకు తెలిసిందల్లా ఇది సహజమైనది మరియు సృష్టి ప్రారంభం నుండి అన్ని జాతుల్లోనూ ఇలా జరుగుతూనే ఉంది, దీన్ని మార్చలేము.

మా పిల్ల ఎల్ జి బి టి ఐ అన్నది మేము ఎలా తెలుసుకోగలం?

పిల్లలు తమ లింగాన్ని బట్టి ఎవరి పట్ల లైంగికంగా ఆకర్షితులవుతున్నారన్నది గుర్తించగలరు లేదా వారు తప్పుడు లింగంలో పుట్టినట్టుగా భావిస్తారు. మీ పిల్లలతో వారి ప్రారంభ వయసు నుండే వారి సమస్యల గురించి మాట్లాడండి, దాంతో వారు ఎల్ జి బి టిఐ అయితే మీకు తెలియబరుస్తారు.

దీనికి ఏం చేయాల్సి ఉంటుంది?

ఇది ఒక వ్యాధి కాదు మరియు అందువలన దీని గురించి ఏమీ చేయాల్సిన అవసరం లేదు. దీనికి వైద్యం లేదా మతపరమైన సాధువుల వద్దకు వెళ్ళనవసరం లేదు, ఇలా చేయడం వల్ల పరిస్థితి విపమించవచ్చు. మీ పిల్లలని బాగు చేయడం కోసం చేసే ప్రయత్నం ప్రతికూలంగా వారి ఆరోగ్యంపై ప్రభావితం చూపుతుంది. మీరు వారిని అర్థం చేసుకుని, మరింత ప్రేమని వారికి పంచండి. మిమ్మల్ని మీరు ఎడ్యుకేట్ చేసుకుని ఇతరులని కూడా చేయండి. సమాజం ఏమంటుందో అన్న భావంతో సిగ్గు పడకండి. మనం వారిని అంగీకరించాలి మరియు మనం ఎవరు అన్న వాస్తవాన్ని అంగీకరించాలి. వివాహాల ద్వారా లేదా అంధవిశ్వాసాల ద్వారా ఇతరుల జీవితాలను నాశనం చేయకూడదు. ఎల్ జిబిటివ ప్రజలు ఎల్లప్పుడూ సమాజపు ఉనికిలో ఉన్నారు. వారు అసహ్యించుకునే వారు కారు మరియు సమాజానికి ముప్ప కాదు. నిజానికి వారు ఒక ఆస్తి. వారు పరతులు లేని ప్రేమ మరియు అంగీకారం సేర్పడానికి వచ్చారు. వారు ప్రేమని సమాజంలో విస్తరించేందుకు వచ్చారు. వారు ఆడవారికి, వికలాంగులకు మరియు భిన్నంగా కనిపించే వారికి మరిన్ని హక్కులని తెచ్చారు. తెలివైన వారు మరియు ప్రేమించే వారు, వారు మీ కుటుంబానికి ఒక బహుమతి వంటి వారు.

నా బిడ్డ జీవితం ఏ విధంగా ఉంటుంది?

మీ బిడ్డ సాధారణంగా, సహజంగా, ఆరోగ్యంగా ఉంది. వారు సాధ్యమైనంత ఉత్తమ జీవితాన్ని ఆనందించగలరు. అవును, తోటివారి నుంచి బెదిరింపులు లేదా ఎగతాళులు ఉంటాయన్న భయం మీకుండని నాకు తెలుసు. అయితే, ప్రస్తుత క్షణంలో మీరు పొజిటివ్ గా ఉన్నంత వరకు, మూలం / దేవుడు / ప్రకృతి సానుకూలం చేస్తూ ఉంటాయి. సాధ్యమైనంత ఉత్తమమైన ఫలితం ఆశించడం మరియు మీరు మరిన్ని అవకాశాలని కలిగించండి. వారి వైవిధ్యాల కారణంగా మీ పిల్లలని వెలి వేయకండి.

HIV / AIDS అంటే ఏమిటి?

HIV / AIDS ట్రాన్స్ మిషన్ అసురక్షిత లైంగిక సాంపర్కం ద్వారా సోకుతుంది. మీ పిల్లలు కండోమ్ తో సెక్స్ చేసినట్లయితే సురక్షితంగా ఉంటాడు. HIV ఉన్న వ్యక్తి కూడా మెడికేషన్ చేసి ఒక ఆరోగ్యకరమైన, సంతోషంగా జీవితం జీవించగలరు.

మాకు మద్దతు ఎక్కడ లభిస్తుంది?

నువ్వ ఒంటరి వాడివి కావు; మీలాంటి వారు అనేక మంది ఉన్నారు. ముఖ్యంగా పెద్ద నగరాలలో LGBT కేంద్రాలు ఉన్నాయి, అక్కడ మీకు ఆరోగ్య పరీక్షలు చేస్తారు మరియు సమాజంతో కలిసి ఉంటారు. మీరు పెద్ద నగరాలకు దూరంగా ఉంటే మీరు కూడా మీ స్వంత దేశంలో నుండి హెల్ప్ లైన్స్ కు కాల్ చేసుకోవచ్చు. భారతదేశంలో హమ్ సఫర్ ట్రస్ట్ అని ఉంది, నాజ్ ఫౌండేషన్ మరియు ఇంకెన్నో ఉన్నాయి. పాకిస్తాన్ లో విజన్ మరియు బంగ్లాదేశ్ లో బంధు సామాజిక సంక్షేమం ఉంది. పశ్చిమంలో అనేక ప్రధాన నగరాలలో LGBT కేంద్రాలు ఉన్నాయి లేదా మద్దతునిచ్చే హెల్ప్ లైన్స్ ఉన్నాయి, వీటిని మీరు గూగుల్ లో పొందగలరు. మీకు మరిన్ని సలహాలు అవసరమయితే లేదా సపోర్ట్ కావాలన్న మీరు నా సామాజిక మీడియా వద్ద నన్ను కూడా సంప్రదించవచ్చు.

Urdu

جنسی رجحان کا افشاء

LGBTI کیا ہے؟

زنانہ ہم جنس پرست (لسبین) - ایسی عورت جو دوسری عورتوں کی جانب جنسی کشش محسوس کرتی ہے۔

مردانہ ہم جنس پرست (گے) - ایسا مرد جو دوسرے مردوں کی جانب جنسی کشش محسوس کرتا ہے۔

دوجنسہ (بائی سیکسوئل) - ایسا فرد جو مردوں اور عورتوں دونوں کی جانب جنسی کشش محسوس کرے۔

مخنث (ٹرانس جینڈر) - ایسا فرد جو پیدائشی لحاظ سے سماجی طور پر قبول شدہ جنسی معیار کے موافق نہ ہو۔ مثال کے طور پر، وہ مرد پیدا ہوا ہو لیکن خلقی طور پر خود کو عورت تصور کرے۔ ان کا جنسی رجحان ان کی جنسی شناخت سے الگ ہوتی ہے، لہذا اسے جنسی لحاظ سے مرد اور عورت میں سے کسی کی جانب، دونوں کی جانب کشش محسوس ہوسکتی ہے یا کسی کی بھی جانب کشش محسوس نہیں ہوسکتی ہے۔ مخنث فرد اس جنس میں جنسی باز تخلیط/اصلاح کے لیے آپریشن کروانے پر آمادہ بوبھی سکتا ہے اور نہیں بھی جس میں وہ سہولت محسوس کرتا ہے۔ جنوبی ایشیا میں اس کے لیے ہیجڑا کی اصطلاح استعمال ہوتی ہے۔

بین جنسہ افراد کی شناخت امتیازی طور پر مرد یا عورت کے طور پر نہیں کی جاتی ہے۔ یہ ان کی جنسی خصوصیت بشمول کروموزومس، خصیوں، یا تناسلی اعضاء میں اختلاف کے سبب ہوتا ہے۔ اکثر و بیشتر پیدائش کے دوران دوجنسہ بچوں کی جنسی تخلیط کی سرجری انجام دی جاتی ہے تاکہ انہیں مجموعی طور پر سماج کے لیے زیادہ قابل بنایا جاسکے۔ اسے اب حقوق انسانی کے بیجا استعمال کے طور پر جانا جاتا ہے اور ایسے بچوں کی جنسی اعضاء کی قطع و برید بلا اجازت اور خطرناک ہے۔ بین جنسی افراد کی شناخت مختلف درجے کے جنسی یا صنفی شناختوں کے تحت ہوسکتی ہے، جو ان کی نشونما کے ساتھ ارتقاء پذیر ہوتے ہیں۔

یہ کیوں ہوتا ہے؟

سائنسی برادری کو اس بات کا کوئی پختہ ثبوت نہیں ملا ہے کہ ایسا کیوں ہوتا ہے۔ ہمیں یہ معلوم نہیں ہے کہ آیا یہ حیاتیاتی، ماحولیاتی، جینیاتی یا نفسیاتی وجہ سے ہوتا ہے۔ ہمیں ابھی یہ معلوم ہے کہ یہ قدرتی چیز ہے اور دنیا کے آغاز سے ہی تمام انواع کے اندر پایا جاتا ہے اور اسے تبدیل نہیں کیا جاسکتا۔

ہمیں کیسے معلوم ہوگا کہ آیا ہمارا بچہ LGBTI ہے؟

آپ کے بچے کو خود معلوم ہوجائے گا اگر اسے اپنی ہی جنس کے کسی فرد میں جنسی کشش محسوس ہو یا انہیں محسوس ہوکہ در حقیقت ان کی پیدائش غلط جنس میں ہوگئی ہے۔ ان امور پر اپنے بچے کے ساتھ ابتدائی عمر سے ہی کھل کر بات کریں، تاکہ اگر وہ LGBTI ہوں تو وہ آپ کو اس کے بارے میں بتاسکیں۔

اس سلسلے میں کیا کیا جاسکتا ہے؟

یہ کوئی بیماری نہیں ہے اور اسی وجہ سے اس کے لیے کچھ بھی کرنے کی ضرورت نہیں ہے۔ کسی عامل یا مذہبی رہنماؤں کے پاس جانے کی ضرورت نہیں ، کیونکہ اس سے صرف مسئلہ خراب ہی ہوسکتا ہے۔ اپنے بچے کا علاج کرنے کی کوشش سے صرف اس کی صحت پر منفی اثر ہی پڑے گا۔ آپ کو صرف اپنے بچے کے ساتھ زیادہ محبت سے پیش آنا چاہیے اور یہ سمجھنا چاہیے کہ وہ کس کیفیت سے گزر رہے ہیں۔ خود کو اور دوسروں کو معلومات فراہم کریں۔ اس بات کی شرمندگی میں نہ پڑنے کی کوشش کریں کہ سماج کیا سوچے گا۔ ہمیں صرف خود کو قبول کرنے اور ہم جو کچھ ہی اس کی سچائی کو تسلیم کرنے کی ضرورت ہے۔ ہم دوسرے لوگوں کی زندگیوں کو شادیوں سے متعلق شرمندگی کا احساس کرواکر یا غیرحقیقت پسند بن کر تباہ نہیں کرسکتے۔ LGBTI والے افراد کو ہمیشہ سماج سے خارج کردیا جاتا ہے۔ وہ گندے نہیں ہیں نہ ہی وہ سماج کے لیے خطرہ ہیں۔ درحقیقت وہ ایک اثاثہ ہیں۔ وہ غیر مشروط محبت اور قبولیت سکھانے کے لیے دنیا میں آئے ہیں۔ وہ محبت اور شمولیت کے معاملے میں معاشرتوں کے نظریے کو وسعت دینے کے لیے دنیا میں آئے ہیں۔ وہ عورتوں، معذور افراد اور ان لوگوں کے لیے مزید حقوق کا باعث بنیں گے جو مختلف ہیں۔ وہ عقلمند اور پیارے ہوتے ہیں، اور آپ کے خاندان کے لیے ایک تحفہ ہیں۔

میرا بچہ کس قسم کی زندگی جی سکتا ہے؟

آپ کا بچہ معمول کے مطابق، فطری اور صحت مند ہے۔ وہ ممکنہ حد تک بہترین زندگی گزار سکتا ہے۔ ہاں مجھے معلوم ہے کہ آپ کو یہ خطرہ ہوسکتا ہے کہ انہیں ڈرایا دھمکایا جائے گا یا مختلف ہونے کی وجہ سے ان کا مذاق اڑایا جائے گا۔ تاہم، جب تک آپ موجودہ وقت میں مثبت سوچ رکھیں گے اور پیدا کرنے والے /خدا/قدرت سے جڑے رہیں گے آپ بالکل ٹھیک رہیں گے۔ ممکنہ حد تک بہترین نتیجے اور اپنے لیے زیادہ ممکنہ چیزوں کی توقع کریں۔ فرق کی وجہ سے اپنے بچے کو علاحدہ نہ کریں۔

HIV/AIDs کے بارے میں بتائیں؟

HIV/AIDs کی منتقلی غیر محفوظ ادخالی جنسی عمل کے ذریعہ ہوتا ہے۔ جب تک آپ کا بچہ کنڈوم کے ساتھ محفوظ جنسی عمل کرتا ہے اس کے محفوظ رہنے کا امکان زیادہ ہے۔ یہاں تک کہ HIV کے ساتھ بھی کوئی فرد دواؤں کا استعمال کرتے ہوئے صحت مند، خوشگوار زندگی گزار سکتا ہے۔

ہم کہاں سے مدد حاصل کرسکتے ہیں؟

آپ اکیلے نہیں ہیں؛ آپ جیسے بہت سے لوگ ہیں۔ خاص طور پر بڑے شہروں میں LGBT مراکز ہیں، جہاں آپ صحت کی جانچیں کروا سکتے ہیں اور میل جول بڑھا سکتے ہیں۔ اگر آپ بڑے شہروں سے دور ہیں تو ایسے ہیلپ لائنس موجود ہیں جنہیں آپ اپنے ملک میں کال کرسکتے ہیں۔ ہندوستان میں ہمسفر ٹرسٹ، ناز فاؤنڈیشن اور دیگر بہت سے ایسے ادارے ہیں۔ پاکستان میں ویژن اور بنگلہ دیش میں بندھو سوشل ویلفیئر سوسائٹی ہے۔ مغرب میں زیادہ تر بڑے شہروں میں LGBT سنٹرز یا امدادی ہیلپ لائنیں ہیں جنہیں آپ Google پر تلاش کرسکتے ہیں۔ اگر آپ کو مزید مشورے یا مدد کی ضرورت ہو تو آپ سوشل میڈیا پر مجھ سے بھی رابطہ کرسکتے ہیں۔

PART 4: LET'S CHANGE THIS

Your mind will bring up all sorts of false beliefs. Your job is to identify them and return back to love.

11) CLEAN YOUR SUBCONSCIOUS

Removing guilt, shame, insecurities and promoting self-love.

Acknowledge the guilt and shame that comes with being LGBTI. We as South Asians know of the unnerving amount of pressure we receive to get good grades, a better job and a socially acceptable heterosexual relationship. A lot of pressure is put on South Asian children as a whole and being gay forces us to feel conflicted and torn. So how do we release the suffocating guilt and shame we feel every time our mother calls? Accept. Accept who you are. Rather approve of who you are. Accepting is passive whereas approving is more action based. When you accept, you just resort or succumb to something. But approving requires our active involvement and inner work to say, 'Yes I am who I am, and I do not need to conform. I approve of who I am, because who I am is neither right or wrong, it is simply what it is. 'I' being a beam of pure positive light who is worthy. I approve of myself. I acknowledge and congratulate myself. I applaud the person who I was born as. And you can choose to either applaud or ridicule me, but my validation does not depend on that. I am happy and content in the knowing that my creator, from whence I came from, loves me deeply and approves of who I am.'

HOW TO RELEASE GUILT?

Feeling guilty makes us think we are wrong. We seek love and think the only way to get it is by punishing ourselves. This starts a pattern of self-punishment and self-blame, otherwise known as guilt. Guilt is a mask over negative core beliefs acquired during childhood. These core beliefs are: I deserve punishment, I deserve to suffer, I don't deserve to be happy, and I don't deserve to be loved. Core beliefs will be explored towards the end of this chapter. But for now, let's accept this belief pattern exists.

Guilt is a momentary emotion and to get rid of it, we must acknowledge that it is causing us great harm. We must realise that it is not serving us and is self-abusive. Guilt and shame are negative emotions fuelled by negative thoughts. We must be willing to release them. To turn them around we need to affirm to ourselves that we deserve to be happy and that we deserve to be loved. In any given situation which brings up guilt or shame, first, learn what your responsibility was within it and then take a firm stance to change your thinking of it in the future. Judgements and assumptions about yourself keep you a prisoner to guilt. Looking at the past trying to change it will do you no benefit. Neither will self-hatred and self-blame do you any favours. Simply giving yourself unconditional love will release you from the bondages of guilt and shame. Guilt is the opposite of self-love. By shifting your perspective on what you are beating yourself up on guilt will be released.

Brené Brown says don't be afraid of shame or failure. Shame is the internal dialogue which thinks we are never good enough. Shame and guilt are separate. Shame is the focus on oneself, whereas guilt is the focus on one's behaviour. Shame is 'I am bad', guilt is 'I did bad'. Shame is linked to addiction, violence, depression, suicide, and eating disorders. Secrecy, silence and judgement are the three key things that make shame increase. Empathy is the antidote of shame.

Most of us have shame and guilt because of our sexuality. We may question whether we were born gay because of some bad deed done in a past life. We may ask if we should be punished for that which we think we have done.

The definition of Karma is:
'Every action comes with a cause and effect.' So good things come to those who commit good deeds and bad things to those who commit bad deeds.

However, karma is more complex then that. There are two types of karma, instant karma and karma that comes back in later lives.

According to the Law of Attraction and Abraham Hicks' teachings, the word karma has been used incorrectly.

'You are eternal beings and your consciousness is ongoing. When you re-emerge into the non-physical, you let go of all resistance. Then when you decide to emerge into the physical, you do not carry the past with you. You do not carry your negative concerns from lifetime to lifetime.' Abraham Hicks

So no one has any pre-planned karmic lessons in this life.

Personally, I feel uncomfortable with karma being something that you get in this life in accordance to your past deeds. My mum has for instance said that I am gay because I did bad deeds in a past life. But I believe we are eternal consciousness and over time when we go back to being non-physical our slate is cleaned so to speak.

I believe we chose this life to expand and learn. We all have instant karma. When we do bad things (because of negative thoughts) bad things will happen to us there and then in this lifetime. Just in the way, if we are angry and driving, we attract angry drivers who honk and shout back at us, instant karma works in the here and now, depending on our mindset and how loving we are.

It is; of course, better to feel good as good things are more likely to happen back to us. To expect the best outcome and feel good about oneself and one's experiences is paramount.

Otherwise, we give away our power and become victims of life. I understand that elite Brahmin priests used the law of karma to enforce the caste system through subjugation and self-acceptance. I also understand that it may have helped people accept themselves and their circumstances. For instance, Brahmin priests may have said a child is a beggar in India because of some bad past life karma. But victimisation may make this child stay in abject poverty forever. Indeed, in India this is what I saw whilst travelling, living and backpacking. However, in Hindu scriptures, it is written that it is up to each person to help elevate the pain of those who are less fortunate then themselves and not to continue the suppression. Whether this happens in real life is another thing.

'You are extensions of Source energy in varying degrees of alignment.' **Abraham Hicks**

We are all part of creation, but not all of us are connected to it in the same way. Some of us are more connected to Source through our positive thoughts, feelings and words. Others, however, come from a place of lack declaring 'I can't do this' or 'there's not enough for everyone' and are fairly disconnected.

This negativity literally pollutes the environment around us. There should be a tax against it. People should be encouraged to clean up their vibrations each morning. For it can have momentous effects on this planet and beyond. Whether this is done through prayer or meditation depends on the person. However, it must be remembered that prayer and religious practices will not work if people are not positively committed to them. For there is no point in going to the Gurdwara or Mosque to pray if you don't want to get out of your negative mindset to blossom and flourish into love.

In her mindset-shattering book, 'You can Heal Your Life', Louise Hay urges us to remove all negative self-talk from our lives. She asks us to remove all limiting beliefs from our mind. By maintaining a 100% positive outlook, our life can be transformed. A good trick she gives to combat negativity is chanting 'I love myself, I am worthy of love, I am love' a thousand times a day. You have the power to choose thoughts that can allow you to attract the best life possible. Think of the best outcome and live in the high-vibration of love and you cannot go wrong.

This is because all thoughts are not created equal. A thought that comes from a field of unity, togetherness, or love is far more powerful than a thought that is emerging from a field of fear, doubt and worry. The vibrational intensity of it is simply higher. Thoughts that come from negativity emit a lower amplitude, beta range. Meditation and prayer are both high-frequency intentions and thus are more powerful. So fewer people vibrating at a higher frequency can make a difference. If a certain amount of people meditate, sing, pray or chant its effects vibrate into the larger community.

For instance Ashoka, the great Indian ruler sent enlightened monks to different crime ridden cities around India. The impact they had was phenomenal; crime rates lowered drastically. Similar tests showing the same results have since been done around the world. In the summer of 1993 transcendental meditators in Washington DC helped reduce crime rates by 23.3%.

JEALOUSY

The gay scene is full of jealousy. Heck, the whole world is. But what exactly is this emotion? Jealousy occurs when we are not connected to our self, our higher self. We believe that there is a lack of abundance for all, including us, and the success of another hurts us, as we want the same feeling as them. What we tend to forget is that we live in an abundant Universe with limitless possibilities. The gay scene as it is marginalised has more of this emotion in it. The more marginalised you are, the more subjugated you feel and the more jealous you can become. I see it as a scale, where people fit themselves according to how they see themselves fairing up. For instance in the Western world the straight, white, middle-class male sits on top of the scale, then we have the straight, white, middle-class female, you can insert varying degrees of marginalisation thereafter based on colour, race, religion, social and economic status and sexuality. The ethnic LGBTI person fairs quite low on the scale. Now if you buy into this mechanism of social construct and are not consciously aware, it can be very detrimental for you.

Whenever someone else gets that promotion, praise or partner you can fearlessly envy them. This is the main curse of the gay scene, and of our LGBTI South Asian community. Everyone wants the limelight for themselves and will do whatever it takes to get there. It is not constructive and indicative of a healthy life, nor will it help our cause to continue. United we stand stronger. Agreed?

We are one.

Jealousy is when you separate yourself from the 'one'. You believe that you are not part of the one, whole collective consciousness. This is the ego's illusion mixed with insecurities. We should be happy for someone else's success in their career, relationship, family and personal life. If we want what the other person has, such as a romantic relationship, then we need to be on the same vibrational energy of appreciation as them. We should appreciate their happiness, joy and success as though it was our own. Only through doing that do we attract more of the same to ourselves.

Jealousy is a means of testing where you are spiritually on the emotional scale and a great indicator of the inner work that is required. Ideally, we should be less concerned what others are doing and where they are. We should remind ourselves that there is abundance everywhere, and our appreciating of such things will invite it into our life too. Happiness is measured from within. Thus we need to work within ourselves. We can never know the journey of another person, what they have had to endure and whether what appears to be success, happiness and joy is not just a façade. We don't walk in their shoes, so we will never know. They do not necessarily have a better life. For the grass isn't always greener on the other side.

When you feel someone has something that you should have had you tap into poverty consciousness- falsely thinking there is not enough for everyone. By doing this, you end up lowering your vibrational frequency by reaffirming that whatever you are jealous about is not in your life at the moment. It is the surest way to prevent good stuff coming into your life. We must remind ourselves that we are all on different journeys, and comparison is SUICIDE. This is an ABUNDANT Universe and the possibilities are limitless but only if we tap into them by believing so. And on a deeper level, all physical experiences are temporary and come and go. Nothing is permanent, neither you nor I, we are constantly evolving, transforming and transmuting. Focus on your own journey, bless all those around you and carry on bringing greatness into your life by expecting it!

SELF-ACCEPTANCE

Acceptance, in general, raises your vibration (and thereby increases your connection to Source). Accepting the perfection that you are allows the miracle of manifestation to materialise. When we look at the absence of what we are, or what we don't have, we lower our vibration and self-worth. We conclude that we are unworthy of all that we want as we don't have it. If we were worthy, surely we would have it by now. However, we must remember that we are the creator of our own reality. Nothing outside of us is bestowing happiness to us. Everything is self-induced. Acknowledging the fact that I'm doing it all, I'm allowing it or denying it, brings clarity and power back to ourselves. See worthiness implies that it is up to someone outside of us to decide when we deserve something. When it is not like that. The key is to love and accept yourself. Successful people understand this fact and talk about what they want not what they don't want. They talk about what is coming into their life and not what has happened. They congratulate others as doing so raises their vibrational frequency thus allowing more good into their life. They are appreciative and thankful. They realise the only thing they can do is be JOYFUL and content.

HOW TO GAIN SELF-ESTEEM?

How do you gain self-esteem when you have been used to gaining approval from others? First, appreciate that being appreciated is not bad. It's ok if someone loves you. But soon as you get dependent on someone else for attention for your own connection to Source, you make life very difficult for yourself. Verbalise the awareness of your own connection and thus the ability to give yourself self-esteem. When you feel good, acknowledge it. 'I feel full; therefore I must be in vibrational harmony with who I am. When I am well connected to who I am, I feel great and when I am not I don't feel great.' When you feel down, let those around you, family, friends or partner know that you are going to spend some time with yourself until you feel the release of your resistance (and negative mood). Then you will feel better. Deal with it on your own first; don't ask others to bring you to joy. Connection is a personal issue. Feeling better is the most important part. If you find yourself feeling a negative emotion reach for a better feeling thought. Know what you do want and focus on that wholly. For focusing on your current lack of self-esteem will just bring more of that to you.

When it comes down to dating, and not receiving replies to your messages it is better not to get down about it. I remember the rejection I felt every time a guy did not reply back to me or blocked me on Grindr. It was literally weakening my inner confidence as I allowed it to get hold of me. However, I realised great wisdom and acceptance from it. What is meant to be will come at the right time, and that desperation was not attractive. The Universe gives not what you want but what you feel. So when you are in a state of incompleteness, you attract similar people who reject you as you reject yourself. It is exactly the lesson you need. If you are awake, you will realise you don't need to bow down for anyone's love. Focus on what makes you feel good and distance yourself from things that make you feel bad. Create/attract spaces with conscious like-minded people. This will be the biggest gift you give to yourself.

WHAT ARE YOUR LIMITING CORE BELIEFS?

I have spoken about certain emotions that arise such as guilt, shame, jealousy and lack of self-esteem. But from where are these emotions triggered? What is their root cause? Limiting or negative core beliefs are the soil from where these emotions arise. Beliefs are subconscious, impactful experiences that happened during our childhood. They become our core beliefs, when they are repeated time and time again. Examples include, 'I am unlovable', 'I will be hurt if I get close to someone', or 'there is no point to life'. When we experience these beliefs, they become deeply rooted. Many times we ignore things that invalidate those beliefs whilst looking for proof that validates them. This belief then becomes the foundation of the life we live. Limiting core beliefs are thoughts that are thought so often the subconscious mind takes over. They become unconscious, and we are unaware of them. To become aware and find our core beliefs we have to be aware of things that upset us. The sadness we experience from a limiting belief is the Universe's way of helping us find what is buried in our subconscious. Notice what is upsetting you and then actively and consciously question the reason why you are upset to whittle down these thoughts to your deepest core thought. (An exercise to identify your limiting beliefs is in the Action Sheet that follows this chapter).

HOW TO CHANGE A BELIEF?

To change a belief, you need to change the way you think about beliefs and reality. Beliefs are not fixed but flexible. A belief is a thought that you keep thinking, which creates a frequency that shows evidence in the physical form. That physical proof strengthens this belief. It is a thought backed up by confidence, faith and assumed truth. The reality of what you believe to be true has nothing to do with the actuality of what is true. Objective truth and fixed reality are different to what we believe to be true. They are the actual truth without the ego's interpretation. Beliefs thus can be changed especially if they are detrimental to us. The frequency of our desire and belief need to be an exact match in order to manifest the life of our dreams. For instance, if you want a perfect relationship, but your limiting core belief is that you don't deserve a perfect relationship, this belief will block this manifestation. Hence why certain things don't manifest. (Steps to change and heal beliefs are outlined in the Action Sheet that follows this chapter).

SHADOW WORK

If we choose to focus on positive aspects of our life only to escape a negative emotional state, the positive focus can become a mode of resistance. It is then better to stop focusing positively and to go directly to the core of the negative emotion to release it. This is called shadow work. Shadow work is understanding what you don't know about yourself. It is a technique of diving directly into the issue you have in order to heal it. It allows you to come to terms with and accept why you do certain things or why certain things hurt you. It is an inquisitive way of learning why an issue is good for you, whether it serves you or is worth having at all.

There are mixed reviews about shadow work. Many spiritual teachers discount looking at the negative side of your psyche because by putting attention onto it, it is more likely to manifest. They think by focusing on things that need to be cleared from your subconscious, you will find more things to clear from your subconscious. However, this is based on a narrow view of consciousness, resistance and the Law of Attraction. Integration and wholeness of both our shadow (negative side) and light (positive side) are important as otherwise our subconscious will keep trying to bring up what we deny. Shadow work is making unconscious, conscious and unacceptable, acceptable.

Someone who focuses on pure positive focus does not always produce a pure positive vibration and manifestation. We see someone who is purely positively focused who has aura rips, aura tears and imprints in their emotional body. Focusing positively on one thing on one particular day, does not necessarily take into account of your subconscious imprinting (which could be negative). It still has its remnants there. When we face something dramatic like a head on collision, which causes a bone fracture, no positive focus will bring the bone back together by itself. You must see a doctor. It is an uncomfortable process. Of admitting the bone is broken, putting it back in place and having a cast put on it so it can heal. But if we distract ourselves from the fracture by positive focus then we are in a mental and physical tug of war with the aspect that does not want to admit to the reality. So when we try to ignore, get away or escape from something negative, it gets worse. Avoidance is not the solution. So avoiding the shadow side of our psyche is not a way to healing. Don't ignore, suppress or escape from your negative aspects. Don't use positive focus to avoid something that feels negative to you. You must release resistance to heal from it. Thus you have to turn in the direction of it! We already resist our shadow aspects by denying what is unwanted. Suppressing it will only bring its ugly head with vigour and prevent good things coming to you.

Awareness is the next logical step. Like shining a torch in darkness to know what's there. It grounds you and allows you to be authentic. Understand your shadow side to diminish any fear you may have towards it.

‘Positive focus works on everything, except when positive focus is used as a tool to enable your resistance.’ Teal Swan

When we only use positive focus as a get out of jail card, we avoid large parts of our unconscious mind that is focused on past traumas.

The Law of Attraction is the law of mirroring. Meaning whatever vibrations are echoing in your being are mirroring around you. So even if you pretend to be positive, the way you feel is what actually manifests for you. Shadows within you are points of attraction, bringing like experiences to you. They need to be integrated to cease being points of attraction.

Earlier I explained that frequency is very much like a radio. If a station runs at frequency 96.4 FM, you must tune your radio to 96.4 FM to hear it. However, this reality only works if you are one dial but in truth, we are more like a switchboard with multiple dials. The frequency signals that are received by all these dials amalgamate to one overall frequency. By turning one dial higher your overall frequency will improve, but the individual frequency of each dial may not improve with it. Say for example you turned your dial of career higher which raised your overall frequency. Your career dial is now on elation, and you will receive career elation. However, this may not affect all of your other dials. If your relationship dial was and is still on despair, you will still only receive relationship despair. This is where shadow work comes in handy. It fixes the individual dial by repairing it thereby increasing its frequency in alignment to your overall frequency.

The misconception that focusing on shadows will create more shadows stops many from accepting or acknowledging their dark sides. If we take the notion that we are all pure positive consciousness or light then by focusing on our dark side the light does not go away, it is merely obscured. Shadow work simply wipes away what obscures the light bringing the light to focus. Imagine you are held underwater by an anchor. You must turn to face the anchor and unhook yourself from it in order to rise to the surface to safety. Shadow work is very much the same. By focusing on your dark side you are freed from it. The more you do shadow work, the less you will have to do. A healing crisis may ensue if you have been burying loads of issues for a long time. But don't be afraid of it, it's only the body's way of relieving years of negative thought patterns. Say for instance you think you are unacceptable. Many parts of you have been rejected so you may have plenty of shadows. Once doing shadow work a flood of emotions may arise. You may get ill. It would be easy to think that your life has got worse, but the body is merely healing itself. Many people see this and stop doing shadow work. But keep on working on yourself. You will gain freedom, wholeness and peace. Then shadows have no power over you, and thus you cannot be hurt anymore. (The Action Sheet that follows has a shadow work exercise for you to do).

Facebook, Tweet, Pin, Instagram, and Email the message below:

Bollywood Gay Message #11:
I release all negative belief patterns.
#BollywoodGay

Action Sheet 11: Removing Negative Belief Systems

IDENTIFY YOUR LIMITING BELIEFS BY ASKING TWO QUESTIONS:

1) Is the core belief true and if so why is that bad?

2) What does this belief mean to me or about me?

Let's take this example: You come home, and the house is a mess. You feel upset and your first thought is: 'I live in a pigsty'. You feel a sinking feeling in your stomach and sadness follows. Ask yourself why this belief is bad? What does it mean to you or say about you? Keep asking these two questions until you whittle down to your core belief.

Like so:

I live in a pigsty.
It means no one respects my house.
No one cares how I feel.
It is inevitable that people will hurt me.
Suffering is the purpose of life.
Life is a punishment.
It means I'm bad.
I'll be unloved.
I am all-alone -this is the core belief.

Now this belief 'I am all alone' was triggered as soon as you came home. If the house is a mess then your limiting belief 'I am all alone' is triggered.

Be careful of justifying this belief and putting the blame on others, saying, 'Because it makes me feel like people don't care'. 'People should care otherwise, I don't feel loved.' The real answer is if they don't care about you, you are all alone. So when looking at core beliefs don't justify things, but look at what it means to you!

You may find multiple core beliefs. Or you may not agree with them on a conscious level, as they don't make sense to you. Or they resonate so much that they are too hard to handle. So be easy on yourself and take time with this technique.

CHANGE YOUR BELIEF WITH 8 STEPS:

1) Identify your core belief- as explained above.

2) By doing this, you can observe it, decreasing the vibration of that belief and its manifestation.

3) Examine the belief.

4) Beliefs are not true or false. They are either beneficial or detrimental. Make a list of whether this belief serves you or harms you.

5) Decide what you would rather believe. Determine the emotions that are holding you onto the belief. Do you get pity for this belief or does it make you feel better? Does it prevent you from trying new things? Is it worthwhile holding onto this belief? Do you want to change this belief?

6) Decrease your emotional response to this belief by finding alternative evidence to disprove it. I.e. 'I am not good enough. My father always told me this.' Alternative evidence would be: 'My father has a very self-conscious way of being. He's petrified of embarrassments. So when I made mistakes, he felt embarrassed. I simply adopted this belief. I now realise that mistakes are just part of learning and are not embarrassing. Therefore I am good enough'. Look at the belief from a new point of view to really get this point.

7) Look for new evidence for your new belief. Prove what you want to prove. You will find what you are searching for. For example, list your successes. Read, watch and listen to stuff that affirms your new beliefs.

8) Affirmations: often when we automatically change our negative belief of I am not good enough to I am good enough, our internal intelligence realises that this is a lie to what we believe and hence rejects it. Therefore look for thoughts that assist your new belief. What are you good at? I.e. 'I have valuable things to share with people. I am a good singer.' Focus on incremental things you are good at until you come into alignment with the 'I am good enough' affirmation. This is a reason why many affirmations don't work. If they feel false, then you should incrementally improve them. You could say, 'I am starting to feel happier.' Or 'each day I look to things that make me realise how wonderful the world is.'

HEAL YOUR LIMITING CORE BELIEFS:

NEURO-LINGUISTIC PROGRAMMING:

Imagine your life from birth until death as though it is a line. The line can be in front of you, behind you, over you or underneath you. It does not matter if it goes through you, but it should represent your whole life. Now identify a specific emotion or limiting belief you have which you want to release about an event. Let's take an angry situation. Float above your line.

1) Imagine yourself looking toward the angry event at the moment just after it occurred. You are facing toward the past, the event is below and in front of you.

2) Then float directly above the event, looking down at the event, what have you learnt from this event? Can you take these learning's with you to the future?

3) Now go to before the event occurred. Facing towards the future, the event is below you and in front of you. Where is the anger now? Has it gone? To test if it has disappeared go inside the event, in your body at that time and check if you have any anger left. Float back on your line and come back to the present.

SHAMANIC HEALING:

This technique deals with parts of your life where you lost parts of your heart. Firstly let's go back to the traumatic parts of your life where your heart was taken from you, or where you lost your heart, or it was given to others. Close your eyes, the exercise is subconscious, so any images or events that come up go to those. See if parts of your heart have been left back in those moments and collect them. Once you have collected your missing heart pieces from all past events, return to the present. Here you can place them back into your heart. You can repeat the same exercise with situations where others have given parts of their heart to you. Go back to each event that naturally pops into your head and then go about the task of returning their hearts back to them. Tell them that you no longer want their heart, as it is their property. If they refuse to take the heart, you can give it to their spirit guides who will keep it for safekeeping. It is quite a powerful technique.

ENERGY HEALING:

The final technique is clearing your first core imprint by looking at your energy body. Step 1 is locating the pattern and step 2 is deleting the pattern. Close eyes, take your energy 300 feet outside of you where you see, sense or feel divine light. Imagine light coming in from above you, whilst closing your eyes. Allow it to start coming in from the top of your head. It is pure abundance. Allow it to come to your eyes, to see the truth, your ears, to hear guidance, throat to open up to brilliant connection; heart to feel the truth, stomach, hips, legs, and feet. Allow the light to enter you and through each part of your body from the top to the bottom. Allow the light to go through the earth to its centre, where it loves you, and grounds you. Then bring that safe energy back, back into your feet and body to meet the light from above inside of you. Your energy is now grounded, centred and expansive. Light energy is love energy. Expand this energy 360 degrees around you, 5, 10, 20, 30, 40 feet around you.

In this mode, imagine a limiting belief you have, say, for example, lack of money. Then think of a moment in your life where that belief first came up, what age was that? The answer that comes up in first few seconds is the answer. See we absorb most of our negative belief patterns during 1-7 years of age as they imprint in our body and affect our entire lives. Did you duplicate that energy from your mum, dad or someone else? Now imagine where in your body you feel heavy from this incident. What is the main emotion tied into it? Negative emotions cause physical 'dis-ease'. This spot you have identified as heavy, give it as much light energy as possible. Clear and transmute it across all time, dimension and reality. The energy you have accumulated from above and below, centre it on this spot until you transmute it, thereby healing it. What was your mum's main story about money? What was your mum's main emotion about money? At what age did you duplicate this pattern? Point to the heaviness of this part on your body and give it all the light you can. Clear and transmute everywhere you are living your mum's story.

Any other emotion you have to this topic clear and transmute it too. What was your dad's story about money? There is not enough? What was your dad's main emotion about money? What age did you duplicate your dad's energy about money? What's your main emotion about money? Point to where it feels heavy, tight or contracted? Bring a lot of light to that space, clear and transmute it! Fill in with positive energy, by bringing in light energy. Ask yourself what will it take for you to always have a positive viewpoint about money.

Do this to all thoughts, events, and emotions, as often as possible, to clear away all your negative blocks that prevent abundance in your life. ☺

EMOTIONAL FREEDOM TECHNIQUE:

Check out my video called Removing Emotional Blocks on my YouTube Channel and website www.myspiritualsoul.com. It will help you turn negative belief patterns about any topic into a positive one!

HOW TO FACE YOUR SHADOW:

Sit in the negative emotion. Observe the real reason why you feel this emotion. Fully sink into that feeling of lack. The lack that limits you. Sit in the eye of the storm and surrender to it. It's ok to feel negative emotion. Sink into it and realise it is impermanent. Why has it arisen? What can be learnt from it? If you ignore or push away negative emotions, you won't be able to feel positive emotions fully, for they are but two sides of the coin of life.

Put your daily work in. Meditate, pray, exercise (yoga if you want) and be in the present moment. It may not seem like anything, but I guarantee the daily work will add up to an avalanche in your favour. Do your **DAILY WORK!**

'They may want to contain you. Control you. Make you into their puppet of subversion. However, a strong, powerful, independent-minded, creative, love force like you can never be contained. When love pumps in your veins, and you know your mission on this earth, you are a force to be reckoned with. You seek neither approval nor applause. You're unapologetically your authentic self. Keep giving love. Keep embodying the light that you are. Shine brightly and keep the hope alive. We are all counting on you, and silently cheering you on.'

12) STEP BY STEP GUIDE TO AUTHENTICITY

For all of you who message me: 'There is no quick fix to anything'. There is no quick advice/tip to coming out. There is no quick sort my life out for external approval or acceptance. There is continual sustained internal work that needs to be done for a long length of time before results will show up. The internal work is life long- if not many lives long. Don't be disheartened by this. For every step on the journey will bring fruits. Happy, joyful, loving improvements to your life. It is totally worth it. Thus start the internal journey today by being authentic to yourself.

'The truth will not kill you, but quite the opposite.'

Stand in your light; shine bright, for it will bring you positivity and joy. When I filmed that infamous video of my mother and me in Punjabi, it went viral. It was filmed with love and intended to help people. And as you can see we received only but love back. It is a prime example of how living in your authentic truth does not kill you. Rather it brings others who also live their truth toward you.

WHAT DOES BEING AUTHENTIC REALLY MEAN?

When we are authentic, we are powerful, and we don't care what other people think about us. We are aligned and blended with the whole of which we are. In this state, we don't look for the disapproval of others or find evidence for it. But of course, we are human and thus we go in and out of alignment. When out of alignment we must realise that the disapproval of some is all to do with them. All you can do is to rediscover your own power each time. You do this by unapologetically being who you are. That is where your authentic self resides. Feel fabulous in that moment. Be it as often as you can. With practice, you can be there all the time. But first, make peace with what is. This releases resistance allowing you to be who you truly are.

Authenticity is not something we have or don't have. Rather it's a daily practice of how we choose to live. It is about choosing to be honest and allowing our true selves to be seen. It's a desire for more genuine connection. It's about playing it unsafe and choosing to be real over being liked. It means stepping out of our comfort zone. Authentic people accept their strengths and weaknesses. They connect deeply with others because they are transparent, vulnerable and genuine about how they feel.

When we are in the presence of an authentic person, our intuition lets us know. We gravitate toward people whom we perceive as honest, genuine and sincere. We love people who radiate warmth and are down to earth. We gather around the people who can tell it as it is and laugh at themselves in the process.

'Given the magnitude of the task at hand - to be authentic in a culture that teaches us that being imperfect is synonymous with being inadequate - I decided to use my research to better understand the anatomy of authenticity. What emerged from the data as the most powerful elements of building authenticity were understanding that authenticity is a choice and a practice - having the courage to be vulnerable, and engaging with the world from a place of worthiness rather than a place of shame or never enough.' Brené Brown

Putting yourself out there and being authentic can be quite frightening. However, it's still better than hiding yourself and your gifts from the world. Your unexpressed ideas, opinions and contributions don't just go away. Rather, they gnaw away at your sense of worthiness and pride. We all have different aspects of ourselves that we show to those around us. We may act one way in front of our family, in a different way in front of our friends, and yet another way in front our work colleagues. This is normal as we all create distinctive personas depending on the setting were in. This makes defining our authentic self-difficult. Thus it is a daily practice of being emotionally honest, and allowing ourselves to be vulnerable that shows us who we really are.

Being authentic to how you want to feel.

Danielle LaPorte's book 'The Desire Map' explains how trusting your gut and owning who you are is the most important thing you can do. She explains that feeling good is the whole point of life! See authentic people generally feel better about themselves as they are themselves at any given moment. They are more resilient and less likely to turn to self-destructive habits for comfort. They tend to be focused on the choices they make and more likely to follow through with their goals. So if you are feeling unhappy, stressed, bored or uninspired, it could be a sign that you are not acting authentically.

HOW SHAME BLOCKS AUTHENTICITY?

Shame often prevents us from presenting our true selves to the people around us. We see ourselves as flawed and unworthy and thus unable to be ourselves around others. The shame we feel because of this further prevents us from being our genuine selves. We sacrifice our authenticity to control how others perceive us and get caught in a cycle of shame, or the fear of being shamed. We move further away from our authentic selves as we tell people what they want to hear. Unable to speak our mind honestly in an effort to please others we feel more shame for not taking a stand for what we believe in.

CAN VULNERABILITY LEAD TO AUTHENTICITY?

Vulnerability is being willing to express the truth of how we feel at every given moment no matter what. By being vulnerable, we are willing to open both our strengths and flaws to the world. This is a clear route to being a more authentic you. If the word vulnerability sparks off the impression of weakness and frailty, the term openness can be substituted instead. Openness sounds a lot softer and inclusive. Being open to who we are and to who we are with, in essence, is what vulnerability is about. Openness is truth telling. But truth telling is not just the darkness, the tough truths. It is also the happy truths, the expression of joy. The 'I love you', 'I want this job' or 'this is the best thing I ever did'. Sharing joyful truths is not a narcissistic act; nor is it a divisive thing. For sharing your joyful truths helps create a positive impact on people.

Brené Brown has done a lot of research on vulnerability. Indeed she says vulnerability is the measurement of courage, not weakness. Vulnerability is the core of fear, anxiety, shame and difficult emotions. But it is also the birthplace of joy, love, belonging, creativity and faith. So it's very problematic when as a society we lose the capacity to be vulnerable. It's when something good happens but instead; we think of the worse that might happen. We live in a culture which tells us there is never enough. We are not good enough, and we are not able enough. Many numb the emotion of vulnerability with addictions such as drugs and alcohol. But when we numb the dark emotions we also numb the light emotions like joy. The only solution is vulnerability.

Connecting with one another is the reason why we are here on this planet. Shame is the emotion we feel when we fear being disconnected with others. Shame makes us think we are unworthy of connection. People who have a strong sense of love and belonging believe they are worthy of it. They have the courage to be imperfect, compassion to be kind and ability to connect with others as a result of authenticity. They let go of who they think they should be to be who they really are. They embrace vulnerability as what makes them vulnerable makes them who they are.

HOW TO BE TRULY AUTHENTIC?

Authentic people allow themselves to feel emotions as they arise without suppressing them. They experience life challenges from a place of love, forgiveness, and gratitude. Authentic people speak highly of themselves and others as they understand the importance of the energy behind their words. They believe they are worthy of love and peace and so care more about their own opinions than that of others. Authentic people create their own rules and thus have the courage to live their lives based on what they believe is right. This inner confidence gives them the strength to share their guilt and shame leaving people with no means to exert their power over them. Authentic people are more focused on being true to themselves and thus less concerned about rejection from others. Being authentic is a daily practice of embracing your truth and sharing it with the world. Great confidence and inner peace come from not having to hide who one is from others.

So find your power and say something that frightens you, do something that you are afraid of, or go somewhere where you feel uncomfortable. Practice being out of your comfort zone and being more true to you. Is there a dance class you want to go to but are afraid of? Do you want to say something to someone who has hurt you in the past but are afraid to speak about how you feel? Are you afraid of travelling? Go backpacking! The more you exercise this muscle the closer you come to becoming your greatest version. Authentic people are some of the most powerful people as they expose themselves. They leave no ammunition to be attacked with. Open yourself up to the world. Get more intimate with yourself. Don't be afraid to wear your heart on your sleeve. Surrender to allow more into your heart space. Let go of the defence and allow the relationship with yourself plunge onto a whole new level. Speak what's on your mind without the fear of judgement. And you will find, when you open up to people they open up to you.

Remind yourself regularly that your feelings are justified. The way you feel matters. It may not be comprehensible or acceptable to others, but the way you feel matters. It's not about your thoughts or actions, but your feelings about a particular situation or event. Sit in that feeling, understand that feeling, allow that feeling to resonate so you can understand the core of it. Never run away from a feeling, especially if it is negative. There is great learning in feelings. Once you are done, the feeling will automatically improve. Whilst experiencing the feeling, however, know that it is impermanent and know that there is learning in it. Pray for guidance and help, meditate for calmness and serenity and do some exercise to move the energy through you. Because stagnation is not good for the body or soul.

'We shouldn't strive for perfection. We should strive for authenticity.'

Embrace the truth of who you are. This is the lesson LGBTI are here to teach the world. Most people live inauthentically, doing as society expects of them without questioning what they actually want to do. Ideally, we would all like to 'come out of the closet' and live the lives we've dreamt of. I understand that this might not always be feasible due to our circumstances. Some of us may fear being hurt in the process. Thus it is paramount we are honest and true to ourselves first and to those who we feel comfortable telling. Having marriages of conveniences with someone of the opposite sex, deceiving family and friends does no favours to yourself or the partner you are with. As already mentioned: if you expect the best possible outcome, then that outcome is more likely for you.

Personally, I'm so grateful for all the experiences I have had in this life, in this body, on this earth since my birth. All the struggles, heartaches and joys have been wonderful experiences to learn to be the person I was born to be. I see many people live unconsciously like robots, doing as society tells them. They accomplish their education, excel in their career, get into a relationship, make money, and buy a house, car, etc., without nurturing or even knowing their spiritual self. Void of connection, miserable, frustrated and anxious, these people live materialistically, judgmentally and with great suffering. On the other hand, there are plenty of awakened folks who cultivate their soul daily and shine brightly in an otherwise dark world. The great thing is, as the planet goes through its consciousness shift, the former now question their worth, value and meaning in this Universe. Even as they approach their 30s, 40s, 50s, 60s they realise that the capitalist ball and chain way of living, does not allow them to be happy in their daily life. And it is up to us, my dear friends, to shine brighter than before, to be that example, and when asked to direct them lovingly.

We need to be authentic to ourselves first. None of us is perfect, and we need to embrace that. By showing our flaws to the world, we are showing our truth. To simply hide and be someone else in public and someone else behind closed doors separates us from our own divinity. By accepting our flaws, we accept our divinity.

Start by being authentic today! Facebook, Tweet, Pin, Instagram, and Email the message below:

Bollywood Gay Message #12:
I choose to live my highest truth.
#BollywoodGay

Action Sheet 12: Living Your Truth

Using the example below live your authentic truth by writing your own coming out story. The more you perfect this by visualising the positive outcome you want, the higher the chance your coming out story will be received with love. You can then either read it out to your parents or simply use it as a template.

Dear Mum and Dad,

There is something I think you should know because it's a major part of my life. I am Lesbian, Gay, Bisexual, Transgender, Intersex (**pick the one that defines you**). It does not change who I am or the person you have grown up to love and cherish. I'm still the same; only I'm attracted to the same gender, both genders or feel as though I am a different gender (**choose the one that defines you**).

I think you deserve to know this, as I cannot go on lying to you and most importantly to myself. I want you to be involved in every aspect of my life. I know this must be hard because you probably imagined a life for me in your head but I promise there is a better life waiting for me. Being honest with you is the first step. I feel relieved sharing this with you after all these years, holding this secret inside me. I just want to live a happy life and not hide who I am.

I know you might be thinking what people or relatives will say, but the truth is it's our life and if we are happy and content the opinions of others won't matter. All I know is I love you, and you love me too. I will always be the same person, the one you held in your arms, the one who was naughty in school and the one who shares every laughter and sadness with you. I'm sorry I wasn't able to tell you to your face, but I hope this letter helps ☺.

Love always,

Your Name

(NOW TRY THIS EXERCISE ON THE FOLLOWING PAGE)

Dear Mum and Dad,

Love always,

'As your vibrational energy rises, you may lose contact with old behaviour patterns and systems. Old friendships may part, to new beginnings.'

13) CONSCIOUS GAY MEN

'I want to be connected as much as possible to that which is God.'
Oprah Winfrey

You can consciously make the decision about the kind of person you want to be and the kind of people you want to surround yourself with. Energy is addictive and absorbs into our bodies. Thus it is crucial to surround ourselves with positive influences. Remove negative images, media and people from your life. They bring you down and will have an adverse effect on you. If you indeed want to be a conscious gay man, then you need to be resilient about this.

Many years ago I made the decision to unfriend or hide posts from negative people on Facebook. It was bringing me down and affecting my unconscious mind. Instead, I liked pages of spirituality, love, positivity and good news. This automatically started benefiting me each morning on my news feed. I started writing positive posts and watching Abraham Hicks on YouTube daily, at breakfast, on the commute to work and on my breaks. I felt uplifted. I would motivate others, and encourage them to be more positive. I decided to be an example of love and compassion.

If friends, family or colleagues are bringing you down, first look at your own inner voice and actions, for you are attracting or bringing out the negative side from them in the first place. Thus there is a need to fine tune or reprogramme your vibrational energy. Once you are vibrating pure love energy on a regular basis, through daily meditation, prayer and exercise you will notice that either the negative folk no longer cross your path, or that their consciousness increases too. They will be elevated to their highest self and truth just basking in your beautiful presence. If they do ever bring up negative, critical, or bashful conversation, you can simply redirect the discussion onto more positive things.

I do this at dinner parties often, when people begin to moan about their life or complain about others. I say 'so tell me about the best experience you've had at work'. Recently I was at a dinner party with a guy who worked on road shows with celebs. He was moaning about how high maintenance they all are, and I quickly changed the subject by asking him to focus on the funniest experience he had whilst working there. This can uplift a mood, a conversation and bring light in the dark. You are your own candle. Light it and shine bright today.

We come to Earth to learn how to let go. Letting go is the wisdom we come to seek.

We are a mix of souls on this planet. Old and new souls combined. Some more restless. Some at ease. Some desire to wake up now, on a mission to succeed. Others are content, in flow, and some are in pain, twisting with woe. Nothing is right, and nothing is wrong. We are who we are, and all we can do is follow our instincts. That tells us whether what we are doing is right. When things feel right and feel good, that is when we know we are on the right path.

Your vibe attracts your tribe.

In new age spirituality, there is talk about new souls (lightworkers) who are incarnating on earth with a soul mission. As we go through growth in life and question why we are here as a collective consciousness, we broadcast a desire. In the 1960s there was a lot of war and suppression, which gave the desire for a new earth. This desire was answered by a brand new type of consciousness.

WHO ARE THE STAR CHILDREN?

Star children or star seeds are highly evolved beings that have lived elsewhere in the Universe. They come in three forms: indigo, crystal and rainbow. Named such due to the auras they emit. They are here to teach us due to their evolved spiritual consciousness and help take us spiritually forward during the Aquarian age.

Indigo children were born to parents of the 1960s hippy era. They are born in the late 1970s-1980s and have come to change the world. They came down looking for a fight as a warrior. 'I will not conform to your rules' is their motto. They are willful and difficult to raise but also hypersensitive. Their task is to pave the way for other souls. Often brought up in dysfunctional families, these children have lots of mental health issues, due to feeling different to others. Addictions and depression can be common with indigos, and unless they are supported, they will find it hard to live on this planet. But once their energies are balanced, they use creative ways to break through archaic systems and pave the way for the crystal children.

Crystal children are usually born between 1990-2010 to indigo parents. They don't have boundaries of their own and are very sensitive. They bring a new state of consciousness for humanity, that of sensitivity. The only way we can evolve is by supporting each other. Crystal children vibrate on the 5th and 6th dimensional realm meaning they are very loving. Their crystal aura assimilates to the auras of those around them allowing them to connect more deeply with others. Their prismatic energy is very clear allowing them to take the energy of the person they are with making them excellent energy workers.

Rainbow children are thought to be the builders of the New World born between 2010-2030 to crystal parents. They vibrate at the 9th dimension of consciousness, the dimension of collective consciousness/oneness which means they are here to serve the earth. Natural healers and instant manifesters they use their psychic abilities to read people's feelings. Rainbow children come to earth with no karma from the past because they do not continue from any previous cycle of reincarnation. This is also why they are high in vibrational and physical energy. Rainbow children love unconditionally, have open hearts, and don't fear strangers. Their open heart chakras heal everyone they come into contact with by giving out rainbow coloured energy. They are our earth angels.

Essentially star children are an evolutionary species here to raise the consciousness of the planet. If you are LGBTI, you most likely belong to one of the subcategories above.

There is nothing to be found outside; there is no external happiness, joy or love. It's all within.

Conscious gay men understand that the Universe constantly has their back. If things don't go to plan, there is a reason for it. See the Universe is always bringing you inline with your purpose. When we steer away from our purpose and are on the wrong track, the Universe nudges us back onto the path we are meant to go. So don't resist if a certain career path doesn't work out, or a certain goal is left unachieved. You are meant for greater things. Different things. Things that fulfil your purpose and make you smile. Things that will fill you up with joy and make you shine.

The same is true when you are knocked off your feet. You feel down because you were not aligned with your true self. The true self is always connected, happy, knowing and wise. When you are unhappy, you are looking outward for your happiness. Thus the Universe nudges you to realise. When this happens recognise that you were not connected to your higher self, you were in the ego mind and in a place of scarcity. For when we are connected, we are happy. Happiness or rather joy is the indicator of your alignment to Source. However happy and in love you are, the more aligned you are. When you are aligned everything is perfect, everything works out just fine, and you are at ease, in flow.

Conscious gay men understand the importance of balance. We are sociable beings, built to have regular communication with others. From cave man societies to now, we need to huddle and cuddle regularly. Now, of course, being marginalised from society can make us lonely. Conscious gay men know to avoid addictions such as alcohol, drugs and sex and go for more positive pursuits. They balance their personal and private time making time for exercise. If we are balanced in these areas of our life, we are going to do just fine. When we substitute one area for another or avoid whole parts of ourselves, then we are in trouble. It is very important to maintain good friendships with people and to meet with them regularly to avoid feelings of exclusion and separation. Thus go find your tribe. Apps such as Meetup or Eventbrite are great at finding things to do. You can also join societies and clubs to feel more included in your life.

Who Am I to Judge? I make mistakes. I am human. Who am I to judge? I am imperfect. I get angry. Who am I to judge? I know my truth. I know what I have gone through. So who am I to judge?

The wisdom that comes from opening our perspective makes us realise that we should not judge others. Whatever path another is following is due to a mix of their own history, lessons and purpose and has nothing to do with our own. Sure we can learn from it and be inspired, but critical and judgemental we cannot be. Each comes here for their own homework, earthwork. We can never know what a person is going through unless we walk in their shoes. Thus when people talk about gender fluidity, sexual spectrums and those around us judge, we should say, 'who are we to judge? Who am I to judge? I am imperfect and wounded like any other. I have not walked their path.' When someone loves someone so much that even after their breakup they still carry on loving them. Who are we to judge? I am tired of all the judgemental LGBTI folk that are out there, who often out judge my own straight critical family. It's not healthy that we don't support one another, that we like each other to fall, that we bitch and gossip and bemoan. Conscious gay men are aware of their own faults. They understand the real lesson in life, to identify their wounds and heal from them, by applying love. They never kick a person who is already down, or if they accidentally or purposely do, they realise soon after and try in the attempt not to judge. We need only try to be better human beings, and that is enough. The desire to be better will ensure it happens.

Start seeing the vulnerability and softness in everyone. We are all humans. We all bleed the same. We all have issues. We all want to be happy and loved. I applaud those who try to better themselves, try to help others, or who bite their lip when someone says something unkind to them. I applaud those who identify their faults, but harness that with self-love, and bring their pure vibration back to life. Let's look at ourselves before pointing the finger at others. Instead of laughing, ridiculing and mocking one another, let's say you're a human, and you deserve the best. Let's try to be kind.

'Ego- Edging God Out.' Dr. Wayne Dwyer

If the whole purpose of spirituality/enlightenment is to eradicate the ego then why do we have it in the first place? The ego is the mind, the chattering mind. The mind that says me, myself and I. I want this. It feeds on scarcity, fear, lack, jealousy and insecurity. It also is the part of ourselves that helps us to realise our true self. Much like yin and yang, we need the opposite to know the truth.

Just as the newborn baby needs a sense of ego so it can proclaim its own self. In much the same way we need the ego to know our higher self. Imagine leaving a baby by itself, helpless, staring at a mirror; it would not know where the mirror ended, and it started. It needs the ego to separate itself and to realise it is its own being. Only through maturity and time do we learn how the ego has deluded us. Unlearning the ego is our life path.

'It's so easy to give other people credit for the way they behave.'
Abraham Hicks

When we are in our ego mind, we blame everyone for everything that goes wrong. We forget that it is us who have attracted the way they behave to us in the first place. According to the vibration we offer we attract certain behaviours from others. If we are in a negative mood we bring out the negative in others. If we are in a positive mood the positive aspects of that person's psyche is mirrored to us. The way people behave towards us also matches our expectation of them. People raise or lower their behaviour according to expectation.

Only once we accept this fact and recognise how we feel, do we take responsibility for what is happening around us. By focusing on the good characteristic of difficult people, we activate those in them and see it in their kinder attitude towards us. But if we keep looking at their negative characteristics believing them to be true they will be true. We should not use the truth of something as our criteria for focus. There are all sorts of things that are true that we don't want active in our vibration. For instance, if you think it's hard to be gay, then you will bring difficult situations into your life. The evidence will back it up and make you think it's ultimately true. However, there are many truths. You cannot look at lack and be in alignment with who you are. It is far better to see the best in others and yourself and activate that in your consciousness to manifest it in the physical.

COMPASSIONATE LISTENING

Thich Nhat Hanh, a Buddhist monk and peace activist, teaches the value in listening compassionately to difficult people. Compassionate listening is listening with love. He says when arguing with someone rather then listening to respond, listen by giving them love. You do this by imagining love flowing from your heart to theirs. It really helps to dissipate any anger and quickly shifts your conversation to a positive solution. Compassionate listening is the way to go. As is metta, whereby you practice giving love to everyone through your daily meditation. Do this especially for those you struggle with by praying for their suffering to lessen and heart to open.

'Forgiveness is the fragrance the violet sheds on the heel that has crushed it.' Mark Twain

Conscious gay men understand the value of forgiveness. They forgive themselves because they are human. They forgive themselves because they are imperfect. They understand that each mistake is a learning. A learning to dissolve the ego and return back to love. They forgive others too. They understand that just because someone committed a gross crime against them, it does not mean that a few weeks, months or years later they have not repented, become fully enlightened, or transformed for the better. Thus give people the benefit of doubt by seeing the good in them. This is the only way to bring peace and harmony onto this planet.

Never limit yourself to the countless, infinite possibilities the Universe provides. And forgive everyone including yourself today! This allows the miracle to happen.

It was just over a year ago when I learnt the real value of forgiveness. I had been practising forgiveness with my father for quite a while now, releasing pent up resentment and tension from years of emotional distance. My relationship with him had become quite good by then. But what really helped me master this technique was when one of my relationships came to an abrupt end.

The lesson I learnt from my ex-boyfriend came when he said, 'Mani why are you hurting yourself', in response to my anger at his neglect. This resonated deeply as I realised only I had the power to love and hurt myself. He was just the object, means or instrument through which I was allowing my pain to simmer. I forgave him instantly. I knew I had not been a great partner too and had to an extent brought about the tension and subsequent end in our relationship. (We are still good friends).

The second incident was when some members of my extended family were homophobic to me. It hurt that these people were unkind when I had tried to be nice to them. I have to admit I had posted a couple of things on social media about how family issues had made me upset, and this was used as fuel against me. I realised people choose their own paths, and it is up to them to change for the better if they want to. I could not preach or expect acceptance from them. I had to accept me!

Once I did this, I felt transformed. An energetic shift of miraculous things started to occur in my life. As I began to exercise the forgiveness muscle, my life itself began to improve. I no longer blamed others for the way they made me feel but took ownership of it myself. I also began to understand other perspectives and opinions. I was most importantly kinder to others and myself.

So as you can see forgiving others is great for ourselves. It does not mean you forgive and forget and carry on getting abused by these people. For I still keep distance and choose not to mix with certain relatives. It just means you let go of what happened so it no longer has a hold on your mind or body! Indeed forgiveness is the gift we give ourselves. Resentment has a way of remaining in the physical frame and causing illnesses as explained by Louise Hay- You can Heal your Life! A must read for everyone!

You choose who you interact with, but release all the anger, judgement and resentment from within. That is what true forgiveness is!

The spiritual text, A Course in Miracles teaches that forgiveness releases the ego's hold on a person. The ego believes that it is separate from God, which causes great pain. We mimic this pain every time we perceive ourselves separate from others or our dreams. Through forgiveness, we learn that we are all one and that by not forgiving one person we are holding the entire Universe at ransom. As we forgive each person around us, and we forgive ourselves, we come closer to the realisation that we are in fact one with God.

Instill love. Remove Hate. Instill forgiveness. Remove resentment. Instill Joy. Remove unworthiness. Instill hope. Remove fear. Amen.

Pray for those who say they hate you. Give love to those who hurt you. Hurtful people are suffering. They see not beyond their ego veils. They reflect their pain on to you. They see the outside as the object of their suffering. Forgetting that it is only them, and always them, that are at the root of their suffering. Pray for those who say they hate you; ones who are ignorant and afraid. Give love to those who hurt you.

SPIRITUAL DIMENSIONS

I have been throwing the word dimension around in this book so far without explaining it. There are many different spiritual dimensions or realms that co-exist at the same time. Understanding them will help to explain the spiritual evolution each being takes and help us learn what the planet is currently undergoing. This planet has so far existed in the third dimension. The third dimension is more physically oriented than the higher dimensions which are more etheric. Manifestation in the seven dimensions (of many more) occur in the following way:

3rd Dimension Spirit -> Thought -> Emotion -> Effort -> Manifestation

4th Dimension Spirit -> Thought -> Emotion -> Manifestation

5th Dimension Spirit -> Thought -> Manifestation

6th Dimension Spirit -> Manifestation

7th Dimension Spirit = Manifestation

The 4th dimension is precisely what the book 'The Secret' teaches. The problem many people have with 'The Secret' is they give up too quickly and don't put enough emotion and visualisation into the process. Earth and most of its inhabitants have already entered the 4th dimension. Things no longer take a lot of time or effort to manifest. The way we feel will mostly determine the outcome we manifest.

For example, if we feel afraid we will manifest scary situations and if we feel excited, we will manifest situations to be excited about. The time taken for things to manifest is shortening. What we feel and what we expect to happen will be more important than exerting physical effort to bring things to us. Focusing on feelings means that all that is left to heal emotionally will more likely come to the surface. Whatever we have ignored, suppressed or forgotten about will come up to the surface, and our fears will materialise for us to deal with.

If we had the 5th dimension on Earth people would be walking disasters. We are not ready to think a thought and manifest it right away. That is why the current matrix of this planet was wired to 3rd and now 4th level dimension to provide a buffer period before desires manifested. I mean can you imagine thinking your baby will fall down the stairs, and they do at that very moment! We have to be very positively focused before getting to that stage. Of course throughout human history, we have had enlightened beings who have been at this level of consciousness. Jesus Christ was vibrating at 5th dimension, and that is why is it often referred to as 5th level Christ consciousness. He would simply see a sick person as healthy and instantly manifest wellness into that person's being.

According to Mayan and New Age spirituality Earth was meant to shift into the 5th dimension from 2012 onwards. This would happen gradually, with the frequency of the planet being increased slowly up until that point. Going further than that would be optional. We are now in the 5th dimension, however, it is up to each person to decide whether they want to be part of it.

Now, none of this would happen automatically. There are many spiritual forces assisting the Earth to increase its frequency. However, it's up to each individual to do their internal work to be able to assimilate to it. People who resist the acceleration will experience mental and physical dis-ease. If we try to hold on to our old ways, the Universe will make life more and more intolerable. Our hidden fears will come out and force us to confront them which will cause further mental strain and difficulty assimilating to the earth's changes. The only way to overcome this is to work on our unhealed issues to become complete in ourselves and empowered.

THE ILLUSION OF TIME AND SPACE

Time and space are flexible. You can experience synchronicity (unexplained coincidences happening repeatedly) and realise that everything is interconnected. Through such events we realise the power of thoughts and understand how everything is intertwined, the past, future and present are all happening at once. It is imperative to be aware of the now. In the now, all things exist. When we worry about the future, we create anxiety. Guilt arises from thinking about our past mistakes or our unresolved issues resulting in depression.

When you realise this, you may experience other vibrations, dimensions, realities, or frequencies of energies. You may see other colours, lights, space crafts or spirits. This is occurring more and more now because we are becoming clearer as to what is appearing in the here and now. Essentially nothing is linear. All our lives happen continuously, as time is just a construct. At a higher level, you will be able to handle all your lives at once.

Just like a film strip, if you look at one frame you will see your current life. But if you take the film further away from you, you see all your lives at once. You can then select which life you would like to see close up, and you don't have to be linear about it. You can go from strip 1 to 5 and back to 3. The illusion of time and space helps us to understand the interconnectivity and infinity of the universe and help us enlighten ourselves just like Buddha.

'11:11 is the Universe knocking itself out to give you evidence of your alignment.'
Abraham Hicks

Conscious gay men are open and aware to the messages of the Universe. When they reach a certain spiritual level, having worked on themselves they may start seeing repeating numbers, beginning with 11:11. Each of these numbers has significance. In numerology 1 means a new beginning or the first step. It represents moving into unchartered waters. Something epic is about to happen. It means that whatever you are thinking at the moment is manifesting. You are connected to your higher self so be careful of your thoughts, for as you think you are manifesting quite instantly. This is because you are connected to your highest vibration. You are moving from the 3rd dimension to the 5th dimension and beyond. Time begins to cease. More synchronistic (together happening at the same time) experiences start to happen. What you think becomes.

Have you ever thought about someone and suddenly they call or text? Or you see their name in certain places, or meet people by the same name? Do you bump into someone who you have been thinking about all day? These are not coincidences, but synchronicities. Your dominant thoughts align with your life and become your dominant experiences. The illusions of the world will begin to disappear. You realise the infinite possibilities that exist. You realise that the only thing you can't do is what you think you can't do. But if you think you can do it then you can. The number 11:11 signifies that your thoughts will rapidly manifest into your reality. You are also open to higher entities who may contact you or help you. This is because those in higher vibrations, or higher dimensions are now in alignment with you. Thus you can communicate with them, channel them or feel them.

The number 11 in numerology represents spirituality, intuition, sensitivity, honesty, patience, idealism and compassion. When we see the numbers 11:11 the Universe is urging us to listen to our intuition. We are being awoken to the countless opportunities that are now available to us. Seeing this number sequence is a way for the Universe to tell us to pay more attention to the synchronicities that are happening around us.

The Universe tries to guide us through signs, however, it is up to us to be aware enough to notice them.

Noticing the number 11:11 also signals that we are undergoing accelerated soul growth, meaning soon we may find ourselves living the life we had previously only dreamt about. We have cleared enough of our unconscious mind that we may now find unexpectant people and events coming into our lives when we need them. 11:11 also indicates that our twin flame or what people most commonly label as soulmate is near by. (More on twin flames in Chapter 15).

Other numbers will then start appearing such as 22:22 or 3333, 444 and so on. Each has different meanings, as can be Googled online. The way I check there meaning is to search for '444 angel number' or '2222 numerology' and you will get your answer. The Universe is always communicating with you, and this is especially true when in alignment. So become a conscious gay man and revel in the mysteries of the Universe. They are waiting for you.

It's up to each person to learn their lesson in any given situation. We gain wisdom according to our own spiritual advancement. If we are highly connected and knowing, we will charge through blocks and flourish with ease. Remember anything is possible, nothing is lost. We only ever gain. Look within and not out. Peace will be there.

Facebook, Tweet, Pin, Instagram, and Email the message below:

Bollywood Gay Message #13:
Happiness is an inside job.
#BollywoodGay

Action Sheet 13: The Awakened Gay Man

HERE ARE 8 TIPS THAT HELPED ME GET OUT OF DEPRESSION:

1) In the morning, as you wake up, in the shower or whilst having breakfast say at least one thing you are grateful for.

2) Have a gratitude journal which can further entrench this mindset as shown below.

3) Try not to complain or bitch to friends, instead talk about your achievements and successes.

4) Look for things to be happy for whilst travelling to work- the trees, birds and children.

5) Say thank you to those who serve you at cafes, restaurants and shops.

6) Answer the phone with excitement.

7) See the positive lesson in difficult times.

8) When inclined to play the victim or feel pity- reverse that by listing all the things that are going well for you right now.

WRITE DOWN 5 THINGS YOU ARE GRATEFUL FOR EACH DAY:

I.e. The scrumptious food on my table
The fluffy clouds and the funny shapes they make
The beautiful cooling breeze
My warm cosy bed I never want to get out of!
The ability to be me.

1. _____
2. _____
3. _____
4. _____
5. _____

If you want to be more conscious then why not try out a **30-DAY POSITIVITY CHALLENGE**. I challenge you for the next month to only use words of love, gratitude and positivity! See how it transforms your life when you talk to others or yourself! Watch how spirit literally comes forth from those around you. Divine messages will come from those who surround you.

FORGIVENESS EXERCISE:

Write a letter forgiving all the people you still have a grudge with. Read it out aloud in front of a mirror before tearing it up and if safe burning it outdoors.

'In closing my eyes, I see.'

14) MIND, BODY & SOUL

Many gay people focus only on their physique and forget about their mind and soul. This is the reason many addictions and mental health problems exist within our community. Obviously, you will agree, with us being marginalised many times over and given the communities we come from, looking after our mind and soul is just as important as our body. But saying that, many within our communities, not loving themselves, forget their body altogether and binge on fatty foods and diets that induce 'dis-ease' and obesity. We need to learn how to balance our physical health alongside our mind and soul. Also remembering that what we eat and how we cook it is just as important as doing some physical exercise! I'm going to give you the lowdown because you will be surprised with the amount of unhealthy LGBTI friends and boyfriends I have had. It's time to shape up!

You are what you eat!

If you love yourself, you would lovingly select the kinds of food you eat. We are told to drink 8 glasses of water a day and eat 5 fruits and 5 vegetables daily. Of course, these are guidelines, and each person's body is unique and requires subsidence in varying degrees. The key to a healthy body is to keep its PH level alkaline rather than acidic. Fast food, meat, soft drinks, fish, dairy, and alcohol all contribute to an acidic PH within the body; whereas fresh fruit and vegetables, contribute to an alkaline PH level.

As you grow more spiritual you become more sensitive to everything around you. Food intolerances such as gluten or allergies you never had before may start to creep up. This is a way of your body telling you what it can no longer tolerate, as it doesn't serve you anymore. You might be cleansing yourself of toxins.

All bodies are different, and we all know what feels right for us. So focus inwards and see if the food you eat is indeed the food that your body craves and needs to flourish. Do you feel sick often? Or are you a healthy happy person? Food has an effect on all of this. If you come from a high-vibe and understand that your body craves food that it needs to nourish it and that by having it your body will be healthy, then you will.

FIRSTLY LET US START WITH FLUORIDE

Fluoride is purposely put into the drinking water of some countries who falsely proclaim it gives healthy bones. Many other countries ban this process because fluoride is toxic. It is a by-product of manufacturing and companies wanting a way to get rid of it managed to get the government to put it in water. It is also put in toothpaste allegedly to give us healthy teeth. Now if you're a spiritual person, you will be aware that fluoride calcifies the pineal gland, also known as the third eye (6th Chakra). The pineal gland is located in the space just in between the eyebrows and slightly above it on the forehead. It has been known to be sacred for thousands of years from the ancient Egyptians to ancient Indians. It is from where we gain intuition, access higher realms of consciousness and gain knowledge of the truth. Now governments pump fluoride into water and toothpaste in order to calcify this gland and to block its functioning abilities. It's a form of control and submission.

The pineal gland is also known to have several functions such as secreting melatonin which aids in sleep and regulation of the endocrine system. Calcification of this gland happens early on, hardening and losing its functionality. Food additives such as artificial sweeteners and radiation from electronic devices may also contribute to pineal calcification.

DECALCIFYING THE PINEAL GLAND

To prevent calcification of the pineal gland from fluoride, we need to avoid it in our water and food. Eating organic food and drinking or cooking with liquids that don't contain the fluoride is advised. I would also limit red meat, fizzy drinks and artificial foods. So to tackle this, I recommend drinking filtered water from a filter that removes fluoride, chlorine, metals and particles. Now most filters you get on the market, especially the low-end ones do not filter out fluoride. So you have to check selectively and purchase one that does. I use Gentoo which not only removes the fluoride, chlorine and aluminium but also alkalizes the body. You can also buy more expensive options of filtering water from the tap.

If you can get carbon filters for your showers, I would also recommend that. This prevents further calcification to the pineal gland by absorption of it through the skin. However, to remove the residue of calcium already present in the body I recommend raw cacao. Adding it to smoothies or to cereal works best! Meditation, yoga and chanting also help decalcify the pineal gland by stimulating the gland through resonance in the nasal bones. As the calcium crystals are broken up in the gland, the increased secretions can wash away the calcification. Check out the Action Sheet at the end of this chapter for more information.

VEGETARIANISM/VEGANISM

Eventually, on the spiritual path, you may question whether to be vegetarian or vegan. Ahimsa is the ancient Indian philosophy of non-violence. When you understand the laws of cause and effect (karma), you will naturally lean towards love for all. Given that the modern animal slaughtering system is deeply flawed and full of suffering you may want to separate yourself from this. Animals are injected with hormones, antibiotics and kept in overcrowded sheds in dire conditions before being killed in the cruellest of ways. The fear-educed endorphins they release are assimilated in our bodies as we consume them along with all the other nastiness the food industry pumps into them. Meat, fish, dairy and eggs are generally treated in this way. For instance, dairy cows are injected with antibiotics and hormones to make them produce more gallons of milk for us.

Interestingly, channels such as Abraham Hicks and Bashar state that certain animals enter into soul contracts with humans to be consumed as food. They claim that animals are more intuned to universal consciousness and understand that death is not the end. Just like in tribal societies where animals were or are ritually sacrificed and consumed for the Gods, animals in today's age offer themselves for human consumption. They claim that the same is true of those who offer themselves for scientific and cosmetic testing. If we dine whilst in a high vibe state, the meat/fish we consume will also represent that higher vibration. They further claim that the physic abilities of animals will be realised in due course, which may put off humans from killing, abusing and testing such wonderful creatures. Thus use your own intuition to decide what's right for you.

Plant-based foods are not treated any better either. Companies genetically modify food, inject fertilisers into their molecular structure and feed it to us. Why do you think we have so many allergies today? It's the body's natural way of saying enough. Cancers, illnesses, and painful 'dis-ease's unknown many decades ago are common today. Be very careful of what you eat. Go organic if you can and try a raw food diet to detox and cleanse yourself.

Don't forget to check the products you use. Are they tested on animals? Are they laced with chemicals or metals? The skin literally absorbs whatever is placed upon it. Natural cosmetics, sprays and soaps are the way forward. Demand this from your supermarkets. Write letters and complain or shop at natural stores like The Body Shop!

SUGAR

Sugar, which is made up of glucose and fructose molecules, is a poison because of the way in which our bodies break it down. When we metabolise fructose in excess, our liver turns that energy into liver fat, which leads to metabolic 'dis-eases'. Sugar is known as the biggest addictive substance on the planet (it is similar to caffeine but much worse). It is more addictive than drugs like cocaine. Sugar is added to practically everything, whether we like it or not. It is added to bread, cereals, sauces and even water, so avoiding it can be difficult. It makes our blood sugar levels rise with consumption and then drop rapidly soon after. This means we can have an energy slump and most often a feeling of depression thereafter. A bit like a rocky roller coaster, people go through high and low mood swings and crave the food that tires them out ultimately. For example, after eating something sugary such as a piece of birthday cake our body releases stress hormones. These stress hormones raise our blood sugar, providing us with a temporary energy boost but later make us anxious, irritable and shaky. Added to this sugar addiction can also cloud memory, make us lose concentration and clarity in daily life.

Sugar causes blood glucose to spike and plummet leading to mood swings, headaches, fatigue, and cravings for more sugar. Every time we feed our craving for more sugar, the temporary good feeling dies a few hours later, leaving us wanting more. Sugar also interferes with our immune function and increases the risk of obesity, diabetes and heart 'dis-ease'. It accelerates ageing, causes tooth decay and affects behaviour and cognition in children.

Many processed foods are marketed as low-fat. To substitute for the lost flavour manufacturers add salt and sugar to it to make it taste better. Fructose-heavy fizzy drinks are also terrible for you. Coke for instance contains lots of sugar and sodium. These foods should be consumed in moderation. Resort to drinking filtered water instead. Even the squash flavours you can add to water, the ones with no added sugar are lathered in aspartame which is a brain cancer causing sugar substitute. The likes of Monsanto are to blame for the manufacturing and distributing of these kinds of toxic foods. It is safe to say that in the future we will be even more aware of what is put inside our food and demand for better farming and manufacturing practices. GMO foods, artificial flavourings and fatty fast foods will need to be replaced with organic, healthy raw produce which again will elevate not only your vibration but your consciousness with it.

Those who avoid sugar tend to feel more emotionally balanced, energised and have no cravings for it. Some use jaggery or gur as it's known in India, which is a far better substitute for sugar. Jaggery is a raw form of sugar with many minerals and health benefits. However, if you are diabetic or wanting to lose weight, then it's not recommended. You also don't need to stop eating fruit to lower sugar levels and calories. Fruit contains natural sugar and fibre and is in fact very low in calorie. This means that the body can identify when it is full and stop you from over-consuming. On top of that fruit contains essential nutrients and vitamins vital for the body.

TAMASIC, RAJASIC AND SATTVIC FOODS

When I was doing my yoga teachers course in India, we were taught about the three types of foods: tamasic, rajasic and sattvic. The latter, which is also the name of one of my friends, means pure. It is a state of mind in which the mind is steady, calm and peaceful.

Tamasic foods include meat, fish, fertilised eggs, onions, garlic, mushrooms, alcohol or any food that is not freshly prepared. Such foods have a sedative effect on the mind and body and cause mental dullness and physical numbness. In times of pain, they can be consumed as they alleviate suffering.

Rajasic foods comprise caffeinated drinks, dark chocolate, spicy or salty food and unfertilised eggs. Many rajasic foods were obtained from harming other organisms and thus result in aggression or irritability to those who consume them. They stimulate the mind and body and are considered neither beneficial nor harmful to the person.

Water, cereal grains, legumes, vegetables, fruit, honey, nuts, unpasteurized milk and its products like yoghurt are all sattvic foods. As they are often obtained without harming other organisms, they contribute to a healthy mind and body. It is therefore recommended to consume these health-giving foods on a regular basis.

DRY BRUSHING

Have you tried to dry brush your body before a shower to get rid of dead skin cells? The benefits of dry brushing are profound. Brushing the skin regularly stimulates the lymph vessels (which are part of the body's immune system) helping the body detoxify itself naturally. Dry brushing is one of the simplest and most natural ways to exfoliate skin and keep it soft. It clears oil, dirt and residue from the pores. Dry brushing helps improve pores on the body and increases energy and blood flow as it increases circulation.

You can dry brushing daily before you shower. Use a firm, natural bristle brush with a handle. Begin at your feet, brushing the bottom of the soles and legs in ten long, smooth strokes for each section. Continue working upwards towards the heart and chest area where the lymph system is located so it can be drained of toxins. Now work on the arms, starting at the palms and brush up each arm as you close in towards the heart. Brush each section of skin ten times then continue on your abdomen and back and face with a more delicate brush. Brush lightly, a soft and smooth stroke often works best. Your skin may turn slightly pink after brushing, which is normal but it should never become red or sting.

COLD SHOWERS

Our ancestors had it right cold showers are miracle workers. As soon as I learnt of their benefits a few years back, I started having them daily. I tend to first shower with warm water to get myself warmed up in the cold British weather and then towards the end of my shower turn the dial to as cold as I can handle for a minute or two. It feels great afterwards as you feel more alert. The deep breathing in response to our body's shock to the cold water helps us keep warm, as it increases our overall oxygen intake. Cold showers release a rush of blood through our entire body thereby increasing our heart rate. This gives us a natural dose of energy for the day. Hot water tends to dry out the skin, whereas cold water tightens the pores and external skin preventing them from drying out. Cold water also acts as a seal preventing dirt from penetrating the skin and scalp. It can make hair look shinier, stronger, and healthier as it flattens the hair follicles increasing their ability to grip the scalp. Blood circulation is improved as the cold water encourages blood to surround our organs helping to combat circulation issues. As cold water hits the body, its ability to get blood-circulating leads the arteries to pump blood more efficiently, therefore boosting our overall heart health.

Cold showers also aid in weight loss. The human body has two types of fat tissue, white and brown. White fat accumulates when we eat more calories than we burn and sticks to our waist and thighs. Brown fat, however, is considered healthy as it keeps us warm when our body is exposed to extreme cold conditions. Cold showers promote brown fat activity within the body thus preventing white fat causing weight gain. A quick cold shower after rigorous exercise at the gym can also relieve muscle soreness. Cold showers have been shown to relieve depression, increase tolerance to stress, and even 'dis-ease' due to the cold receptors in the skin sending an overwhelming amount of electrical impulses from the nerve endings to the brain.

OIL PULLING

Oil pulling is something I got into after having bleeding sensitive gums. It's an ancient Ayurvedic cure to gum 'dis-ease', pain or bleeding and removing toxins from your body boosting immunity. It also helps in cavity and gingivitis prevention, sinus issues and gives you stronger teeth and gums. It can alleviate sleep problems, headaches, hangovers and skin issues (acne, psoriasis and eczema). To oil pull slosh 1 tablespoon of cold-pressed olive or coconut oil in your mouth for 10-15 minutes (don't swallow, whatever you do), then spit it out into a bin. Brush your teeth normally afterwards. I do it daily, and it helps keep my teeth white.

THE IMPORTANCE OF REGULAR EXERCISE

A lot of us who experienced discomfort with Physical Education at school avoided exercise like the plague. It reminded us of macho bodies and all the pain we experienced growing up. We need to change that. Choose an exercise you enjoy and do it either with friends or alone regularly. It will help relieve pent up emotions. Do it because you enjoy it, not because you want validation or acceptance from others by having bigger muscles. So do sports activities that are fun, enjoyable and push you. I do yoga daily.

TAME THE WILD HORSES OF THE MIND

Now that we have balanced our diet and exercise regimes, it's time to tackle the mind, which is ultimately linked to the soul. We need to remove negative patterns from our own mind so that we are healthier. So any negative self-talk, criticism, or judgement needs to go out the window. Are you a constant worrier? Anxious all the time? Then you need to relax and be in the present moment. Have fun and laugh. Don't take life too seriously. If you are thinking about the past, you are depressed, if you worry about the future you live in fear or anxiety, and if you are in the present moment, you are at peace. Realise that in this red-hot moment you are well. You are breathing, conscious and aware as you are reading or listening to this book.

SLEEP

The amount of sleep we need depends on our body. Some people need a few hours, and some need more. It's not the hours that we need, but it's the depth. A deep, restful sleep that makes you feel alive when you wake up is far better than many hours of shallow sleep. If you cannot sleep then lay in savasana position (also known as corpse pose- lay down on your back with your arms and legs stretched out) and do Vipassana meditation (focus on your natural breath for a minute before turning your attention to scan each body part from the top to bottom for any sensations you feel, without giving any sensation preference). Or drink turmeric milk which from its ancient Ayurvedic healing properties is a great relaxant. A teaspoon of turmeric into hot milk is what I drink, and it tastes delicious!

WHAT ARE CHAKRAS?

I've been throwing the word chakra around for a while in this book assuming you know what I am talking about. If you don't, here's a quick summary. The word 'chakra' is derived from the Sanskrit word meaning 'wheel'. A chakra is a whirling, vortex-like, powerhouse of energy. Within our bodies, we have seven of these major energy centres and many more minor ones. It is through these seven chakras, in which energy flows through. If this energy becomes blocked, it can lead to illness. Therefore understanding the chakra system to keep the energy moving is imperative for good health.

The first chakra is called the base or root chakra. It's red in colour, and it is located at the perineum or base of your spine. The chakra closest to the earth is focused on earth grounding and physical survival. It is associated with our feet, legs, bones, large intestine and adrenal glands. It controls our fight or flight response and if blocked may cause paranoia, fear, procrastination or defensiveness.

Secondly, comes the sacral or navel chakra which is orange and located between the base of your spine and navel. It is associated with the kidneys, bladder, lower abdomen, circulatory and reproductive system. It deals with our emotions, desires, pleasures, sexuality, procreation and creativity. If this chakra is blocked it may manifest as emotional unbalances, obsessive behaviour and sexual guilt.

The third chakra (solar plexus) is yellow in colour and can be found just above the navel area. This chakra can affect our digestive system, pancreas, adrenal gland and muscles. It is the seat of our emotional life, and thus feelings of joy, sadness, and anger are associated with this centre. Our personal power, ambition, sensitivity and ability to achieve are stored here. If blocked this chakra may manifest as frustration, anger and lack of direction or a sense of victimisation.

The heart chakra is the fourth in line. Its colour is green, and it is located in our heart. It is the centre of love, compassion, harmony and peace and believed to be the house of the soul. The fourth chakra is associated with our heart, lungs, arms and thymus gland. When we fall in love, the unconditional love moves to the emotional centre where our fourth chakra is located. If blocked it can show itself as immune system, lung and heart problems, or manifest as inhumanity, lack of compassion or unethical behaviour.

Chakra five is blue in colour and located in the throat. The throat chakra allows for communication, creativity, self-expression and judgement. It governs the neck, shoulders, arms, hands, thyroid and parathyroid glands. It is concerned with healing, transformation and purification. Creative blocks, dishonesty or general problems in communicating ones needs to others result from the blockage of this chakra.

The third eye (pineal gland) is the sixth chakra and can be found at the centre of your forehead. Its colour is indigo and is used to question the spiritual nature of our life. It is the chakra of question, perception and knowing. It is concerned with inner vision, intuition and wisdom and holds our dreams for this life and recollections of other lifetimes. If blocked may cause problems such as lack of foresight, selective memory and depression.

The seventh chakra (violet) is the crown chakra and is located at the top of your head. It rules the central nervous system, cerebral cortex, and the pituitary gland. It is concerned with information, understanding, acceptance and bliss. It is known as the gateway to God and thus often called the chakra of divine purpose and personal destiny. Blockage of this chakra may manifest as psychological problems.

There are various ways of balancing the chakras once unbalanced. In the Action Sheet that follows this chapter I explain how to balance the sixth chakra. If you want to know more about balancing the other chakras, then I suggest watching the video 'How to Balance Your Chakras' found on my YouTube Channel.

SOUL?

What is the soul and how do you connect to it? It is connected to the essence of you, and it is separate. It is that which is infinite and whole, connected to the oneness that is the universal force energy called God. When you begin to go beyond your crazy chattering mind and obsessive attachment to the physical body, you realise that at your essence you are love. Meditation can help you realise the wisdom of this. Also, being in nature or looking at the stars can help you understand this. Realise the smallness of this ego body and vastness of the Universe that is. Also, by following the food regime and keeping healthy your connection to your actual self will come naturally. Eating foods such as raw cacao will open up your third eye and give you that intuition to your higher self that you needed. Following a detox of raw food or after a while of continual yoga practice, the world will unfold as never before. The veil of ignorance and attachment to falseness will fade gradually. You are now connected to who you really are at your core. Your essence. Your soul.

External beauty is impermanent. Once the physical self-ages, decays and perishes all that is left is your essence. That is the real you. It is all that really matters. Understand that which is truly you. It will ease your suffering. It will take you to joy. In realising the impermanence of it all.

Facebook, Tweet, Pin, Instagram, and Email the message below:

Bollywood Gay Message #14:
Self-care is the only way to bring real change on this planet.
#BollywoodGay

Action Sheet 14: How To Nourish Yourself

Want to do a detox? Get rid of all the crap from inside and outside your body? Then do a month or more worth of cleansing!

I RECOMMEND THE FOLLOWING THINGS TO TRY OUT:

- **Raw cacao** (add it to smoothies to clear out your system)

- **Filtered water**- Gentoo jug- takes a few weeks/months for fluoride to clear out of the body

- **Daily meditation**

- **Try a cleanse or detox**- such as a raw food diet.

- **Colonic irrigation** is a great way of getting rid of decade's worth of toxins that have stored in your colon. Not only does it release pent up emotions, pain and trauma but it also gives you a healthier digestive tract.

- **Get a spiritual healing.** Shamanic healing, crystal healing or otherwise. This is a regular of mine to clear me of past baggage.

You know when your pineal gland (third eye or 6th chakra) is open when it pulsates or twitches and allows you to see different perspectives.

HERE ARE 6 TIPS TO ACTIVATE THE 6TH CHAKRA:

- *Tip 1: Indigo is colour of the sixth chakra- wear clothes of this colour, surround yourself with this colour, or take an indigo Epsom salt bath.*

- *Tip 2: Go for a chakra healing near you. Your lower chakras may need to be opened and balanced before you can access higher chakras.*

- **Tip 3:** Chant the mantra Aum as this opens the third eye/pineal gland.

- **Tip 4:** Take an iodine supplement to decalcify it.

- **Tip 5:** When meditating focus on your third eye point between eyebrows and forehead.

- **Tip 6:** Buy crystals that work on activating the third eye e.g.: lapis lazuli, sapphire or sodalite-communicate with these stones and ask for them to help you open your third eye.

START A REGULAR EXERCISE ROUTINE

Starting a regular exercise routine is imperative to a healthy life. The key thing is that it has to be enjoyable and give you physical benefits. For instance, if I don't do yoga on a daily/regular basis my whole body stiffens, and I get aches and pains! I don't know how people survive without stretching daily! This keeps me on my routine.

GO TO A MEDITATION RETREAT TO LEARN THE BASICS OF MEDITATION

If you already know a bit and want a free retreat try out www.dhamma.org. I go there a few times a year. I also conduct my own retreats for LGBTI people a few times a year so head over to my website and sign up to the newsletter to know more www.myspiritualsoul.com.

'You will break and then all that will pour is love.'

15) SOULMATE? YES, PLEASE!

Are you ready for a soulmate relationship? The kind you envisaged as a youngster? A Bollywood youngster at that? The dramatical runaway kind of romance in Hindi films where parents refuse their child's romantic choice but agree to it later? How did all that change when you found out you were LGBTI? Did insecurities, guilt and shame make you lust for sex instead of love? Or did you give up on love altogether? What 'love' message are you giving out to the Universe? Are you settling for less?

I always wanted a relationship. I felt like I was constantly in the single swimming pool and wanted to jump over into the couples' section of the pool. I was like a dog to the bone. Desperately searching for love but acting out of fear. I would attract men who weren't ready to commit and could only give me physical connection. I kept swimming with unhealed men who were not evolved enough for a relationship. I came to learn that in shear desperation the very thing that I wanted was being repelled from me. I was acting out of fear thinking there was not enough in the world. I didn't believe a relationship would come naturally in its own time and that I had to force it to happen. I was reacting out of fear as opposed to being inspired to act out of love. Inspired action happens when we are in alignment. When we trust the process and believe abundance is our birthright.

I came to believe that most gay men were not into relationships, were promiscuous and unable to love. I have since learnt that this was an untrue generalisation. Whatever you are in alignment to you will see. If you look for something you will find evidence for it. Like if I have a stomach cramp and I search that in Google I am sure to find countless life threatening 'dis-eases' in the results. In the same vein, as soon as you start looking for possibilities they will come to you. So since I got into a relationship I started to meet many couples, and South Asian LGBTI couples at that. It is very beautiful indeed. Recently at a gay couples birthday party I was so happy to meet loving, mature and wonderful gay South Asian couples. What I am saying is, there is hope.

'Planning for love makes you loveable.'
Danielle LaPorte

You have to prepare yourself for the 'one'. You do this by loving yourself fully, for people who love themselves attract people who love themselves back. You may feel like you love yourself already, however, we all have deep-rooted complexities that need healing. Check out Action Sheet 9 and 11 on how to love yourself deeply and how to remove those pesky limiting beliefs.

It's important to look for the internal qualities you want in a partner as opposed to just external characteristics. Look for good heartedness, love, understanding and connection as opposed to how good he looks or how much money he makes. Let the Universe take care of that part. It's always a vibration match when two souls meet. You attract what you are and thus focusing on being the best version of yourself is key for a successful partnership. The main thing is feeling encapsulated in love and feeling supported and cared for.

Step by step- person to person your soulmate will manifest.

If you don't know what you want, simply make a list of all the things you don't want. Past relationships, failed flings, or bad family dynamics can help you determine what you absolutely don't want in your life. Once you have the idea of what you don't want in a partner, you can piece together what you do actually want. We are all ultimately window-shopping with the partner(s) we bring into our life. We are simply feeling if they are good for us and whether they hold the qualities we seek in our ideal mate. So don't be disappointed if it doesn't work out right away, as you are just fishing around. Your ideal mate is waiting out there somewhere. If you remember this, the edge off of dating will lessen, and you will ease into relationships.

ARE YOU READY FOR THE 'ONE'?

I know there is no set time for falling in love, meeting the 'one' and having the relationship of your dreams. But ask yourself are you actually ready? Are you ready physically, emotionally, sexually, mentally and spiritually? Now as I write this, I don't mean a regular hang out type of relationship. I mean the actual 'one' you have been waiting your entire life for.

Do you have the physical space to allow this person into your life? Are you independent from family obligations? Emotionally have you worked on yourself, released childhood hurt and anger? Are you trying to heal yourself? Or do you put the entire onus on your perspective partner declaring, 'They will heal me. Once I have them, they will make me happy'. This is the wrong way to view relationships. For inner contentment comes from within and not without. One has to have done a lot of the groundwork themselves before they meet a perspective healed partner.

Many gay men are stuck in their sacral chakra, which is associated with obsessions, lust, sexuality, and sensuality. Due to issues of guilt, shame and lack of internal stability and security, they express connection to others through sexual acts, reducing their wholeness to that act alone, unable to emotionally connect as is possible in higher chakras such as the heart chakra. They are unable to see another as a whole being and instead reduce them to exert their sexual desire, which of course reduces their own wholeness too. We attract people with similar thought patterns and similar emotional blockages when stuck in the sacral chakra. Then desperation, lack of self-love and worthiness, fear, anxiety, coupled with false thoughts of a perfect, unobtainable partner all lead to relationship hopelessness.

WHAT/WHO IS A SOULMATE?

The word soulmate comprises of 'soul', which is the eternal part of you and mate, which could be a marriage partner, a friend, a worker or counterpart. Thus a soulmate is not limited to a romantic partner. Quite often, soulmates agree to incarnate on earth and help one another grow and learn. They may continue incarnating in several lifetimes until particular lessons are learnt or soul contracts are fulfilled. The end result is to balance your karma (through forgiveness and compassion) so you can further progress on your soul mission.

So in reality, any type of relationship can be used for growth. Think about some of your closest relationships with family and friends. Have your experienced a connection deeper than usual with a particular family member or friend? Does a certain friend or sibling understand you like no other? There are countless soulmates out there for us all, and can appear in romantic or non-romantic relationships.

A soulmate's duty is to help us align with our true self. Soulmates mirror our deepest unhealed wounds so that we can heal from them. A real soulmate will help us see our wounds and they will heal automatically through simply identification. But they are not always meant to be happy feelings for us. For instance when we are unconnected to Source our ego can take things literally and get hurt. In this state we believe that our partner is the reason for our unhappiness, as we look outward for serenity. We forget that we are responsible for our own happiness. That is why we choose certain soulmates to come into our lives at any given moment to jolt us back to our true, pure, fulfilled selves. This happens by them annoying us so much that we go from a misaligned to realigned relationship with Source through our healing process. The quicker we let go of the anger and blame we hold the sooner we return back to our pure loving self.

DO SOULMATES ACTUALLY EXIST?

A soulmate is not always what you think it is. In some circumstances people create a certain vibration where the soul that is attracted reflects back to them what they need to learn to be the fullest representation of themselves. Thus anyone you interact with in any given moment is a soulmate. They reflect who you are at that moment so you can understand yourself and return back to love. For instance, you could perceive a soulmate to be your enemy as they reflect your negative vibration and cause great turmoil in your life. They are in fact your soulmate forcing you to look at your deep-rooted negative complexes and release them. It is soul contracts we make to be nudged back to self-actualisation, however many miss this mark and blame their soulmate for their misery. A soulmate is simply someone who reflects the difference between your current reality and your actual reality that which is pure love energy. That is why it is essential in order to have a positive soulmate experience to be in a positive mindset. You should therefore use every relationship as a soulmate one so you can be the fullest version of yourself.

'Love is when what you want is never important. But what the other person needs and wants is always paramount.' Pastor Wintley Phipps

Essentially there are thousands of soulmates; each with the purpose to help you realign to Source. If you are hurting, then you are not connected to yourself. For when we are truly aligned with our true self, to God, Nature, Universe, Source, etc., nothing brings us down, we see the lesson in everything, and understand the multi-dimensionality of each situation. Soulmates are inherently good experiences but can be experienced as bad when we are off the path, the path that connects us to God.

For example, say you are disconnected from yourself, you do not see your own inherent beauty, and therein dismiss the inherent beauty in your partner. You may scream, shout or do something untoward to them, which offends your partner. (Of course your partner's energy must be misaligned if they are offended by your actions and words. If they were aligned they would see the beauty within you, and focus on the good you have. They would not challenge you but give infinite compassionate love, which would diffuse the situation). Negativity has generated within you, and thus karma is full steam ahead toward you. You do not see this as your soulmate and blame them for your problems. This can be extremely painful for both of you as the argument may bring up past traumas. This is a bad soulmate experience, but one which is inherently good for you (as it reminds you that you are disconnected from Source and forces you to grow). As humans it is near enough impossible to be connected to Source 100% of the time, so we must forgive ourselves for this. If you realise your fallacy quick enough, that you indeed were disconnected to Source, that your ego was at play making you react angrily you will release your karmic debt in the situation and grow spiritually.

A better example would be that you try to see the good in all, especially yourself and your loved ones. You obviously are human so it's ok to get off the path and get annoyed. Your partner is also similar as you attracted them into your life in the first place. You have regular positive practices in play to align your energy to Source and you look for positive aspects about yourselves, compliment each other and are grateful for your life. So if you have an argument, and your partner reacts with love then all things resolve easily. However if they get upset, then hopefully your compassion and gratitude muscle, which you pump daily, soon kicks into place to diffuse the situation. You see your different viewpoints, apologise together and learn from it and move on! This is a great soulmate experience. I know which one I would rather have. People who are like this have this kind of relationship experience on a regular basis. It is healthy, progressive and full of wisdom. I urge you to evaluate the kind of experiences you have with your loved one(s), because unless you improve them, they will keep coming up again and again as negative. And you unknowingly play victim, when the power lies within you from the start.

WHAT ARE TWIN FLAMES?

The concept of twin flames developed among the ancient philosophers, mystics and sages. At the moment of a soul's creation, it was split into two halves, each exploring a different aspect of spirituality or duality. On one side was the divine masculine spirituality and on the other side was the divine feminine spirituality. A twin flame is essentially the other half of your soul. Thus what the general population terms as a soulmate is, in fact, a twin flame.

When you are with a twin flame, you feel complete. However, as they reflect the inner you, the relationship can also be quite challenging. It is unconditional love and a deep bond that helps twin flames to continue when things become difficult. A twin flame is like the ultimate soulmate. Though there are many soulmates, there is only ever one twin flame.

If you believe your twin flame is out there, it means that you will meet them in this lifetime. Otherwise, you will not, as not everyone is meant to meet their twin flame. For twin flames don't always incarnate at the same time. Often one chooses to incarnate in the physical whilst the other remains non-physical assisting from the higher realms. In time, as your soul progresses, you may reunite with your twin flame on the physical plane. Your twin flame may incarnate in the same or opposite gender, but spiritually they will always compliment and balance your energy.

SOULMATES VS. TWIN FLAMES

We are in a new era in human evolution where our relationships will begin to heighten our spiritual evolution. Our lovers will not simply fit into our lives, or be someone we merely love, they will, however, actively contribute to our soul's growth. You will experience the same soulmates many lifetimes, either as romantic partners or as friends and family members. They will guide us to grow and prepare us to unite with our twin flame.

Soulmates are known to be from different soul groups, allowing for tremendous growth. They can serve as heart centre catalysts to open you up and assist you in your ascension process and spiritual evolution. Soulmate relationships have the primary purpose to further learning by adopting new traits, sharing and growing together in love and harmony. A soulmate is united to you when you reach the point of maturity, where you are ready to enter into a real and true relationship of the soul.

Twin flames are a different story, and we are seeing more and more twin flames reigniting; coming together again, for their own special and unique purpose. They are male and female energies separated, but which were once as one. They originate from the same soul family and share the same energetic blue print. They are the yin to your yang and the dark to your light.

Your twin flame can also be considered your soulmate. However, the main difference being that they are your soul's counterpart or other half. It's important not to fear when your twin flame or soulmate will manifest, but rather allow the Universe to guide you to those who will help you be the truest version of yourself.

Twin Flames vibrate at a higher frequency than soulmates because they are the ultimate example of polar opposites. They are two individual souls that complement, understand and connect with each other. They emit the same frequency of vibration, which accounts for a strong feeling of energies when they are physically around one another.

HOW TO ATTRACT A TWIN FLAME?

You attract your twin flame into your life by dramatically improving the relationship with yourself. You do this by treating yourself better, improving your self-worth and committing to your happiness. A twin flame's intention is to bring positive focus towards you. So to attract a twin flame you need to accept and be positive towards yourself too. Spiritual people tend to be the most focused to get a twin flame relationship but are more likely to have this much later on in life, because they are obsessed with self-improvement. We want contrast and crappy relationships to expand and learn. Self-improvement means that we need to improve ourselves and there is something inherently wrong with us. It means we are not thinking positively about ourselves. That is why a twin flame relationship won't manifest. Stop trying to change yourself to make someone love you. Start accepting and loving all your flaws, and then you can attract the twin flame that does the same.

Approve of yourself. You don't need to change yourself to meet a twin flame. Appreciate yourself. Feel complete in yourself. You have to love yourself, and be ready for it. You have to actually feel it and know what is going on in your heart. Romantic partners reflect how you feel about yourself. If you are unhappy, miserable or on a lower level of vibration, you most likely attract a similar partner. Romantic relationships are mirrors. They mirror the deepest unhealed wounds within you. If you don't find yourself attractive, the people you attract won't find you attractive either and/or they won't find themselves attractive. How can you find men who will love you if you don't love yourself? You need to have done a certain amount of groundwork within you to be able to have a prosperous relationship. Of course issues have roots and even when we have done a lot of groundwork, the ugly roots reappear. It is an on going process. But at the least resolve issues with your family and parents. Forgive them and give compassion to them by understanding they did what they thought was best at that time. This is because parental issues have a way of showing up in relationships. So go fix your relationship with your mum and dad.

Now I do not say that all this groundwork has to be done in this life before you meet your twin flame. Many matured souls come fully equipped and prepared to tackle life's challenges head-on.

Many don't. Those who are already mature may have learnt as much as they needed to in their past lives to become fully aware. They only need a few knocks here and there to centre themselves and unlearn the trauma of reincarnation to remember their infinite unity to Source energy and allow universal knowledge to pour through them.

You will meet your twin flame when you realise that they are not missing. When you achieve vibrational alignment with that which is you, your twin flame will manifest. Remember no one can complete you. That you have to do yourself. Don't look for the right person, rather make yourself the right person. Then the right person will be drawn to you depending on the work you have done on yourself. If you are looking for someone to complete you, you will attract someone who is also looking for you to complete them. But if you look for someone who is committed to their own happiness, you will meet the same.

If you haven't been able to meet your twin flame thus far it is simply because you have been beating the drum of what you don't want. Perhaps you are projecting what happened in the past such as betrayal, deceit or lying into your current reality blocking your love to manifest. Perhaps you don't think its possible to manifest your twin flame or that you are unworthy of them. If you chase something, then it will run away from you. Being impatient about wanting a relationship, means you don't give the Universe enough time to bring it to you. The ideal relationship you want is out there. You have to be patient. Expecting a miracle is the surest way of manifesting it. So expect that your twin flame is on their way. Most importantly feel the energy of love as often as possible. When you see romantic couples on TV or in public praise them and match up to their vibrational frequency as opposed to feeling jealous about it! On a daily basis be on the brink of appreciation by focusing on all the positive aspects of your life.

Reaffirm to yourself that you are the attracter of what you want and you can attract it from anyone you want to attract it from. Pick someone you think is right and start attracting the qualities you want from them. Choose someone who has a majority of things that you like. For satisfaction on every level is not possible. Expansion from learning and growing, however, is great. Choose someone who is also willing to keep up with who they are becoming whilst wanting to grow. If they want to see what you want to see, you will surely close the gap between you.

HOW DO YOU KNOW YOU'VE FOUND YOUR TWIN FLAME?

You know when you've found your twin flame when you feel a deep sense of peace and feeling of returning home. It may feel as though you have known this person your entire life as you feel comforted in their presence. You understand each other, even though you have never met and a level of intimacy will be present. You may have dreams or visions of them before meeting in this lifetime. Meeting a twin flame feels like coming home to long lost energy. After meeting, you may have memories of other times and places from other lives. Your twin flame will mirror your issues and concerns. You compliment each other's skills sets, talents and capacities. You are the ultimate embodiment of yin yoga.

You may be of different ages, same or opposite sex, vastly different backgrounds, opposing religions or cultures, but feel incredible unity and oneness with this partner. You feel each other's symptoms, emotions and illnesses, even when far away and not communicating. It may physically and mentally hurt when you are away from each other. When you are with them and your relationship is in balance you become stronger, more powerful and capable. You feel united in the mission to serve others or the world. Your unconditional love is like no other. Your twin flame may have a habit, quality or baggage, which normally is a deal breaker for you, but you overlook it willingly, and work through it with your partner. You meet them when least expecting it after being forced to measure some form of self-acceptance. You attain a level of friendship on top of the sexual attraction between you. To harmonise and balance you push each other's buttons so you can become the highest version of yourself. Friends, family and others are affected, humbled and deeply moved by the relationship and feel something cosmic is happening in the union and are sometimes threatened by this. The growth, lessons, and person you become happen much more rapidly, and powerfully with your twin flame, then any other time. You come to realise that previous relationships or soulmates prepared you for your twin flame. Your twin flame may even embody a number of characteristics of previous mates. Finally you feel you have been waiting for them your whole life.

Your twin flame is YOU.

When you unite with your twin flame, you may feel a familiarity between you as though you are looking at yourself in the mirror. It feels as though you have met before as you recognise each other's soul. Synchronicity brings you together; your heart chakras open as your souls unite as one. An acceleration of spiritual ascension activates the memory of your soul's life mission awakening you to higher levels of consciousness. Both twins feel as though the other has completed them. However, the feeling of being completed by someone is, in fact, the recognition of the self in the other. You are your own twin flame.

HOW DO YOU KEEP YOUR LOVE ALIVE?

Normally after 6 months of being with a partner the euphoria dies. Reality sets in and you tell yourself that you didn't see the 'real person'. In the beginning of a relationship chemical reactions force us to have positive focus towards our partner. These dissipate with time, meaning we need to consciously focus positively in order to retain that euphoric feeling. However most of us focus by default on what is bothering us, the negative aspects of our partner which in turn reduce our passion and enjoyment chemicals. In 'Enchanted love' Marianne Williamson tells us that during 'the falling in love phase' we actually see the 'real person'. We see their soul. The euphoric phase of the relationship was in fact reality from a spiritual perspective. As humans we do not have the personality structure to handle that much love. Euphoria is in fact the right state of mind. During the initial stages of our relationship, we see our partner as God would, pure and perfect. Then judgement kicks in with the unforgiving mind. We focus on their personality not their spiritual self. To their external flaws and not their internal perfection. The 'real' perception of our partner is then lost to us. So many times the people we love the most receive the greatest judgement from us. We look at their faults and see why they are not good enough, rather then seeing their inherent beauty. Regular spiritual practice can help us sustain our partner's true self by focusing on their innocence rather then their guilt.

Having a serious spiritual practice built into your relationship dynamic can be transformative. Whether you practice gratitude, forgiveness, meditation or prayer, bringing love into the relationship rather then criticism will keep that euphoria alive. A relationship is like a seed, you must water it, give it good energy and nutrients so it can blossom. At first it will be a weak little shoot, which will get stronger with time. Build trust with your partner which of course starts with learning to trust yourself. Insecurities that sprung up from being hurt in the past, having your trust broken, issues with your parents or childhood abuse will need to be healed. Projecting the past into the present, thinking everyone will hurt, lie or abuse you will weaken your relationship. Conversely you have to behave the way you want your partner to treat you. Be faithful, loving and truthful. A relationship is a two-way thing, as the other person is a reflection of you. So if you don't want your partner to be texting and bothering you when you are out, asking you where you are and what you are doing, you also need to not be doing that. If you want your partner to be more romantic you should be more romantic as well. Communicate honestly, sensitively and express how you feel about issues. Persevere to work through issues with love rather then fear. Learn to be each other's best friend and be there for one another. Keep your passion alive by complimenting one another regularly, show affection or do something romantic like buying each other a rose. Plan your future together by using the words 'we' instead of 'I'. Use positive terminology, instead of calling disagreements, arguments call them 'heart to hearts' for words have vibrations. Finally try to resolve your issues before going to bed and come from a place of love when doing so.

AM I JUST SETTLING?

There are no hard and fast rules to relationships. They are unique and personal as each person brings their own individual concoction of issues to deal with. I've heard some people say: 'If he doesn't move in with you in the first year, it's never going to work out.' Or, 'If he doesn't tell his parents about you, he's not serious.' This is all nonsense. Never listen to anyone else's advice or even really seek it (unless your life is in danger and there is violence or abuse). Follow your own inner guidance system and if it feels good to you, it's probably right.

Relationships are valuable teachers. Ask yourself what are you learning about yourself in the relationship, as it exists so far? Are you learning what your true preferences are? The purpose of a relationship is to reflect to the other(s) in the relationship what they need to understand to be more of themselves. Everyone in a relationship is in a relationship to help the other(s) to be given the opportunity to be who they are more and more. If you don't know what a relationship is meant to do, you will have trouble in them. For it means you don't have a clear relationship with yourself regarding who you are, who you want to be and what your highest excitement is. Once you have figured this out, the Universe and the components that make up the machine within it will synchronise to bring all that you desire into your life.

When you experience negative behaviour in another person, ask yourself what is it in me that is reflecting through this experience? For example, a woman with an abusive relationship pattern will keep attracting partners who control her life making her feel terrible. She does this because her inner belief about herself is 'I am unworthy, not good enough, and I hate myself'. This belief was present in her before she met her partner(s) making the two a match. That is why working on self-love and self-worth is key to finding the relationship of your dreams.

If you don't change your discordant vibrations, you will keep coming up with partners with the same behaviours with which you treat yourself. You will keep running into and encountering negative patterns. But if you commit to staying with one situation long enough to improve the vibration within you, your relationships will dramatically improve. Either you will no longer be a match for this negative relationship and your partner will fade smoothly out your life, or when you change your vibration, you will no longer be a match to the negative behaviour in them and your partner's negative behaviour will no longer be part of your experience.

It is however, quite normal to lose our connection to Source and for our vibration to lower. Our job is to return to our connected and compassionate self and to be able to see the positive aspects of our relationship. Tune into your feelings. If you are out of alignment for a short while but through gratitude, affirmations or meditation you can go back into appreciating your partner then all is normal. But if on a continual basis you feel uneasy, hurt, upset or not connected then you know that the relationship is not how it should be.

WHAT ABOUT MARRIAGE?

Marriage is the process of letting everything unhealed come to surface to heal to make the relationship continue. Our partner becomes the reflection of all the good and bad things about us. But many people scared of their own reflection end their relationships. Rather ask yourself, 'If my partner is behaving in a certain way, what is it in me that is making me a match to that condition and how can I change that thing?' Your marriage partner can be the most dominant thing causing you to heal all that is unhealed about you. The marriage vows 'I am going to promise myself to you' itself means that in order for us to stay married I have to correct all of the things that are uncorrected within me. I am willing to heal my unhealed wounds for this relationship to flourish. If we are out of alignment, our relationship conditions are going to be uncomfortable. Get into alignment and realise that marriage can be the same as promising yourself to the shortcut to expansion or nirvana.

TANTRIC SEX

Tantra is an ancient Hindu tradition of beliefs, meditation and ritual practices that seeks to channel the divine energy of the Universe into the human experience to be liberated from the cycle of reincarnation. The intimacy part of tantra heals our relationships allowing us to have satisfying relationships with the people around us. Through tantra we learn how to connect deeply, allowing great healing to take place within us. The ritual of tantric sex is what most know about, however, there are many other forms of it too. Tantric sex is a slow form of sex that's said to increase intimacy and create a mind-body connection that can lead to powerful orgasms.

Essentially you could get enlightened through tantra. But the reason why it doesn't happen is because people are afraid of intimacy. Enlightenment is seeing your true self. When we get intimate, we shed the veil that prevents us being close to another. The key is to get intimate with yourself through masturbation and then with your partner.

To use tantra in lovemaking, instead of focusing on your sexual organs, focus on your heart chakra. By focusing on your heart, not only do you prolong ejaculation but through connecting deeply with the person, you gain a sense of sacred sex. If you stare the person in the eyes and focus on your heart chakras, the experience can be explosive. Having rehearsed in this, you can move your gaze to your third eye centre and experience the fireworks that ensue. Practice makes perfect! (The Action Sheet that follows explains how).

Tantra opens the chakra energy system, known as kundalini, within the body. Kundalini is released from the pelvis, up the spine through movement, breath, meditation and sound. Once this energy is released, it can heal lifetimes of mental limitations that accumulated within the body. It can also aid in regaining our natural spiritual gifts such as clairvoyance and the ability to connect with others.

SO HOW DOES TANTRA CHANGE ALL THIS?

Tantric sex can teach us how to use the totality of this union with our partner during sex. Our physicality is not the sexiest thing about us. A truly sensual person has a presence about them that is absolutely captivating and enthralling. The way they look us and touch us can leave us spellbound. What their body looks like is quite irrelevant; simply breathing and touching this person can send chills and orgasms throughout our bodies.

We are energetic as well as physical beings. When we touch our lover, with deep affection and delight rather then just for the sake of it, they sense this. When you are in the present moment electricity permeates from your fingers into your partner's entire body. This sexual energy returns back to you as you both become the givers and receivers of tantric energy. We are meant to connect with one other on a deep level. Human beings do not do well without feeling a deep connection. Often when disconnected we wrongly label this as being needy or desperate. But deep down we know we are capable of phenomenal connection, and when we feel this connection, our life gets better. Our depression and anxiety disappear, as we notice the joys in life. We appreciate each other and feel a deep level of contentment and happiness.

When we bring in everything that we truly are into our intimate experiences, we go from simply having sex to having an experience involving our minds, emotions and feelings. This is vital for the overly sexualised gay world where men are obsessed with having sex with everyone. When we learn to connect more deeply, physical sex, promiscuity, porn and one-night stands will be a thing of the past. We will unify as Gods and become enlightened.

Physical sex, or promiscuous sex depletes us of our spiritual energy. As we orgasm with anyone, without checking in if their energy aligns with our own, we allow negative resonances from their auric field to our own. We literally pick up their negative auric imprint and intoxicate our being with it. If sleeping with multiple partners in a short amount of time, we may start to feel not like our self. Say for example the sexual partner you've chosen is someone with low self-esteem issues. That person's issues become entangled with your emotional self, and all it takes is one encounter to weigh you down for the next 2 -3 weeks. To remedy this and allow the sexual bonding to wear off it is good to withhold from sex for a few weeks.

On the other hand, incredible things can happen in your life when all your chakras are activated. When sexuality is approached from a spiritual perspective, it becomes a sacred, ego-less approach to sexuality or more importantly an ego-less approach to your partner. It can be utilised as an instrument to experience higher realms of spirituality. This is only possible if both partners follow this path together; otherwise, they will grow apart. Check out the Action Sheet that follows for a tutorial into tantric sex.

MANIFESTING THROUGH AN ORGASM

When we orgasm, we align to Source and feel life force energy (spiritual energy) flowing through our bodies. Therefore manifesting during climax is one of the most powerful ways to attract what we want. Alignment occurs between the perception of our physical reality and non-physical reality allowing Source energy to run through us. During orgasms, our ego is dissolved, allowing us temporary enlightenment. There are two types of orgasms, explosive and implosive both of which can be healthy and unhealthy.

In an explosive orgasm which is what men experience, energy moves out of the body. This is the best type for manifestation as vast amounts of vibration is emitted to the Universe. However being a shallow form of orgasm it depletes your energy. An implosive orgasm is where energy moves inwards so it is retained within the body. It is natural to women, and aids in healing or unity work by pulling your partner's energy into you. It restores the body and soul and nourishes through increasing energy.

Ultimately our craving for orgasm is relief, release and oneness. We all need to learn how to give and receive love on a continual basis and remember that what we focus on during the moment of orgasm is what we will conceive in reality. With a partner, we need to think and feel what we want manifested in our life. It is imperative to be careful of our thoughts and feelings during sex and orgasm. In the minute of orgasm accumulated energy is released, which can be harnessed to manifest our reality. In those seconds before and during orgasm change your focus on emotionally and mentally the very thing you wish to manifest. Use it for more bonding, unification or oneness with a partner or use it to advance your career or for personal success!

It's beyond the physical- your top, I'm bottom paradigm. It's beyond the body and I, ego, self. It's beyond all of that. It's pure selfless unconditional love. A deep understanding and care for the other. A connection which erases the separation between you and I. It is love. Unconditional love. Where all that matters is deep concern and consideration. The desire to look after this person and be there for them. The realisation of the purity of their soul. Their selfless love for you. And above all the personal realisation that you are beyond this physical body. You are pure potential energy ready to burn bright as you intended to. Undressed the veil of ego. Naked you stand in your glory. All thanks to this realisation. This person. But more importantly due to your own inner work. Your own ability to see clearly. Time and patience. And removal from the madness outside. Which fixates on the body and feeds on insecurities. You have transcended. And oh how wonderful it is.

Facebook, Tweet, Pin, Instagram, and Email the message below:

Bollywood Gay Message #15:
Expecting a soulmate is the surest way of manifesting one.
#BollywoodGay

Action Sheet 15: Twin Flames

Whilst soulmates can come in many forms, twin flames come only as one. Thus the romantic ideal of a twin flame is what we actually aspire to be with. Here's how to manifest yours:

SELF-ACCEPTANCE EXERCISE:

Choose one thing you don't accept about yourself. Discover what that one thing is and write a long list why that trait is beneficial. Feel better about having that trait. Find approval for it.

I.e. I am emotionally unstable:

I give others permission to be who they are.
I gain self-awareness and growth from it.
People can be vulnerable around me.
I am real.
Buddha was emotionally unstable.
Crisis can lead to self-discovery.
My relationships are never boring.
I don't hide anything from my partner.
It gives my relationships growth.
I have a good guidance system due to my emotions.
I am healthy, as I don't suppress anything.

When you realise that you are the reason for your own happiness, you let your partner off the hook. They are no longer the reason you smile. They no longer need to be your puppet, that you get annoyed with when they don't make you feel a certain way. They are independent, free and add to your life their own happiness and not yours. While you do the same.

BELOW ARE 3 SELF-AFFIRMING STATEMENTS TO REMEMBER:

1) You deserve love, and you are not a sexual object to be used, nor are you unworthy of closeness.

2) What you do to others is what you internally do to yourself. So treat prospective partners as loving beings and take it slow, date, be friends, and don't focus all on sex. You want a relationship then act like that's what you are doing.

3) Unlock your higher chakras by meditation and yoga or another means so that you feel self-secure and stable. Finally love yourself and everyone

HOW TO HAVE TANTRIC SEX:

1) Start by breathing in unison, make eye contact, and share positive words with one another.

2) Now, lightly touch each other with your fingertips, awakening the nerves thus heightening sensations. Come close to each other's genitals, without touching them.

3) Purse your lips open allowing your breath to flow from one another freely, pressing your lips at the end to form a sensual kiss.

4) Practice giving each other a tantric body massage by taking it in turns to lie face down, while the other lightly massages the non-erogenous zones before moving onto the erogenous zones.

5) Finally, practice loving sex, where you look into each other's eyes, both feeling secure, grounded and connected with the other.

DELIBERATE SEXUAL BONDING:

Normally sex bonds couples for an average of 2-3 weeks, however, deliberate bonding extends this to 2-3 months. Deliberate bonding blends your spiritual essences together and awakens your telepathic and empathic abilities. It also aids in healing the body, balancing emotions and opening the chakras. Here are 4 tips to deliberate bonding:

1) Just before climaxing with your partner, focus your attention on the part of your body that needs healing. When you do this, spiritual energy activates its healing there.

2) To create stronger bonds with each other imagine your energy entering your partner's heart space during sex. Feel this connection and repeat 'I choose to bond with you' as you come to climax.

3) Create a rainbow bridge from your heart to theirs mentally, which enhances your telepathic abilities.

4) As you climax lightly press the tip of your tongue with theirs. This connects the energy cycle that flows creating a deeper bonding experience.

'If you have life you have purpose.'
Caroline Myss

16) HOW TO LIVE WITH PURPOSE

The higher self is like a dove. Flying high, rising and knowing. Seeing the way ahead, before the physical self-realises. Connect to it.

How do you live a purposeful life? By finding your purpose of course! We all have a purpose. But how do we find it? You find your purpose when you're not put in a position where you betray yourself, negotiate your sense of integrity and compromise who you are. It just feels right.

For all those who say, 'I don't have a purpose', I say: we are all born intuitive. We all have an inner guidance, inner voice. Thus not only does everyone have a path or purpose, they already know it.

SO HOW DO YOU FIND YOUR PURPOSE?

You find your purpose by following your joy. We chose our purpose before being incarnated. We have a close relationship to what our purpose is as a child. Our adult purpose is an evolutionary byproduct of what we enjoyed doing as a child. But parents and teachers get in the way and tell us what to do. In school, if a child dislikes and is bad at Maths, they are given a Maths tutor. But if they enjoy and are good at music, why aren't they given more music lessons? If we allow children to specialise in what they love, they are more likely to become geniuses in those subjects. I don't know about you, but I haven't used most of what I learnt at school as an adult. Rather we should be equipping our youth to care about what feels better for them. We should tell them to follow their joy. My advice to those who read this book is not to let anyone tell you otherwise. As you feel good, you navigate towards where you need to get to like a compass. Of course, your path will sway, but it will ultimately take you to where you need to be, and only you know where that is, only you can follow your bliss. The best livers of life are those who have fun. Have fun in whatever you are doing and your purpose will shine out of you.

We all have a purpose we came to experience in each life. It is imprinted in our soul. However, to realise it, often we have to experience the absence of it. For example, say your life purpose is to realise unconditional love. To experience it, you must first experience the absence of it. You must experience conditional love. The experiencing of conditional love allows you to realise that in fact what you most desire is unconditional love. This is the reason why most of us experience the opposite of what we are actually here to experience first, so we can realise it. This is why some of us experience discrimination in order to feel acceptance. LGBTI folk may experience exclusion because their life purpose is to feel inclusion. Going through the opposite of what our life purpose is, helps us to realise it. One way of understanding your purpose is to focus onto that which has caused you the most pain. For instance, I always wanted a relationship and only received one-night affairs. In the same vein, I always wanted a permanent career. I pined for it. Imagine that painful feeling and sit in it. Imagine that you are in that experience and identify the feelings that arise. They may be a lack of acceptance, conditional love, restriction, fear or feeling unworthy. This is your negative core imprint. Thus your life purpose is to experience the opposite of that: acceptance, unconditional love, freedom, love and feeling worthy. Be aware, however, that the opposite of one emotion can be different to different people. For example, the opposite of panic may mean calm to one person but trust to another. A good way of figuring out which emotion is the opposite of your negative core imprint is to look up the antonym in a thesaurus to find out the word that most resonates for you. That will be the purpose(s) your soul has in this lifetime.

Another way to find your purpose is to align to who you are. Most people are misaligned to their true self. They are a concoction of fear and love. They feel frustration, anger or hate and at the same time feel joy, love and union. They want approval, or validation and only utilise their small uncreative egoic mind. However, once they are connected to love on a regular basis, through, meditation, prayer, yoga, gratitude and reflection they are closer to who they truly are. They realise the infinite possibilities of creation. When you tap into your higher self, which has no barriers to who you are, you find all sorts of creative outlets for living and earning from a life you have always wanted.

'When you follow your highest excitement, without expectation of the result, you unlock the infinite tools of the Universe to fully support you.' Bashar, channelled by Darryl Anka

The funny thing is, when you are happy for long periods of time, your purpose finds you. It naturally unfolds in front of you. It nudges you in the back and says, 'Hey why not try this out'. Or peers from way out there and says, 'Hey come on over here. Try this exciting new thing out.' Your purpose never leaves you. Only you leave it. Blinded, head down, eyes closed, fingers in ears, you fail to hear its sweet call. Your purpose is within you, around you and in those that surround you. Your purpose never leaves you, fails you or closes its doors. It's always patiently waiting for you to wake up, see it, open your hands and grasp it. It's always in the reach of your hand, the softness of your cheek, the fragrance by your nose, and the whisper in your ears. Close your external eyes, and look within. It's there the loudest.

Let me give you an example from my life. All my life I sought approval from my parents and peers. I achieved tops A*'s grades, went to a top university and got a top notch job. However, that was not fulfilling me. The UN was a bore. It was a desktop 9-5 job that did not serve my creativity. I was regurgitating the same reports over and over! However through the setbacks, through the Universe saying 'No, you are not meant to do this, for your inner vibration resonates at a higher frequency than lack, fear and roboticness', I began to see creative outlets for what I wanted. Only once truly connected to Source, through daily Abraham Hicks marathons on YouTube did I understand what I was meant to do. Various tarot readers, psychics, palm readers and clairvoyants with the help of signs from the Universe directed me to this path. What I'm saying is this: get happy and then act. Get happy and then do. Get happy and then be. Just get happy. It's only from a higher frequency that you can truly know who you are. Once you are tapped into God-force energy, your whole life pans out. Get happy now!

HOW DO YOU KNOW YOU ARE ON THE RIGHT PATH?

You know when you are on your right path when you don't let yourself down anymore. You don't negotiate your sense of integrity or heart. You have no need to compromise, as what you are doing feels right. You feel fulfilled and like yourself. The right path is your calling. Everyone has it. Ask yourself what would you do if you had three months to live? What if fear was not involved and money was not an issue? That there is your calling. It can be either 'big' or 'small' it does not matter. Have no judgements or expectations and give up the need to know what happens tomorrow. Just follow your dreams. Be fully present and appreciate all that is in your life right now. The right path will then be laid out in front of you.

Most people, unfortunately, live in permanent dissatisfaction. What they fail to realise is that purpose is not necessarily about where you are going and what you're doing- that's outer purpose. Inner purpose is more important; it's your purpose to be in this moment. Aligning your life fully with the present moment, so you are no longer out of alignment with who you are. This is our true purpose. So go beyond dissatisfaction and be at one with yourself.

WHAT IF YOU ARE IN A TOUGH SITUATION AND LOST YOUR JOB?

If you are in a tough situation or have lost your job it is because you had your life focused on a path that didn't belong to you. Instead of being connected to Source and taking guidance from your higher self you focused on your limited egoic self. You may have held onto rage that didn't belong to you, disconnecting you from your essence. Perhaps you didn't realise a lesson and hung onto the pain.

Maybe you stopped living your purpose. Maybe you thought you had made it or achieved it already. The moment you think you have made it, it's over. When you start taking your talent, gift and passion for granted that's the moment you stop living your purpose. To think yes I'm earning this much, I've done this degree, or I have acquired this job, is to stop your life purpose in its tracks. This is when a tough situation can appear. However, when you start appreciating your talent, your talent will help you manifest success.

We are, however, never on a wrong path. We simply go through a detour when we are disconnected to who we are. We are always growing and developing into our life purpose. When we are disconnected, we experience tough times, which are there to help us to reconnect with our self more deeply. You have to keep your passion alive, keep growing, keep expanding and keep assimilating into your life purpose.

'Don't waste your life living someone else's life.' Steve Jobs

Create your own unique vision and share it with the world. Some people may say what you are doing is pointless. But once you are in the flow of your life purpose and things start to come together in time with patience, they will be calling you for advice!

When you first start people may not think it's possible, and they may doubt you. But keep going. Be the seer who manifests your dreams. It's those very people who have failed in the attempts to live their life purpose by giving up too early, and succumbing to mass consciousness, who discourage you in your path. These very people try to shatter your dreams and tell you to work in an environment which is safe or devoid of creativity.

Most of us live for others. Trust in yourself and let go of society's expectations of you. Stop comparing yourself to others. Connect with mother earth. She will guide you to your true life purpose. Follow the thing that makes you feel most alive. Once you let go of all distractions, you will be able to hear your purpose. What are passionate about? Forget about money, awards and recognition; that will come. Instead, write a list of what you would love to do. How do you feel about each point? Now focus on the point(s) that gives you the most joy. That is what you must pursue. Reconnect to your heart space and do it because you love to, not because you have to. The only thing that matters is who had the most fun.

'When you do what you love, time seems to stop, and you remain youthful (your physical body thinks only a few minutes have elapsed). When you do what you dislike, time drags, and you age.' Bashar, channelled by Darryl Anka

Often we are obsessed with the end result. We forget about the journey. The newness of the moment. You spend two years arguing, worrying about a project, annoy everyone and arrive at the intended result. But is this seen as a successful result? Firstly you upset all those around you, your unconscious mind, which is always connected to all, gave out negative pollutants and toxicity to the Universe meaning the result carried the same energy with which it was birthed. The way you feel during the journey is the most important part. We as humans have screwed up this important detail. We think in the having of the new car or relationship we will be happy. We plead, pray, obsess over the new phone and when we get it we are happy for a few weeks until it gets scratched, starts playing up and we forget its newness. We then go chasing a new material possession. What we must remember is that we should think about how we want to feel first. We have desires, goals; end results in mind because we think in the having of it we will feel happier. So tell yourself I want to feel happy, that is my intention. During the process of achieving your goal keep reassessing. Do I feel happy doing this? If not then stop; because the achievement of the goal will be scented with bitter sweetness. Nothing is worth pursuing which makes you unhappy in the process. Be in the moment and realise how you want your life to feel. Don't go jumping from one goal to another, dismissing your entire life and ending up deeply miserable and unhappy. The way I want to feel in my life is: connected, free, abundant, creative and conscious. If anything I do contradicts that, then I simply let go of that goal, or change my attitude to it!

A new world order is on its way. But are you ready for it? Most people are sick of their regular 9-5-work life. Grinding for low pay and privileges. The fear mentality, which created a submissive working class, is a thing of the past. With depression and social separation at an all-time high, people are looking for a new way. Anything is possible. You don't need to work hard to make money. Indeed you don't need to 'work' at all. Become an entrepreneur. Work according to your own demands. Be your own boss. When you tap into the universal energies that be, you realise abundance is your birthright. There are unfound forces waiting to be tapped into. You can be that creative, positive, powerful force you always wanted to be. You can relax and enjoy your life and live simpler. Get a house in the country that you made yourself. Go backpacking. Anything is possible if you open your mind and become your own boss. Try it- I am.

Tell others how to find their purpose and live the life of their dreams. Facebook, Tweet, Pin, Instagram, and Email the message below:

Bollywood Gay Message #16:
By following my joy, my purpose unfolds.
#BollywoodGay

Action Sheet 16: My Purpose Is:

If *money* and other *restrictions* were not a *hindrance*, what would you do as a *profession*?

_____
_____
_____
_____
_____
_____

What gives you the *most joy* in daily life?

_____
_____
_____
_____
_____
_____

What makes you *happy*?

_____
_____
_____
_____
_____
_____

If you had *one year* to live, what would you do *differently*? How would you *live* your *life*?

_____
_____
_____
_____
_____
_____

Are you more of a *homely* person or *outdoorsy* person?

_____
_____
_____
_____
_____

Do you like *interacting* with *people* and/or being with *nature* and *animals*?

_____

_____

_____

_____

_____

How do you want to *feel* each day?

_____

_____

_____

_____

_____

What has always been your *dream*?

_____

_____

_____

_____

_____

_____

_____

_____

_____

Purpose can be as *humble* as working an honest living, to as *extravagant* as being a new world leader. Where do you fall on this *spectrum*?

_____

_____

_____

_____

_____

'It's our goal to reflect the value of God.'
Oprah

17) BE A POSITIVE ROLE MODEL

'Your playing small does not serve the world. Who are you not to be great?'
Nelson Mandela

As it has been up until now, LGBTI individuals of any ethnic group have generally remained closeted. This is slowly changing in the Western world with the Caucasian community, however, us Asians are still lagging far behind. Stuck in shame, and guilt or afraid of what others will say, we shy away from our important assigned task.

We are in desperate need of positive LGBTI South Asian role models. We need to be in the media, out and proud. There are youngsters struggling with their sexuality, parents of gay children who are lost, concerned friends, judgemental family and confused elderly who all need positive role models to look up to. They need South Asian role models, people who look, talk and walk like them. Those who speak with the same accent and language as them. Because let's face it, our community likes to compare. And if they see Aunty Ji with her Punjabi son on TV and being gay is ok, then it will be ok for them too. We need to help one another, and we need to do it now.

I decided to take the platform. By no means am I perfect. No one is. I am in my late 20's, and I make mistakes all the time. I get angry, annoyed, frustrated and can be horrible! I know all of this lovely wisdom stuff I preach but don't always remember it during the heat of the moment or during bad times. My poor partner and family get the brunt of my sharpness and scorn. However, I learn quick, and I try to see the wisdom in everything. I get over things fairly fast and don't allow them to simmer for too long. The good thing about knowing things is that you can inform others of them if asked. You simply cannot be 100% perfect 100% of the time. You will fall, and you may become nasty. That is why it is important to have done a lot of your own inner work. To have a regular spiritual practice or a practice which grounds and balances you. This way when the times are tough, you can flow through them with ease, or with as much grace as you can. I think having a partner really helps to bring up years of hidden wounds to the surface to look at and heal. I mean ideally you want to be a walking talking example to the world, but let's face it unless you're a Buddha or angelic being, you are going to falter, and falter a lot. Therefore never doubt yourself. All you can do is try. This human physique with its ego mind is a pain to deal with. It needs to be constantly whipped into submission or gently soothed so that it can allow your soulful love to shine.

We were assigned to speak the truth and be our authentic selves unapologetically. Once a soul has gone through self-acceptance, actualisation, and realisation, the next logical step is to be an ambassador for others.

'I have come to create teachers not to gather disciples'. Yogi Bhajan

I invite you all to be positive role models now! I contacted Stonewall, the national and international UK LGBT organisation and urged them to do more for South Asians and ethnic minorities. They responded. I volunteer as a Role Model for their Schools programme; I appear on posters in schools, and I train staff and children alike on LGBT issues. I also volunteer for Diversity Role Models and do similar work for them, speaking in schools up and down the country demonstrating that you can be South Asian and LGBT. See all you need to do is Google and email various organisations and ask how you can volunteer or support them. You can volunteer in front or behind the scenes or just donate your time or money. When you make a choice to help others, the Universe will show you ways of doing it. Whether it's an email, a friendly call, a tweet or inspired thought, the Universe will help you be the role model you aspire to be. You simply have to say 'Yes' to yourself.

HOW TO CREATE A MOVEMENT?

I am not here to work alone, and neither are you. We are here to be an army of spiritual, activist and social leaders. Let's begin. So how do you create your own movement? How do you be the momentum you need to create positive change? Here are my top 10 tips:

1) Figure our what movement you want to do? Do you want to advocate for gay rights, women's rights or for education?

2) Imagine yourself doing what you love even if you are currently in a totally unrelated job. Feel the way you would feel if you were in that job and visualise doing it daily.

3) Never give up, but don't be desperate. Miracles happen in their own time. Just expect them to come. And be happy

4) Embody the message of your cause. Be a walking, talking representation of the movement you desire to be part of.

5) You have the seed within you to create this movement. The mere conception of it in your mind means you have the power to materialise it.

6) Figure out in which way you would contribute to this movement. Are you artistic or logical? Would you raise money or protest?

7) If you want to take your message to the masses, you need to be moved by your message. So why are you passionate about this cause? What moves you about it?

8) Treat each person who is attracted to your movement as the only one. Treat them as though they mean everything to you. And watch your movement expand.

9) External movement comes from internal movement. Embody your movement. Watch, read and surround yourself with inspirational people and content that allows you to blossom to the person needed to be this movement maker!

10) Finally remember, when you align to what you want to do, those who also align to it will come to you. Be patient.

> *'I am, I am, everything that I need to be*
> *I'm smart enough*
> *Brilliant enough*
> *Young enough*
> *Wise enough*
> *I have been through enough*
> *I'm the perfect*
> *Perfect*
> *Perfect*
> *Person for my assignment*
> *No one can do it for me*
> *I am an unrepeatable miracle*
> *And in my imperfections*
> *I'm perfect for this assignment.*
> *'Take a deep breath in'*
> *I get a thousand second chances*
> *And when I get to 999*
> *I get to press reset.'*
> **Lisa Nicholls**

So many of you message me, 'Mani I would love to help you with the work that you do. I would love to be of service.' But most who message are in the closet, want to remain anonymous or are afraid. I mean yes you can be a role model online, or in certain private spaces, but you're still not living your truth. If it is safe for you to come out then please do, even if you initially think it isn't. If you live in a western country with LGBTI rights and have adequate protection and support from the state, you may want to consider being a public role model. We do need more out, proud, loving and self-accepting LGBTI role models. We need an army of LGBTI who are not afraid to show their true self. Who don't have marriages of convenience. Who don't marry someone of the opposite sex. Those who shine in their light knowing the Universe will always protect them.

Being a role model does not mean you have to be the next Gandhi or UN Secretary General. Being a role model can be as simple as someone who lives their truth and is kind and compassionate as much as they can be. A role model is someone who inspires, or brings joy into the hearts of others. Simply walking out the door and making the choice to live your own life with love and with honesty is being a role model. An internal light switched on helps illuminate the world. Once you stand in your own glory, others will follow. They will be inspired to live their life and not the life expected of them. Not only gay people but straight people will see how you choose to live authentically and with vigour.   They will be inspired to leave dead careers, relationships or to speak honestly to their friends and family. Too many of us live double lives, sheltering our true emotions from those that matter to us the most. We have become mere shadows of ourselves.

However, if you want to be the next Mother Teresa, I would not stop you. If I am totally honest, I would like all of you to shine as bright as possible and break through barriers of selfishness and indulgence. The way the world is right now we need as many good people as possible doing things in a big way to bring about peaceful change. I want Nelson Mandela's, Martin Luther King's, Buddha's, Christ's and all other types of game changers to present themselves. We need to all work together now! The world is going through a spiritual shift, and we need to return it to light. Far too many of the world's children starve, mothers die and fathers are killed. Let us shine today.

It takes real guts, real motivation, and real dedication to be a leader. You have to face your failures, your imperfections, and your failings. You must forgive. Forgive yourself and others completely. Be grateful, humble, and at one with yourself. This is a process. It can take days, weeks, months or years. Some are already well equipped for role model leadership. Lightworkers, those who are incarnated on Earth without karma. Those already self-actualised. Those who do not need the daily incantations of mantras, meditations, prayers or downward dogs (yoga). Your duty my friends is to shine bright and be an example in a big way. Be seen. Write, talk, do workshops or simply be in love with all.

Those of us who are not there yet, may need to put in the elbow grease. That doesn't matter. I have put years into self-development and actualisation, and I can truly tell you each step of the journey helps bring more inner peace, wisdom, clarity and happiness. Taking a few steps on the path to liberation will not only benefit you but will benefit humankind in general. You owe it to yourself and to your brother, sister, mother, father, lover, friend and foe.

However, don't get caught in the trap I did of preaching!!! It is no good to anyone. It's irksome, and people run away from preachy preaching know it all's. Accept your mistakes. Be true to yourself and be the light. Shine in your purity and example and let others be inspired. Try not to shine a spotlight onto someone's imperfections. Simply live in joy, forgiveness, gratitude and positivity. Those who are ready to shine will come to you asking for advice and guidance on how to live a happy life. Other not so eager souls may run for the hills, thinking you are a weirdo. Forgive them.

Their time will come. It is not your duty to convert, to force or to show the truth. Allow the universal forces and divine timing to work its magic. Your task is you. To be a magical wizard of internal love and let it spiral out.

'I believe you're not given a dream, unless you have the capacity to fulfill it.'
Jack Canfield- Chicken Soup for the Soul.

We can only show you the door. But you, yourself must walk through it. Activists are not to be put on a pedestal. The work alone is independent and self-orientated. We may show you how to unlock the door or damn it, break the fricken door down. But give us not all of the credit. Because the actual work is your own. Muster your own courage and walk.

Facebook, Tweet, Pin, Instagram, and Email the message below:

Bollywood Gay Message #17:
I am here to play big. I am here to shine. I am a role model.
#BollywoodGay

Action Sheet 17: Shine Bright. Be The Light.

List **5 role models** that you think are **inspirational**.

1. _____
2. _____
3. _____
4. _____
5. _____

What **qualities** or **traits** do you **admire** in each of them?

1. _____
2. _____
3. _____
4. _____
5. _____

How can you bring these very qualities into **your daily life**?

_____
_____
_____

How could you be a **role model**- either in a small way or big way?

_____
_____

Could you start up a **group**, **social circle**, or just be a positive example of love and light?

_____
_____
_____

Or do you want to play bigger? In the UK we have two organisations called **Stonewall** and **Diversity Role Models** who go into schools and speak about being LGBT. They are in desperate need of ethnic role models. Why not contact them, or find other ways of speaking out about being LGBTI to your schools, colleges, Universities and community centres. Do it safely whilst supported and you will succeed.

PART 5: THE BIGGER PICTURE

'I'm recruiting an army of gay spiritual soldiers, are you ready?'

18) BE THE CHANGE YOU WANT TO SEE IN THE WORLD

'An eye for an eye will make the whole world blind.' Mahatma Gandhi

Gandhi talks about being the change you want to see in the world. I completely agree with him. I have worked in the Human Rights field for many years now and have seen all sorts of contradictions. People want to help the world on one hand but on the other hand, ego gets in the way. I have worked in offices where people literally wanted to pull each other apart.

This is not being the change you want to see in the world. It is imperative for us to all do our own inner work each day at home. In order to show up to the world in a way that advocates peace. Not everyone is awake yet. We will change this over time. By raising our own vibration and coming from a place of service, watch how the world around you spiritually evolves its consciousness.

There is also too much unkindness in the gay scene. There is too much unkindness in life in general. Extended family, so called friends and work colleagues can be very unkind. This is not being the change you want to see in the world. Rather it perpetuates the pain that already exists by being blind to universal truths of oneness and love. It is the robotic autopilot mode of the ego reacting, craving, feeling angry, possessing hatred and ill will to others. It is the: I am unhappy mentality and therefore I will make you unhappy in the process too. We need to stop this auto-piloted mentality.

SO WHAT DO YOU NEED TO DO?

Follow your gut. Follow your heart. Come from a place of inner knowing. Inner connectedness. Inner peace. When one is connected to one's true self, the seated observatory self, one is in the gaps of space, in between outbursts of ego and able to analyse, observe and know the ultimate truth. Tap into this universal wisdom when in silence and then you are good to go! We literally have to come from a place of love and vibrate that out. That is how we become the change we want to see in the world. We want to see love and peace, harmony and togetherness, unity and abundance; thus we must act from that place. Act as though it already exists.

If you want to be the change you want to see in the world, you must envisage that that change has already happened. This is one of the quickest ways of manifesting peace by imagining that the world is already peaceful. Imagine that your country already has gay rights, and gay marriage. Act, believe, and conduct yourself in that manner, without looking for evidence against it. Wholly believe that Section 377 is abolished, and that LGBTI Rights exist in India right now. How would you act if this were the case? How would you behave if your country had gay rights? Would you go and have a marriage ceremony with your partner? If you are able to have a private ceremony go do it now!

In order to be the change you want to see in the world you must raise your frequency. Consciousness and frequency go hand in hand. When you're in a low vibrational frequency, you are in a decreased state of consciousness, and your perception is limited. When you're in a high vibrational frequency, you are in an increased state of consciousness, and your perception is heightened. The lower your vibrational frequency, the less you can comprehend because your ego restricts the flow of life force into your mind and body. The higher your vibrational frequency, the more you can comprehend because you allow a greater life force into your mind and body. Holding a high vibration and radiating unconditional and non-judgmental love raises the consciousness of those around you. Low vibration is sadness; high vibration is happiness. What thoughts are you thinking that cause you to feel good or not feel good? Choose thoughts that help you feel emotionally well about yourself. This enables you to maintain a high frequency even when dealing with those with lower vibrations.

Focus on things that cause you to feel good to hold a high vibration. When dealing with people with low vibration, your job is to be totally present for them and reflect what unconditional love and positivity looks like. Don't focus on their suffering and illness, as your frequency will decrease. That is focusing on negativity. Instead, focus on them being in perfect health. Focus on anything that will bring them more relief. Focus on the truth that they are eternal beings who are powerful creators. That they are not alone, and there is nothing to be afraid of. Jesus used the exact same technique to heal thousands of people during his time. This is called being the light as opposed to preaching which people don't like. Indeed it is unconditional love.

HOW TO GET INTO A HIGH VIBE STATE OF MIND?

When in a low vibe state meditation or sleeping are the best ways to stop negative mind chatter. Observing your thoughts as opposed to criticising or judging them is another alternative. Look at your thoughts but don't invest in them. Watch your thoughts go by like clouds in a sky. You could also write out your feelings, cry or get your frustration out by punching a pillow to discharge negative energy.

Now your low vibe is released there are numerous ways of getting into a high vibe state. You can:

1) Make conscious positive changes in your lifestyle by being aware of your current beliefs, fears and judgements.

2) Play high frequency/vibration music which is any music that makes you feel good. Binaural beats, which are specifically recorded sounds that have various frequencies to induce different states of mind, are a favourite of mine. You could also listen to singing bowls or other natural high vibe music online.

3) Spend time near people, places and things which hold high vibrations such as spiritual teachers, friends, animals, crystals or nature. The latter two maintain their high vibrations continuously, hence why new age people wear crystals or surround themselves around nature.

4) Be inspired. Anything that is inspiring will raise your frequency, so read inspirational books; watch uplifting movies or motivational vlogs (like mines) on YouTube.

5) Exercise, for physical movement causes energy to move through and oxygenate your brain and releases endorphins which are frequency elevating chemicals. So choose one which you enjoy doing.

6) Aromatherapy. Different aromas induce different states within us. Select ones that uplift your energy.

7) Colour has a frequency too. Colour therapy causes you to match the frequency of whatever ingredient went into the colour. Each colour relates to a certain chakra as already mentioned in Chapter 14. Choose a colour according to the chakra you want to unblock.

8) Write a gratitude journal or look for positive aspects as you go about your day. When you look at something with an attitude of appreciation you tap into pure unconditional love energy (same as Source) and increase your frequency.

9) Spend time in water. Light is the manifestation, which holds the closest vibration to that of pure Source energy. Water is second to that. Any time you spend in water you are going to be resonating in a very close frequency to Source itself. So take a shower, bath or swim/paddle in a lake.

10) Practice random acts of kindness. Anytime you are projecting and radiating love you are in high vibration.

11) Enquire. Any questioning you do will bring you to higher levels of awareness and set you free from the illusion of fear. The more you know yourself and get out of the box by being deeply introspective the easier it becomes to hold a high frequency permanently.

12) Laugh and smile. Anything you can do, think, say, watch or be around that causes you to smile or laugh will automatically increase your vibration. Seek out time to have fun!

In short, if you dedicate yourself to happiness and prioritise how you feel you will inadvertently raise your frequency. You simply use the other thing as an excuse to raise your frequency, by accepting its offering to help you. Your emotions are key. The better you feel, the higher your vibration is.

'Dr. Martin Luther King did not say, ladies and gentlemen, I have a complaint. He said I have a dream and because of that dream people galvanised around that and differences were made.' Rev Michael Beckwith

If like Dr. Martin Luther King you too have a dream, you have the power to birth it and make it true. The very fact that you have that dream or vision means that an inner change in consciousness or awakening has already started within you. It's simply a matter of time before it will manifest and start making a positive difference in the world. Thus keep on holding onto that vision. Keep praying and meditating on it and see how the Law of Attraction brings those participants and situations into your life to make it happen. That is why it is imperative to maintain and have a regular spiritual practice or ritual. Your intention will get you to the dream. Leave it up to the Universe and your spiritual guides to work out the tiny details, whilst you keep focusing on the final vision of your dream.

The presence of fear means we think we are doing it alone.

The Universe always has your back. If you have fear, it means you don't have faith in the higher forces that are assisting you each moment and each day. When feeling closed off, in fear or stressed remind yourself the simple mantra by Gabrielle Bernstein, *'The Universe always has my back.'*

Every day I practice universal love or Metta meditation which I learnt through Vipassana meditation retreats. Metta is the ancient Indian Pali word meaning loving-kindness, goodwill, and non-violence. It is the strong wish for the welfare and happiness of others. I practice it by firstly mentally forgiving anyone who has wronged me, secondly asking for forgiveness from anyone I've wronged and thirdly by giving love to myself and everyone.

Why do I do this? Primarily to be a good human being and to be a contributor to universal peace and positive energy. But also because what you do to another is what you intrinsically do to yourself. See on a subatomic level there is no separation between you and I. All that surrounds us, which looks physical and real is, in fact, small particles vibrating at high velocity. This is the frequency of the said physical object! We too vibrate certain frequencies depending on how we feel that day! So why not sit in a comfortable position and imagine love literally vibrating out of your heart into the atmosphere around you.

Also the Universe is like an organism, and we are the minuscule cells within it. The way we are in relationship to our frequency (energy) is the way in which we affect the organism, the whole, the collective. Thus the more of us that can be loving, positive and inspirational on a consistent basis, the better it is for the organism as a whole. Every time you make a change, you are in fact making a change to everything. It's not one incremental change, but an instant vibrational shift to the whole collective. Thus every time you think a good thought, do a good deed or choose to live a better life, you, in fact, contribute directly to the worlds frequency.

'If you want others to be happy, practice compassion. If you want to be happy, practice compassion.' His Holiness the Dalai Lama

Compassion starts from within and towards oneself. Quite often we are very hard on ourselves, comparing our lives to others and getting jealous or insecure about our supposed shortcomings! This is the roadway to suffering and disaster! Being more compassionate to the world and ourselves is done through practising self-love exercises as explained in Action Sheet 9.

Spread love everywhere you go. Let no one ever come to you without leaving happier.' Mother Teresa

The key to developing compassion in your life is to make it a daily practice. We need to open up our heart chakras so we can unblock our energy centres. Not only does this help us be happier but it also makes the world a better place! Oh and I forgot it also helps you on your personal route to enlightenment!!

YOU KNOW WHEN YOU ARE ON THE PATH TO COMPASSION WHEN YOU:

1) Feel happy, joyful and content most of the time.
2) Understand that all is as it should be; the good and bad combined are accepted as they are without attachment.
3) Have healthy, meaningful and intimate friendships that are of a long duration (outside family members).
4) Express unconditional love to all.
5) Are harmonious with nature.
6) Are moved to empathy.
7) Act from a place of service to the world, freely giving and sharing your gifts.

Once we have self-compassion perfected it is time to spread that to those around us. No one is perfect. No matter how saintly we become, there will always be impurities needing to be released. Once equanimous (equal tempered) they will come to the surface. We are imperfect and human. And must realise so is the other. We must forgive them too.

'No one is born hating another person because of the colour of his skin, or his background, or his religion. People must learn to hate, and if they can learn to hate, they can be taught to love, for love comes more naturally to the human heart than its opposite.' Nelson Mandela

We must forgive those who make mistakes and wrong us too. That is why I am passionate about the issues incarceration proposes as they reflect the consciousness of wider society. Imprisonment does not work, for you cannot punish someone without punishing yourself. We don't need punishing; we need compassion and love. We should have compassion for the victim but also for the perpetrator. Putting people with misaligned vibrations into one place creates for more misalignment. Prisoners are in need of healing. We need to work alongside these people and give them compassion. There is an interesting movement in India where Vipassana meditation is taught in prisons up and down the country. It is called 'Doing time, doing Vipassana'. Prisoners for the first time in their life experience the positive benefits of self- development and use it for the betterment of society. They let go of their anger, realise the error of their ways and atone for forgiveness. They should provide Vipassana for free in schools and workplaces to help people. It is happening in some schools and workplaces across South Asia but needs to be everywhere.

'We have a power within us, more powerful then bullets.'
Martin Luther King

As we enter the Aquarian age, the veil of ignorance is slowly but surely removed. People rise up and campaign for an egalitarian society. For socialism, rights for all and peace. This is the way the planet is moving. And it is a joy to see that the spiritual momentum of meditation and yoga taking over schools and workplaces across the world.

I stand in glory as everything works out. I smile in bliss, in knowing. I breathe in the infinite universal knowledge bestowed upon me. I shower love upon you. All of you. May you also come join me in the dance of the yog- of mind and body. We are atoms of vibrations, encircling the brahamic universal plane of existence. You and I. In love.

Facebook, Tweet, Pin, Instagram, and Email the message below:

Bollywood Gay Message #18:
Your greatest gift is your kindness.
#BollywoodGay

Action Sheet 18: Vibrate Love

I want you to have fun! Loads of it. You must have it every day! Smile, laugh, joke and giggle. Fun is the order of the day! I need you to be happy for other people's happiness without it affecting where you are. So start saying **'Omg I'm so happy for your success'**- whenever you see someone succeed in life. Get into that energy base. By doing so, you bring success to yourself and positively change the planet!

I also need you to bring love into your life. I want you to spend 10 minutes a day, releasing all your negativity and forgive everyone including yourself by chanting: **'I forgive everyone who has wronged me'**. Then I want you to chant **'I wish everyone love and happiness and real peace. I wish myself real love and happiness'**. Feel good whilst doing it and vibrate it. So only do this exercise when you feel good!

HERE ARE 7 TIPS ON HOW TO STRENGTHEN YOUR COMPASSION MUSCLE TO ACHIEVE THIS!

1) **Morning ritual**- every morning before starting your day do a simple meditation or prayer. Imagine yourself as a vessel of love that overflows. Imagine yourself generating love, which literally comes from you and radiates out to the world.

2) **Realise the commonalities you have with others**. We are one. The physical separation that the 3rd dimension makes us believe is false. Atomically we are just vibrations of energy all interrelated. When you see yourself in the other- your wisdom and compassion automatically increase.

3) **Look at your own internal dialogue**. Are you kind to yourself? Do you cheerlead yourself? What you do to yourself you do to others. Thus it is imperative you give words of courage, love and respect to yourself!

4) **Buy a rose quartz crystal** and wear it as a necklace. Its crystalline properties literally raise the vibration of your heart chakra, opening you to compassion.

5) **Understand suffering** by repeating: *'Just like me, this person is trying to live a happy, contented life. Just like me, this person is trying to avoid pain and suffering. Just like me, this person has suffered or is suffering in life. Just like me this person is growing and learning about life.'* This simple mantra will help you be gentle with people.

6) **Want others to be relieved from their suffering? Then pray for them**. Pray for your enemies. Pray for their forgiveness and happiness. For one who inflicts pain on others suffers greatly. This is true on a metaphysical, unconscious level. The unconscious mind makes no decree or separation between you and I. If you are aggressive to me, you are aggressive to yourself. It's like the saying, 'holding onto anger is like holding onto hot coals and expecting the other person to get burnt.'

7) **Give unconditional love to everyone**. As you travel to work, send out well wishes mentally to all those you meet.

'I'm not my current situation. I'm not my past. I'm becoming.
In transit. I'm a constant movement of vibrational energy
with unlimited potential.'

19) SPEAK UP- RAISE CONSCIOUSNESS

'There is a time to be quiet and a time to talk.'
Aung San Suu Kyi

How do you raise consciousness? The consciousness of the world is raised once you raise your own consciousness. Sounds like a catch 22 situation right? You thought I was going to give you another answer? No, everything begins with you. What you think, becomes. What you focus on manifests. If you want to see the best in others, you need to start seeing the best in yourself.

Marianne Williamson says it's not about the majority agreeing, it's about the tipping point. Having enough who get it and cause a shift. It's not about the horizontal. About getting as many people as possible to agree to your message. It's not about diluting your message so the masses agree to it. It's about standing in your purity. The purity of the message you want to give. It's not dumbing it down to gain acceptance. So stand in the essence of your message and let the Law of Attraction bring those who get it to you. Once you have a momentum of enough people, a tipping point will occur and your message will be received. Never water down your vision for others. Keep to it. Change throughout history, the abolition of slavery, the civil rights movement, India's independence, was not done by amalgamating the masses and agreeing altogether. It takes the likes of a few well-connected individuals who create momentum through their vision.

'Living a meaningful life is not a popularity contest.'
Marianne Williamson

If all you want is to get a lot of applause from those who agree with you, you won't bring any change. These people already know what you are saying and don't need convincing. Your job is not just to galvanise and get applause from those who agree with you and then demonise those who don't. You are not a true activist if you do that. Take away the judgement you have about others, which separates you. Ask God to allow you to reach out to people who don't already agree. Take away any thoughts that keep you away from being able to reach these people. You have to remove violence from your heart and any judgement you have about someone being homophobic, racist or sexist. Everyone hears everything subconsciously. Everyone can hear what is in your heart. For angry people will not bring peace. The means is just as inherent as the end.

'Dear God please take away from me the judgement I hold against those who I believe do not have the same ideals, opinions and vision as me.'

You only need a few high-vibe (happy, joyful, loving) people to make a big difference in the world. See high vibration has a much higher frequency and impact compared to people who are in the lower vibrations of anger, guilt and shame. High vibration is contagious and can bring positive ripple effects around the world. So if you maintain a high vibe for long enough, you start to spread that to those around you. Thus only a few high-vibe people are more than enough, to combat thousands of those stuck in anger, guilt and shame. Know that you are the difference. Pissed off with the world? THEN GET HAPPY! From that high vibration not only do you gain wisdom, insight and creative solutions, but you also act from inspired action rather than reaction.

> **'People are often unreasonable, irrational, and self-centered. Forgive them anyway. If you are kind, people may accuse you of selfish, ulterior motives. Be kind anyway. If you are successful, you will win some unfaithful friends and some genuine enemies. Succeed anyway. If you are honest and sincere people may deceive you. Be honest and sincere anyway. What you spend years creating, others could destroy overnight. Create anyway. If you find serenity and happiness, some may be jealous. Be happy anyway. The good you do today, will often be forgotten. Do good anyway. Give the best you have, and it will never be enough. Give your best anyway. In the final analysis, it is between you and God. It was never between you and them anyway.' Mother Teresa**

Whenever you see injustice speak up. Whenever you see abuse, report it. Stand up for others. Work together for peace. But do so from a place of love and unity. When one's intention is pure, the outcome will always be in one's favour.

Conduct peaceful protests, spiritual rallies, mass meditations and be bold! Advocate peace through positive methods. Speak your truth, be a strong role model, so that younger closeted South Asians can have an easier coming out. Speak love; it raises the vibration of all those around you. Be an ambassador of peace!

> **'Our lives begin to end the day we become silent about things that matter.'
> Martin Luther King**

Society is experiencing low levels of fear due to mass media consciousness. I say stop watching the news and feeding into fear! The media/news is manufactured to dramatise, sensualise and make sales. The fear is manufactured to make people listen to corporate companies and governments so they can go to war for profit. Billions of people feed into this consciousness of lack, loss and limitation, hypnotised by the newest 'dis-ease' or terrorist group out there. We must realise, what we focus on grows. Focus on fear, negativity, lack and we will have more unrest, violence and 'dis-ease' outbreaks. Realise the capacity within us to deal with this positively. The power is within us; the answer is within us. If a problem is created, then a solution is created too. Not through fear, but revelation, and inspiration. You have to transcend fear or walk in the direction of your faith and take the fear with you to transform it into excitement and love. As I've said before, keep focusing on peace and love, and you will manifest it.

We have forgotten that this is the greatest time in human history. A time with the least amount of wars and conflict. Yes I know it may not seem that way due to the media fixating on small pockets of violence and amplifying them. But the more we focus on that, the more it happens. What you put your attention to grows. In history, whole continents were at war all the time. We have more peace than we ever have had. Stop watching the news or media.

Everyday on my Facebook newsfeed I see articles or posts about homophobic crimes or homophobia in general. It's a constant barrage, and many of my friends retweet, share, comment, dislike and rant about it. Why do so many people spend so much time and energy on individuals or groups who don't like them? Rather than featuring, fostering, nurturing and giving web space to individuals and groups who support them? I simply unfollow their feeds. I do not want negativity on my social media feed. I recommend the same.

The same goes for websites (mostly right winged) and religious followers who don't approve of homosexuality or who are homophobic. Stop giving these people more publicity. The more you highlight them, the more publicity they receive and the more popular they become as your adversaries. In the process, you are causing more harm than good for our cause.

> ### 'If you have knowledge, let others light their candles in it.'
> ### Margaret Fuller

That is why I make it a thing to pump out positivity only. We are the media. The actual media is very one sided. I would always question everything and research it before posting or sharing on Facebook or Twitter. Are you doing your part in sharing positivity only? Are you raising consciousness by sharing the media message of love? Or are you taking humankind backwards by living in fear and negative dramatisation and sharing such messages online?

It is the era of Aquarius, which new spiritual age people believe is the era of awakening. It is what the ancient Indians call the end of kal yug (dark epoch) and coming into the light. What this means is that our vibrations are increasing. As our galaxy makes its orbit to face the star system of Aquarius, the amount of light, awareness and higher connectedness we have increases. It means that the God era where humanity needed Gods to rescue us is over, the guru era where teachers were needed to guide us is closing, and it is time for each to become their own guru. It is time for everyone's internal light to ignite. Just like cans being popped open, we will all eventually pop open and realise our ignorance and understand the truth.

> ### 'Education is the most powerful weapon which you can use to change the world.'
> ### Nelson Mandela

Things are on the change. Even though in schools the term 'gay' is used in a negative, derogatory fashion, the acceptance of LGBTI, partly due to educational and media campaigns in the West, is far more than it was when I was at school. In a recent YouGov poll of 18-24-year-olds, 50% did not self-identify as either entirely straight or gay, but more in between. Whether you can say this is experimentation or growing up, the fact remains, young people are more willing to experiment or shamelessly declare their disconnection of what is a sexual, social norm. This can only be a good thing! In my day, the word gay was never spoken. And no one would dare to declare they were anything but straight. Friends we are onto a winner here. We need to remember that!

NATIONAL COMING OUT DAY

Founded in 1988 National Coming Out Day is celebrated every year on October 11. Let all of your parents know of this date. The date where their child, LGBTI or heterosexual can come to them to disclose what their sexual orientation or gender is at the time. Do this whenever you feel ready, whatever year it may be. Parents need to realise the importance of this date. That their child will not necessarily be heterosexual. Every year on this date I will do a prayer and release that into the Universe to bring courage to those who want to come out and also to encourage parents to keep this dialogue open. I encourage you to do the same.

ARE YOU A LIGHTWORKER?

Are you a lightworker on a mission to save the world? If you are confused about the best way to do this simply remember: if your intention is pure, the outcome will be pure too. If you come from a loving, peaceful, positive place the fruits will reflect that (even if it doesn't seem like that at the time). When we work for the betterment of society, all of the tools of the Universe come together to support us. The Universe is always working for you, protecting you, guiding you and paving the way ahead.

So don't be afraid to ask your Angels, Guardians, Ascended Masters, Divine Gods, Goddesses, and the Universe for constant guidance, direction and assistance. No task is too small. Connect daily and start speaking to them on a regular daily basis. Ask them for guidance, love and direction. They are waiting for your call; you do not have to do it alone.

HOW DO I CONNECT WITH SPIRITUAL GUIDES & ANGELS?

I asked the same question myself a few years ago whilst living in Goa, India. I had been sacked from my job the same day the guy I was dating cheated on me! I was down in the dumps and I wanted to see my Spirit Guides and Angels for guidance. I started talking to them by declaring aloud in my flat that I was not afraid to see them. I wanted to feel their presence and connect with them. I kept repeating this to no avail.

Then one night when visiting a friend in Mumbai (trying to secure a TV show with Bollywood), an angel came to me in my dream. Angels are basically anything you would consider as higher consciousness. You may call them your Spirit Guides, Enlightened Beings, Ascended Masters, God consciousness, etc. and they appear in the form you imagine they would be. They are essentially high vibrational energy and to connect to them you need to be in a similar receptive mode, which means having a high vibe of pure positive love energy around you. You may see them as bright light, sparkling fireflies or actual physical beings. You may be able to see them (clairvoyance), hear them (clairaudience), feel them (clairsentience), or know clearly they are there (claircognizance). These are spiritual gifts, which you can tap into as explained in the Action Sheet that follows.

The angel reassured me that everything would work out as I had planned as long as I remained positive and hopeful. My angel came in the typical form of a winged white robed Greek God/Goddess (I love my mythology). It was neither female nor male and since then I can hear or feel countless angels around me. When I am connected to myself, answers come easily and sometimes I see them in my room, supporting me.

You are a soldier of peace, and you have infinite weapons at your disposal. Use them.

You can also directly converse with spirit like me. The only condition is that you have to be connected consistently. You can ask for things to go a certain way and they will and then ask them to stop too. The night of my mum's video, I spoke to spirit. I said make this video viral and spirit listened. Once things began to go crazy and unmanageable, I said slow down; I need to take things step by step. And surely they did. You can also command the Universe to collaborate with you. But the condition is you have to be connected. You can co-create your life with spirit. The more spiritual work you do, the more your sensory gifts will unlock. The other night I had a dream of many people asking to move to the other side. They wanted to commit suicide due to all their suffering. The reoccurring dream kept me up all night and made me also think I wanted to go to the other side wherein we all come from. A place of peace and oneness. However, a voice came from within me. Very much like the voice that got me out of depression many years ago. I have a purpose on this planet, and I must do my job here. I must help people to realise that they too can be happy and don't have to prematurely move onto the other side. You have the same job, and now is the time to rise up!

Facebook, Tweet, Pin, Instagram, and Email the message below:

Bollywood Gay Message #19:
I speak up for truth. I speak up for love. I speak up for equality.
#BollywoodGay

Action Sheet 19: Stand Up For Equality

Having read the chapter in which ways would you like to **stand up for equality**?

1. _____
2. _____
3. _____
4. _____
5. _____

What *peaceful acts* can you start doing now?

_____
_____
_____
_____
_____
_____
_____

How can you **report abuse** or stand up to someone who is being *abused* without jeopardising your own *safety*?

_____
_____
_____
_____
_____
_____
_____

Be the *media*. How can you **contribute** to the distribution and expansion of *positive posts*?

_____
_____
_____
_____
_____
_____
_____
_____
_____

What *tools* of the *Universe* do you believe in or would like to use for the benefit of your cause?

_____

_____

_____

_____

BELOW ARE 6 WAYS YOU CAN USE THE INFINITE TOOLS OF THE UNIVERSE TO FURTHER YOUR MISSION ON EARTH:

(Such as Spiritual Guides, Angels, Enlightened Beings, Masters, Gurus, Yogis, and God Consciousness).

1) **Keep asking to be guided.**

2) **Declare that you are ready to see, hear or feel them.**

3) **Be in a high vibrational state** by eating healthy organic food, drinking filtered water and maintaining a regular spiritual practice.

4) **Journal**- ask for the energy to write through you.

5) **Listen to your gut instincts** for answers.

6) **Be open and aware** of what is happening around you in the present moment and look or ask for signs. (I ask for Unicorns to know I am doing the right thing).

'With God, all things are possible.'
Dr. Wayne Dwyer

20) MAKE AN IMPACT IN THE WORLD- JOIN THE SPIRITUAL REVOLUTION!

Instead of spending our time chasing after sexual desires on apps, let's use that time productively to make the world a better place ☺

So you've worked on yourself, cleaned your subconscious mind and now what? Usually, when you get to this stage of inner confidence and security, you look around and think, heck I want everyone to strive to be their best too. What about my LGBTI friends and family in the world? Who suffer on this planet. In India, Pakistan and Bangladesh it is illegal to be gay. We need to change that! British Colonial Laws need to be struck down!

By having LGBTI rights in India, Pakistan, Bangladesh and other South Asian countries, we will positively affect the lives of South Asian LGBTI diaspora around the world. The older South Asian diaspora will see that India has LGBTI rights and thus be more accepting of it abroad. They will no longer see it as a Western 'dis-ease' that only white people get.

My aim has always been to be the happiest person I can be. So that I can help you be the same. For when we are vibrating at our highest vibration we are an ambassador for peace. When we come from a place of love, we attract fellow loving beings in our cause for equality and peace. My aim has never been to force the whole world to change and make it accept you. Change can never come through coercion. The world is waking up, but each will do so in their own time. Each is their own saviour and must awaken themselves. Save yourselves. And see how your life transforms. You attract what you are.

That is why we need to work in unison, hand in hand, together, from a place of love. I do not advocate provocation, dramatisation, or head locked battles with community and religious leaders. I want you to go to your places of worship, from a place of love, respectfully arranging meetings, talking to your Imam, Paathi, Pujari and Priest and ask them to help bring light in an otherwise dark world. Take down the purdah and help LGBTI people live their lives with love. We don't want to be converted, changed, manipulated, or silenced, but we want to be an integral part of the evolutional shift in the world. We are just as important as everyone else. Love should be the motivation and unity the intention. From this place, nothing can go wrong. The Universe will open its heavens to pave a path of joy for all. My social media followers are already calling themselves 'Positive Powerful Peacekeepers' going to religious organisations and community groups to discuss LGBTI topics. If safe you can do the same.

> ### 'By helping others, you will learn how to help yourselves.'
> ### Aung San Suu Kyi

Yes, anything is possible. Dream it, believe it, know it, FEEL IT! If people ask you, you can tell them of your plans to live in the country of your dreams with unfound freedoms. You can also talk about your own country becoming a more liberal and freer place for all. Be very mindful of your language and intention. Expect the best possible outcome for yourself. Be 100% positive and hopeful and you will see life manifest in front of your very eyes. I recommend praying or meditating twice a day, regular physical exercise like yoga or running to stay in the present moment and to be watchful of your mind. I can tell you life gets better, and you can be the happiest person you know. But you have to prepare yourself mentally and work at it daily! It was unthinkable in the past that gay marriage would be approved in the USA, and it is. With a group of people with love in their hearts, anything is possible. One day, hopefully soon the same will happen in all countries around the world.

Appreciate your life if you live in a country which already has rights for LGBTI. You are lucky. Stop obsessing about cock sizes, muscles and lack. We are in a privileged position and even if our families disown us or find it hard to understand us, the state provides us with protection and resources. For there are LGBTI in countries where it is punishable by death.

> ### 'Do not wait for leaders; do it alone, person to person.'
> ### Mother Teresa

The purpose of this book is not just about being happy with ourselves; that is the beginning. In many Western nations if not all, the South Asian LGBTI question has not been tackled at all. It is our duty to come out, stand proud, at gay pride parades and community events, to our friends, family and work colleagues to show that we exist and then to have an open dialogue about it. This has to be done from an abundant, Law of Attraction, positive outcome mindset. Know that change will come once we engage from openness and love. Because from what I have seen a handful if any South Asians attend Pride marches. Sure we arrive at night to the parties and drinking, but where are we during the day? Holding flags and being proud of who we are or at home hiding?

The purpose of this book is also to help those who read it in nations unfriendly to LGBTI to empower them from within. To accept themselves, love themselves and know that who they are is absolutely fine. By doing so, from an abundant positive, hopeful mindset, without looking back at the past, or lack of rights in the current physical perception, enormous monumental shifts can happen in no time whatsoever. If we look at the lack and all the bad that is happening to LGBTI around us, we will absorb that vibration of negativity and resentment and bring it to ourselves. Instead we need to focus 100% on the dream that we want as though it has already happened, then people in alignment with that dream will match up and surround us. Eventually, there will be an avalanche of supporters and lovers of equality and hearts will melt. Be love activists. I want you to empower yourself and then each other. Work together not apart. Love is the healing force. Create solidarity and a sense of family. Be the light, the shining example and the happiest people you know. This life is a life of many lives you've lived before. Your mission for this life is clear. Your current birth is about spreading unconditional love, telling the world they cannot change you, accepting yourself and expanding your consciousness.

Create groups, workshops and events. Start small, in your homes, visualise, imagine and sculpt. Call them 'Out of Purdah' meetings where you meet to bring peace, love and connection to spirit. Have fun, support one another and be there for each other. You can advertise on Facebook, Twitter, Meetup or Eventbrite. Do whatever you can, because we need to come together now. We cannot do this alone.

'The best way to find yourself is to lose yourself in the service of others.'
Mahatma Gandhi

These are exciting times. Liaise with the LGBTI community that has settled or gained asylum in the West and ask them to support you to bring change in the East. If all of you flew over to the West and ignored what was going on at home, laws would never change at the pace they need to and younger, more poorer LGBTI who don't have resources, money or methods of getting abroad would be left to suffer. Enough of running away let's face the issue head on! Of course if your life is in grave danger, and you have means or reason to get to a safer place then you must, but still, relay your activism or visionary thoughts from abroad. It is your sole duty to your nation, LGBTI community and planet.

Focusing on the positive and your alignment to Source is not ignorance of what is going on. The media and the world give far too much importance to the negative, the drama, and the fear, to scare us into submission, so that money hungry folk can run the world. I choose to resonate love and peace. As I do this, those who also vibrate the same frequency are attracted to me. My LGBTI community, let's stand hand in hand, and show the world love. Love is the highest vibratory frequency and one person constantly emitting love is far greater than thousands who vibrate lower energies of anger, animosity, hatred and ill will. We are the change. It's not the ignoring of the bad. It's the balancing of it. We need as many people looking at the light, at the tipping point, on the edge of creation, to manifest the vision forwards. It is absolutely essential. We came on earth to have fun and realise our worthiness. The West has told us that war; famine and separation have been the order of world history. However, in ancient religious texts like the Vedas, we know of the Sat yug era (peaceful epoch), where people lived in harmony and peace. They simply thought and felt a thing, and it manifested-food, love, and abundance. We are now returning to to that. It's the age of Aquarius- out of Kal yug. We are going towards the light, and we need people to steer the way. Come steer with me.

'When the power of love overcomes the love of power the world will know peace.'
Jimi Hendrix

A certain proportion of this book's revenue will be donated to LGBTI causes for South Asians, whether that is as grants, loans or scholarships to study in higher education or as bursaries given to escape negative spaces. LGBTI people will definitely benefit! So if you know someone who needs support, or you yourself need support, or you want to progress the LGBTI cause by contributing then email me on hello@myspiritualsoul.com

Finally, I have a vision of opening a centre for highly in tuned psychics, gifted healers and high vibration lightworkers who learn from one another the ancient sacred arts lost to humankind. How we used to heal one another during Atlantean times. I have a vision of sending meditators to borders of war-torn countries. Healing through the power of intent. Sending mental healing vibrations through the atmosphere. Huge energy crystals surrounding them, using the power of crystal grids (patterns made from crystals which expand their energy) to charge love energy so it amplifies. And so it is. I put it out there and allow it to manifest.

If you share in this dream then contact me and Facebook, Tweet, Pin, Instagram, and Email the message below:

Bollywood Gay Message #20:
I will rally for my brothers and sisters. I will make an impact in the world.
#BollywoodGay

Action Sheet 20: How Can I Be Of Service?

WHAT CAN YOU DO TO MAKE A DIFFERENCE IN THE WORLD? IT'S TIME TO THINK BIG AND DO!

Make your own **Out of Purdah Groups** around the globe- where you meet to bring peace, love and connection to the world. Have fun, and support one another. It is very important for those in countries where being gay is illegal so you can support each other like family. Likewise, it is equally important in the West so we can have more visibility and acknowledgement within the general gay populace but also so that we can campaign for the rights of those back home. Our LGBTI friends and family in other countries need us. We are enjoying rights that they are not. It's our duty to support them. That is why a certain percentage of the proceeds from this book will go into that cause itself. Empowering LGBTI people in South Asian countries and countries where being gay is illegal.

Start **Positive Peace Keeper Campaigns**- where you individually or in small groups go to your local religious organisations and community groups to discuss LGBTI topics. Go with a heart of love, of unity and inclusion. Of wanting to help your fellow kind. If you think it easier send an email/letter first. Your safety is paramount, so decide wisely.

My Prayer to the Universe,

I want to help bring light to the world. I want to tap into the infinite possibilities of the Universe. So I can commit to my sole purpose of burning bright for all. I am done with playing it small. I am done with chasing stuff that does not align with my purpose. I am done. I surrender. I surrender my ego. I surrender my limited self. I surrender my fear. At your feet. I surrender. Bow down. I bow down to you. My soul touches your feet of infinite possibilities. I am open and aware. A vessel for your love to pour into and out of. I endeavour to tap into your infinite power and use it to help others. For I am never separate from you, and your power is mine to use for good. I let go of all control or forced direction as I did in the past. Thinking I knew best. I let go of the outcome and trust in your guidance.

Love always,

_____ *(Sign your commitment to the LGBTI Cause)*

'Spirituality is the salvation of the world.'
Marianne Williamson